*John Courtney Murray
and the Dilemma of Religious Toleration*

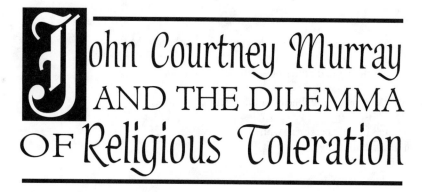

John Courtney Murray AND THE DILEMMA OF Religious Toleration

KEITH J. PAVLISCHEK

THOMAS JEFFERSON UNIVERSITY PRESS
Kirksville, Missouri
1994

© 1994 by Thomas Jefferson University Press, Kirksville, Missouri.
All rights reserved.
Printed in the United States of America.

British Cataloging in Publication Information available.

Distributed by arrangement with
University Publishing Associates, Inc.
4720 Boston Way
Lanham, MD 20706

3 Henrietta Street
London WC2E 8LU England

Library of Congress Cataloging-in-Publication Information

Pavlischek, Keith J.
    John Courtney Murray and the dilemma of religious toleration / Keith J.
Pavlischek.
        p.   cm.
    Revision of thesis (Ph. D.)—University of Pittsburgh.
    Includes bibliographical references and index.
    ISBN 0-943549-26-4 (cloth; alk. paper)   ISBN 0-943549-18-3 (case)
    1. Murray, John Courtney.   2. Freedom of religion—United States—His-
tory—20th century.   3. Catholic Church—United States—History—20th
century.   I. Title
BV741.P38 1994
261.7'2—dc20   94-4765
                                                                        CIP

Design and typography by Tim Rolands.
Cover art and title page by Teresa Wheeler, NMSU designer
Text is set in Berkeley Oldstyle 10/13. Manufactured by Edwards Brothers,
Ann Arbor, Michigan.

∞The paper used in this publication meets the minimum requirements of the American National Standard for Permanence of Paper for Printed Library Materials ANSI
Z39.48, 1984.

For Nancy

Nothing is so fatal to religion as indifference, which is, at least, half infidelity.

Edmund Burke, "Letter to W. M. Smith"

> Turning and turning in the widening gyre
> The falcon cannot hear the falconer;
> Things fall apart; the centre cannot hold;
> Mere anarchy is loosed upon the world,
> The blood-dimmed tide is loosed, and everywhere
> The ceremony of innocence is drowned;
> The best lack all conviction, while the worst
> Are full of passionate intensity.
>
> .   .   .   .
>
> And what rough beast, its hour come round at last,
> Slouches towards Bethlehem to be born?

W. B. Yeats, "The Second Coming"

Well, this development in America of the secular substitute for a traditional religious faith is not something that we can scream and yell about. As a matter of fact, I think the development is inevitable. Both in fact and in law there is no public religion in America today. There is no common religious faith. The law—the First Amendment—that copes with the fact is a wise law. But once one has affirmed the fact and also affirmed the wisdom of the law that copes with it, one still is left with an unanswered question, namely: "Can a political society do without a public religion? ...Society—secular society—must have some spiritual substance that underlies the order of law, the order of public morality and all other orders and processes within society. And if there be no such spiritual substance to society, then society is founded on a vacuum; and society, like nature itself, abhors a vacuum and cannot tolerate it.

John Courtney Murray, "The Return to Tribalism"

Contents

Foreword

GROWING UP IN A SMALL Protestant village in the irrigated farm country of northern Colorado, I learned many things. One of the things I learned was that America was the land of liberty, the place where desperate and aggrieved peoples sought succor, asylum, and, above all, religious liberty. That was what the brave Pilgrims were all about. In fact, that was what Protestantism itself was all about. Nobody but ourselves could tell us what to believe. Well, things are always simpler in childhood. What Keith Pavlischek alerts us to in this beautifully written, powerfully argued volume is that all too many among us cling to an ever so slightly more sophisticated version of this American childhood fable. And those who do not, and have not, accepted the story that usually gets told about religious toleration and liberty in America, are themselves caught on the horns of a number of real, not merely or only conceptual, dilemmas.

We all recall Thomas Jefferson's bouncy proclamation that it did him no harm whether his neighbor believed in twenty gods or no God; it neither picked his pocket nor broke his leg. Jefferson's pocket and his extremities may not have been assailed, but the logic of his version of religious toleration has come under withering fire. For Jefferson surely belongs among those Pavlischek, following Jeffrey Stout, calls the Moral Esperantists. This is a strategy that grounds religious neutrality on foundational or transcendental grounds. Nature and nature's God figure importantly here. For that particular God gave us all the capacity to be rational and all rational beings, presumably, will come to a shared understanding in due course, to common convictions that sustain neutrality as between religious belief or, in other words, religious toleration. Anti-foundationalism has undermined this self-assured universalism.

But the major alternative, the modus vivendi approach, is itself subject to powerful criticism. Those who embrace it hold that political neutrality about religious matters is justifiable on the grounds of prudence—the promotion of civic order and peace being the most prudential grounds of all. Political neutrality here is a means to accommodate a variety of conflicting traditions and commitments sans any faith that commonalities will "converge" on anything other than neutrality itself. Pavlischek unpacks the weaknesses of this approach as well, including a tendency toward "mere expediency" by contrast to solid (or even not-so-solid) principle.

With this background of historic convictions and contemporary challenges cogently displayed, Pavlischek moves to the heart of the matter—his trenchant analysis and critique of the contributions of John Courtney Murray, surely the best known American Catholic thinker, to the debate about religious toleration and liberty. He claims that Murray's struggle with the issue of religious liberty was lifelong and powerfully instructive, in part because, being Roman Catholic, Murray was not so comfortably lodged within the Protestant settlement. Indeed, Murray and his fellow Catholics were placed rather well outside it in the eyes of the majority of our fellow countrymen and countrywomen in the not-so-recent past. One need only recall the fears stoked by John F. Kennedy's 1960 presidential campaign to be reminded of how deep and long-standing is the hostility of the American civic religion to those who are among us but are not quite (or so it seems) one with us.

Murray's engagement with Catholic social thought in the American liberal context is an encounter far less well known than it ought to be among American academics. Murray's story, as told so well by Pavlischek, touches vital matters that vex us yet. Some current commentators go so far as to suggest that we are in the throes of a cultural civil war, in part because the "final" questions that religion ostensibly deals with have invaded the political realm, where nothing can be settled with finality. Why is it so difficult to resolve these questions once and for all? Through the eyes and ears of one of our keenest observers and critics—John Courtney Murray—we gain a deeper appreciation of what is at stake and why those of us who are part of American liberal society—that means every American citizen—will never find a tidy way out of the dilemma. Not, that is, if we keep thinking. Pavlischek helps us to think. For that we must thank him.

Jean Bethke Elshtain

Centennial Professor of Political Science

Acknowledgments

THIS WORK BEGAN WHEN I was a graduate student at the University of Pittsburgh. A word of thanks must go to Roland Robertson, Frederick Whelan, John Chapman, and Walt Wiest, a truly interdisciplinary dissertation committee. I would be remiss if I didn't extend a special word of thanks to Tony Edwards, a masterful advisor who greatly contributed to making this book readable and a bit clearer conceptually. More than that, his confidence in the project—often greater than my own—was infectious. For his timely words of encouragement when things were not all that encouraging, I'll always be grateful. I am also thankful for more recent written comments and discussions with Kenneth Grasso, Robert Hunt, Gerard Bradley, Michael Schuck, Richard Mouw, Michael Baxter, Joan Lockwood O'Donovan, and Stanley Hauerwas, and a special thanks to Jean Bethke Elshtain for her kind words in the foreword. The mistakes, of course, are mine.

Finally, I have been blessed with a marriage to my best friend. Without her sacrifice, encouragement, trust, love, and amazing parental skills I could never have finished this project. Nancy, thank you.

Introduction

THE BASIC INTUITION THAT LED to this book arose about a decade and a half ago when, as an undergraduate, I was introduced to a little book by H. Evan Runner, entitled *Scriptural Religion and Political Task* (1974). Runner's book made quite an impact. I found his observations on the philosophical roots of the rise of religious toleration in the early modern period to be particularly suggestive, albeit somewhat troubling.

The Reformation and the Italian Renaissance, he observed, had brought an end to any commonality of faith that had once been present in Europe. Yet, because virtually everyone was committed to the axiom that agreement on fundamentals was necessary for a stable society, each group, convinced of the truth of its position, was still out to gain the common consent of Europeans. When this proved impossible, Runner explained, resort was made at the Peace of Augsburg in 1555 to the principle of *cuius regio, eius religio*. This makeshift policy, however, only accentuated the local autonomy of the princes and thus contributed further to the division of European society.

This makeshift policy created a problem. Those who thought seriously about the European situation realized, said Runner, that "a mechanical balance of forces was not the solution to the question of European stability" (73). Nevertheless, it was not exactly clear what was to be done. The situation was further complicated because this makeshift policy did not work. The religious Peace of Augsburg was followed by the Wars of Religion, which did not end until the Peace of Westphalia in 1648, which secured recognition for the Reformed, Lutheran, and Catholic communities of Europe. Runner comments:

The Peace of Westphalia remained the basis of European
public law until the outbreak of the French Revolution. The
toleration granted by it was of the old kind, but henceforth
persecution, even of groups not recognized by the treaty,
was the exception rather than the rule. A principal reason
for this tolerant execution of its provisions was not just that
men were growing weary of the struggle; it was something
much more positive. Almost imperceptibly men's minds
had been growing more tolerant. This tolerance was the
expression of a *new outlook* on the world which was rapidly
winning followers, especially among cultural leaders in the
early decades of the seventeenth century.... It was beginning
to appear as though an order of universal agreement, so
necessary for a stable society, could no longer be based
upon a common confession of Christian dogma. Many
leading thinkers were coming to the conviction that if there
was to be a really universal system of law, ethics or religion,
it would have to be based upon such principles as could
readily be acknowledged by every nation, creed and sect.
The ancient theory of universal and necessary truths of
reason, a form of natural law theory, offered itself. In their
great need men fell upon it as upon a savior. (74)

Although I didn't see it then, Runner was giving a sociological account
of the rise of rationalism in the early modern period, one that would in
many ways anticipate that of more recent work done by Richard Rorty, Quentin Skinner, and Jeffrey Stout. Runner saw rationalism as the epistemological
response to the problem of religious disunity and conflict in the early
modern period. "In the concept of Reason," said Runner, "man assures himself with respect to the two basic (and related!) needs of certainty and community" (74). I was thus introduced to the intimate relation in modern
thought between the quests for epistemic certainty and political community.
    Particularly illuminating was Runner's use of Ernst Cassirer's *The Myth
of the State* to buttress his point. There arose in the seventeenth century,
argued Cassirer, a question "that was of vital importance for the development of political thought."

Granted that it is possible and even necessary to demon-
strate a political or ethical truth in the same way as a math-

ematical truth—where can we find the principle of such a demonstration? If there is a "Euclidean" method of politics we must assume that, in this field too, we are in possession of certain axioms and postulates that are incontrovertible and infallible. Thus it became the first aim of any political theory to find out and to formulate these axioms. (Cassirer 1946, 208, cited in Runner 68-69)

The implications of what Runner and Cassirer were saying became clear to me several years later after I had done some work in philosophy of religion and epistemology. The work of antifoundational theists such as Alvin Plantinga and Nicholas Wolterstorff was particularly important, as was that of other antifoundationalists such as Richard Rorty, Alasdair MacIntyre, Stanley Hauerwas, and Jeffrey Stout. The work of these thinkers convinced me that the Rationalism of which Runner spoke, is based on what Plantinga and Wolterstorff were calling "classic foundationalism," which was no longer plausible as a theory of knowledge.

This in turn led me to the dilemma that forms the basis for this work. If, in fact, the arguments for religious toleration that arose in the early modern period were dependent on a foundationalist epistemology, that is, if they were indeed grounded in a belief in "incontrovertible and infallible" first principles, and if the antifoundationalists are correct in calling into question the supposedly incorrigible and self-evident existence of such principles, it would seem that traditional arguments for religious liberty that appeared at one time to be "self-evident" would be seriously flawed. I wanted to know how, given the collapse of foundationalism, an antifoundationalist with religious convictions might argue for religious liberty. How, if we no longer believe in "self-evident" truths, can we establish the "inalienable right" to religious liberty that in America we have traditionally viewed as axiomatic?

To this end, I considered the work of several twentieth-century Christian ethicists who have struggled with the problem. After reading in the primary and secondary literature it soon became clear that one individual stood out: the great American Jesuit theologian John Courtney Murray. Murray's attempt to deal with the problem is easily the best in terms of lucidity of analysis, historical sensitivity, and theological depth. Quite simply, among those Christian ethicists who have struggled with the problem, he is in a class by himself.

And yet I found contradictory emphases in Murray's thought, and in the thought of those who commented on his work. How, for instance, could the great American Catholic defender of religious liberty, the person who was seeking an argument for religious liberty "unencumbered to historical contingency and accommodational ad hockery" (Cuddihy 1978, 77) at the same time be suspected of "historicism" or "situationism" (Goerner, Love, Burgess, Carillo)?

This was further complicated when, after doing further research on Murray, I became aware that there was a bit of a Murray renaissance going on within the American Roman Catholic community. To put it bluntly, I found myself in the middle of an argument among different factions within the Catholic community, each seeking to claim Murray's mantle. How could it be that both "progressives" (e.g., Coleman, Hooper, and Curran) and "neoconservatives" (e.g., Weigel, Neuhaus, and Novak) were claiming him as their inspiration? On the surface, the debate can be seen as a matter of current church politics. The progressives, confronted with a Pope and magisterium they take to be less than progressive, have an interest in emphasizing the "dissenting" Murray: the Murray who challenged the magisterium, the Murray who was unjustly censured, the Murray whose "progressive" ideas about religious liberty were eventually vindicated at Vatican II. The neoconservatives, on the other hand, stress the "conservative" Murray: the Murray who took on the liberal Protestant establishment, the fiercely anti-Communist, pro-American Murray, the Murray who unequivocally would assert without apology that the Roman Catholic Church is the one true church. Because I am not a Catholic, I'm not concerned with solving these internal disputes. Nevertheless, I have become convinced that Murray's mature position on religious liberty, for better or worse, is more ambiguous than either side would admit, and that both sides to some extent trade on that ambiguity.

As I examine these ambiguities in Murray's work, it may appear at times, particularly in the final chapters, that I am doing a bit of Monday-morning quarterbacking. For this reason, I want to make it clear that my selection of Murray had little to do with his Catholicism, or with the contemporary debate over the meaning of Murray's project within the American Roman Catholic community. Rather, I chose him as an example because he grappled with the issue of religious liberty better than any twentieth-century Christian ethicist, Protestant or Catholic. Nobody remotely familiar with Murray's work could conclude that he was an easy target. So if Murray's argument is deficient at key points—and it is—then a fortiori the same can be said for his contemporaries at the same points.

* * *

John Courtney Murray was born in 1904 to a Scottish lawyer and an Irish mother. He attended a Jesuit high school in New York City, where he expressed an early interest in medicine. At the age of sixteen he joined the Society of Jesus. After receiving a B.A. from Weston College in 1926 and an M.A. from Boston College in 1927, he spent the next three years in the Philippines teaching Latin and English literature. After returning to the United States in 1930, Murray studied theology for four years at Woodstock College, a Jesuit institution in Maryland. He was ordained to the priesthood in 1933 and continued his studies at the Gregorian University in Rome, where he received his doctorate in theology in 1937. Murray then returned to Woodstock College where, except for a year spent as Visiting Professor of Medieval Philosophy at Yale University in 1951-52, he taught theology until his death in 1967.

In 1941 Murray became the editor of the newly formed journal *Theological Studies*. For a short period (1945-46), he was also an associate religion editor of *America*. During the war years, Murray was engaged in a debate over the nature and extent of Catholic intercredal cooperation with Protestants and Jews. This issue marked the first of a series of confrontations he would have with Joseph Fenton and Francis Connell. Both helped found the Catholic Theological Society of America (CTSA) and were professors of theology at the Catholic University in Washington, D.C. Connell was elected the first president of the CTSA, and in 1944 Fenton became the editor of *The American Ecclesiastical Review*, the journal from which they and others would launch their assaults against Murray's position on the question of religious liberty.

Murray wrote his first scholarly articles on the issue of religious freedom in 1945. From 1946 to 1954 Murray was preoccupied with the question of religious liberty and was engaged in a running battle with those whose sympathies lay with the *American Ecclesiastical Review*. The debate exploded into open warfare over conflicting interpretations of Pope Pius XII's December 1953 discourse *Ci riesce* (see Pelotte 1976, 43-51). Murray took the discourse to be a rejection of traditional Catholic views on church and state in general and, in particular, a rejection of the views of Cardinal Alfredo Ottaviani, operating head of the Supreme Congregation of the Holy Office. Murray had suggested in a lecture given at the Catholic University in America that Ottaviani's position on church and state had not been consonant with what Murray took to be the more liberal position expressed by the Pope. The controversy terminated with Murray's censure by Rome in 1945, largely through the efforts of Fenton, Connell, and Ottaviani (See Pelotte 1976, 46ff.).

Murray cleared his office of all works on the issue of religious liberty and church-state relations, canceled a book contract, and turned down an offer by the University of Chicago to lecture on religious liberty. At the same time, however, he became more involved in American public affairs. He was appointed by President Eisenhower to serve on the Atomic Energy Commission and became deeply involved in helping to set up the Fund for the Republic, Inc., a project which tackled the question of the relation of religion to a free society. Out of these discussions, Murray's work gained positive recognition among both academics and politicians.

Murray came to national attention with the publication of the book for which he is most famous, *We Hold These Truths: Catholic Reflections on the American Proposition*. The book mostly consisted of previously published articles and Murray intended it to be a primer on the problem of American pluralism. It appeared in late spring 1960, just in time for John F. Kennedy's presidential campaign. Murray was thrust into the national limelight when in December of that year he appeared on the cover of *Time* magazine.

In spite of his increasing popularity, Murray was not invited to participate in the Second Vatican Council and thus was not involved in the pre-Conciliar discussion of religious liberty. Nor was he present at the opening of the First Session of the Council in October 1962. However, largely through the insistence of Francis Cardinal Spellman, Murray received an official invitation to participate in subsequent sessions as a *peritus*, or expert. He was thus destined to play a crucial role in the drafting of *Dignitatis humanae*, the "Declaration on Religious Freedom" (1965).

After the Council, Murray returned to Woodstock, authored a number of articles on the Declaration and addressed a number of other public policy issues. He died of a heart attack in a taxi cab on August 16, 1967, in New York City. He is generally regarded as "the most important American Catholic thinker of the twentieth century" (Miller 1987, 218).

* * *

In the first chapter, I consider the issue of religious toleration as a problem of modern political philosophy and social ethics; more specifically, I show it is a problem of justifying political neutrality toward particular conceptions of the good. I argue that there are two basic ways in which political tolerance of religious differences can be justified. The first is a modus vivendi argument for religious toleration; the other, what I call a "Moral Esperantist" argument, a term used throughout the text as a metaphor for a political view that grounds its argument for religious toleration on a foundationalist basis. Each position constitutes a horn of what I am calling "the dilemma of religious toleration." I conclude the first chapter by considering two broad strategies for slipping between the horns of the dilemma, and argue that neither of them succeeds. I then show that there is something intellectually problematic with the concept of "tolerance." More precisely, I show that there is something odd about our desire to think of tolerance as a virtue.

Chapters 2 through 7 constitute the heart of the book. I show how Murray's work on religious liberty exemplifies the dilemma set forth in the first chapter. While Murray seemed to recognize that foundationalist or transcendental justifications for religious liberty must fail, he came to the conclusion that the traditional Catholic modus vivendi defense of religious toleration as reflected in the "thesis-hypothesis" doctrine was inadequate. Nevertheless, when he rejected liberal Protestant and secularist attempts to defend religious liberty as a natural and therefore transhistorical right, he was obliged to have recourse to collective prudence to make his case. This, I argue, barely separates him from the modus vivendi position of the traditionalists.

In the second chapter I introduce the traditional Catholic position on religious liberty prior to Vatican II's *Dignitatis humanae*, "The Declaration on Religious Liberty." I show how the traditional Catholic position is essentially a modus vivendi argument for religious toleration, and I examine Murray's first exploratory attempt to come to grips with the problem. Chapter 3 deals with Murray's continued polemic against the traditional Catholic position. I examine a number of distinctions to which Murray had recourse, and ask whether they could meet the objections of the traditionalists. I conclude that they don't.

In chapters 4 and 5 I examine in detail Murray's polemic against secularist and liberal Protestant defenses of religious liberty, respectively. I show that in his alternative interpretation of the religion clauses of the First Amendment, Murray set forth a modus vivendi interpretation, justification, and defense of religious liberty, a position that is remarkably similar to the thesis-hypothesis doctrine he also simultaneously opposed.

In chapters 6 and 7 I examine Murray's mature writings on religious liberty following his censure in 1955. I show how Murray attempted to synthesize the conflicting emphases in his polemic against the traditionalist position on the one hand and his polemic against liberal Protestants and

secularists on the other. Chapter 6 examines Murray's work on religious liberty immediately prior to and during Vatican II. Chapter 7 focuses on those
concepts that were central to Murray's mature reflection on religious liberty
following Vatican II. I argue that Murray's own position is seriously ambiguous and suggest that the ambiguity stems, not from any defect peculiar to
Murray, but from the insolubility of the dilemma itself.

Chapter 8 briefly examines the positions of Reinhold Niebuhr, John
Rawls, and Stanley Hauerwas, all of whom seem to see the dilemma and yet
find themselves caught between the horns. My hope is that this all too brief
examination of these scholars will lend further plausibility to my claim that
the dilemma of religious toleration is insoluble.

Chapter One

The Dilemma of Religious Toleration

MODERN LIBERAL POLITICAL THEORY can fairly be characterized by a tolerance toward a diversity of ideals and forms of life within a given polity. Perhaps the most fundamental assumption of liberalism is that government must be neutral on the question of the good life (Dworkin 1985, 191). However, many liberal moral and political theorists are becoming increasingly aware that this tolerant stance has traditionally been justified by appeals to views of human flourishing that are themselves controversial (Larmore 1987, 51). This growing recognition forms the basis of the dilemma of religious toleration, which can be illuminated by considering two standard approaches by which political neutrality toward competing conceptions of the good life[1] is justified.

The first sees the political order as a modus vivendi or means of accommodation among individuals or groups with divergent conceptions of the good. This view tends to be associated with a "convergence defense" of political legitimacy: that is, it seeks to discover a possible convergence of rational support for certain institutions, laws, and public policy from the separate motivational standpoints of distinct individuals or groups (Nagel 1987, 218).

The other view requires that the political order express the liberal's own personal ideal, "in the sense that its highest ideal must mirror or coincide with what are [the liberal's] deepest commitments" (Larmore 1987, 91). It is closely related to a "common standpoint defense" of political legitimacy in which the political order seeks a common standpoint or Archimedean point that everyone can occupy, and which guarantees agreement about what is acceptable (Nagel 1987, 218). While a convergence theory begins with

9

motives that are diverse because they refer back primarily to group- or self-interests, a common-standpoint theory starts from a single, universally held desire that does not appeal to self- or group-interest. This supposedly will guarantee a common social aim.

I will refer to the convergence approach to political tolerance or neutrality as the modus vivendi approach, while I will refer to the common standpoint approach as the Esperantist approach.[2] The latter term is derived from "Esperanto," the term ascribed to a supposedly universal language. Moral Esperanto is characterized by its intent to abstract from the vagaries of particular moral and religious traditions (see Stout 1988, 5). It thus strives to present an ethic that is ahistorical and tradition-independent in that what is unique to a particular religious or moral tradition is to have no weight in political discourse. Appeal is made instead to "principles undeniable to any rational person and therefore independent of all those social and independent particularities which the Enlightenment thinkers took to be the mere accidental clothing of reason in particular times and places" (MacIntyre 1988, 6).

Moral Esperanto currently is spoken in two main dialects: Kantian and Millian. Despite their differences—the latter speaks the language of utilitarianism while the former speaks of others as ends-in-themselves—each understands tolerance toward divergent conceptions of the good within a political order in basically the same way—namely, as expressing the detachment that *ought* to hold universally since it expresses the detachment all rational persons *ought* to have toward a substantial ideal of human flourishing.

For example, if in Kantian fashion it is maintained that the right is prior to the good, that the autonomy of the individual remains the highest ideal, that the autonomous individual should (or can) sustain a certain aloofness from his notion of the good, then political neutrality toward divergent conceptions of the good, including religious conceptions, ought to be a universal norm for the political order that is not contingent upon either empirical/historical circumstances or particular conceptions of the good life. Alternatively, the moral Esperantist might follow Mill's "experimentalist" attitude and argue that the best way to arrive at a firm conception of the good life is to participate in a number of different ones, comparing and rejecting those that are less fulfilling, and argue also that experimentalism would be hampered if government set out to foster only one or some while rejecting other ideals of the good life (see Larmore 1987, 51).

As specifically applied to the political toleration of religious differences, the aim of Esperantist liberalism is to avoid holding the notion of religious liberty hostage to calculations about how to avoid civil conflict over religious differences. It proposes that religious liberty not be tied to such contingencies and insists that religion be tied to a broader understanding of rights in general. Religious beliefs for the liberal Esperantist are worthy of respect, not by virtue of their substantive content, but rather by virtue of their being the product of the free and voluntary choice of rational individuals under "constraints of impartiality"; agents who supposedly choose their ends instead of having their ends as constitutive of who they are (see Sandel 1983).

In opposition to the modus vivendi approach, the Esperantist defense of religious liberty argues for abstention from religious intolerance or repression even in cases in which they might in some way be effective or otherwise good on balance. Esperantists want to ground such abstention on principles that would be absolute, conclusive, and without exception. They seek (and have sought) to regard principles of religious toleration as permanent and universally valid moral principles, and are thus concerned with universality. A defense of religious toleration can be supplied by simple deductive argument: All acts of religious persecution are wrong and not to be done; this act I am contemplating would be of that sort; therefore it is not to be done (see Kilcullen 1988, 108).

By contrast, the advocate of the modus vivendi approach is not concerned with hypothetical universalization, but rather with the likely consequences of a given policy of tolerance or intolerance toward her own group under given circumstances. Religious tolerance may (or may not) become an ideal of the political order depending upon certain historical/social contingencies. The advocate of this approach will take up a neutral political position by abstracting from her substantive conception of the good life, religious or otherwise, but only as far as necessary and only in the political realm. Thus, she does not repudiate her conception nor lessen her attachment to it. Rather, what she takes to be of ultimate significance remains constitutive of who and what she is. Political neutrality, thus understood, becomes a means of accommodation—a means of solving specific problems that arise in the face of conflicting commitments. It is not a standpoint from which one's purposes and commitments are expressed. Such neutrality is strictly political because one's substantial understanding of the good remains paramount in nonpolitical life.

While the modus vivendi view starts from a consideration of consequences, it is not strictly speaking a utilitarian or consequentialist argument in that "it does not presuppose that the goodness or badness of an action always consists entirely in the goodness or badness of its consequences"

(Kilcullen 1988, 112). Nor is it egocentric since it is not merely an appeal to "self-interest" in the narrow sense. "The consequences to be considered may include effects on the progress of the true religion, and may not include effects on the worldly interests of true believers or potential converts—what consequences are allowed to count depends on the moral code of those called on to made the calculation" (Kilcullen 1988, 112).[3]

A number of reasons could move one to urge toleration under this conception: a desire for civil peace following a period of emotional and physical exhaustion of political fighting or even civil war, sympathy for those whose ideals are different yet similar to one's own, the knowledge that one's right to advance and pursue one's own conception of the good, at least in private, will be protected if others also agree to bracket their conceptions in the political realm, the fear that a "friendly regime" will overstep their bounds and distort the true faith. Ordered liberty, under this conception, is achieved by a skillful constitutional design framed to guide self- and group- interests to work for social purposes through the use of various devices such as the division and balance of power (see Rawls 1987, 2).

The distinction between the Esperantist and modus vivendi approaches can be seen if we consider briefly John Rawls' famous "veil of ignorance," behind which the parties in the original position do not know the content of their substantive religious and moral beliefs. Nor do they know whether they belong to a strong or weak religious sect. A modus vivendi approach would lift the veil and allow the parties to know the content and strength of their beliefs. Whether what emerges is a particular policy of suppression or toleration would then become a concrete decision-making problem. Civil intolerance of a particular way of life would not be ruled out a priori. In fact, those who are convinced that religiously and morally deficient ways of life will pollute the environment and corrupt their children would act quite rationally, under this conception, in opposing a policy of toleration. An Esperantist approach, on the other hand, would insist on maintaining the veil, giving what it would hope to be sufficient justification for not allowing the parties to know the content of their religious or moral beliefs in the initial bargaining situation.

The Modus Vivendi Approach as One Horn of the Dilemma

We can identify three fundamental criticisms of the modus vivendi approach to religious toleration. These criticisms are, I think, sufficiently plausible to constitute one horn of the dilemma for an advocate of religious toleration.

First, it is claimed that this view sets forth a defense of religious liberty that is opportunistic and based on mere expediency. Its basis is not moral. Secondly, it results in an unstable political order. Finally, from a different angle, it is often argued that what emerges from the convergence of separate individual and group interests is too thin to provide a common political purpose and that the process by which that thinness is maintained tends to subvert the virtue required to sustain the common good.

The first two criticisms of the modus vivendi approach are made by John Rawls in his article "The Idea of an Overlapping Consensus" (1987). Rawls' position is particularly relevant because he claims his own position escapes the horns of the dilemma. He wants to steer a course between "liberalism as a modus vivendi secured by a convergence of self- and group-interests as coordinated and balanced by well-designed constitutional arrangements–and a liberalism founded on a comprehensive moral doctrine such as that of Kant and Mill" (1987, 23-24).

Rawls characterizes the "modus vivendi" approach as analogous to a treaty between two states whose national aims and interests put them at odds. When the two states negotiate a treaty, each considers it wise and prudent to ensure that the terms and conditions are constructed so that public knowledge of a treaty violation would be disadvantageous for either state. Both parties adhere to the treaty because they both consider it in their interest to do so. Although a state's interest in its reputation as a state that honors treaties is also taken into consideration, generally speaking, each state is ready to pursue its goals at the expense of the other. If the circumstances change, they would do so. Rawls finds this situation analogous to one in which social consensus is founded on self- or group-interests or on the outcome of political bargaining. Such a view, Rawls claims, contrasts with his own view that stresses an "overlapping consensus" because his is a moral conception while the modus vivendi view is not.

We are not concerned at this time with critically addressing Rawls' charge that such a view is sub-moral. Rawls' proposed tertium quid will be examined in the final chapter. At this time I simply want to note that despite his recent rejection of a liberalism based on what he calls "comprehensive moral conceptions," he still admits that his view includes "conceptions of society as citizens and persons" that others may not share. He also seems to have maintained a strong moral-prudential distinction that is usually associated with the "moral point of view" or the language of moral Esperanto. For that reason, his objection has force only if the relevancy and adequacy of moral Esperantism or something similar has been established.

For reasons that will become clearer throughout this work, particularly when I discuss Rawls' views in the final chapter, I do not consider this a particularly devastating criticism of the modus vivendi approach to political neutrality. It is worth mentioning, however, because Rawls' claim that such an approach is sub-moral closely parallels the criticism made against the traditional (pre-Vatican II) Catholic defense of religious liberty. The most fundamental criticism of that position was that it was based on "mere expediency" because it refused to defend a strict separation of church and state and religious liberty as a matter of principle, and reserved the right to restrict religious liberty should a church gain hegemony in a particular polity. To liberal Protestants such a view was considered, at best, sub-moral.

In Rawls' view the modus vivendi/convergence theory is not only opportunistic and hence less than moral; it also tends to promote political instability. The social unity that emerges under this conception "is only apparent as its stability *is contingent on circumstances* remaining such as not to upset the fortunate convergence of interests" (1988, 13, emphasis mine). Again, Rawls claims his own notion of an overlapping consensus differs from a modus vivendi conception in that

> it meets the urgent political requirement to fix, *once and for all*, the content of basic rights and liberties, and to assign them special priority. Doing this takes those guarantees off the political agenda and puts them beyond the calculus of social interests, thereby establishing clearly and firmly the terms of social cooperation on a footing of mutual respect. To regard that calculus as relevant in these matters leaves the status and content of those rights and liberties as unsettled; it subjects them to the shifting circumstances of time and place, and by greatly raising the stakes of political controversy, dangerously increases the insecurity and hostility of public life. Thus, the unwillingness to take these [controversial] matters off the agenda perpetuates the deep divisions latent in society; it betrays a readiness to revive those antagonisms in the hope of gaining a more favorable position should later circumstances prove propitious. (1987, 25, emphasis mine)

Because the modus vivendi approach keeps certain ideals of the good life upfront in the rough and tumble world of politics, it introduces a vice, instability, into the political process. This, it should be noted, is an empirical claim. At times Rawls seems to imply that a well-framed constitution, through the use of various devices such as separation and balance of powers could provide sufficient stability to guide self- and group-interests to work for the common good. Still, one gets the impression that even if a convergence of interests resulted in a stable society it would nevertheless be unacceptable from a moral point of view.

A third objection to the modus vivendi approach is more fundamental and comes from another angle. This has come to be referred to as the "communitarian" position and is represented by theorists as diverse as Michael Sandel, Charles Taylor, Alasdair MacIntyre, Roberto Unger, Benjamin Barber, Stanley Hauerwas, Robert Bellah, and Michael Walzer. The basic criticism here is that what emerges from the convergence of interests is too thin to provide any common national purpose and more importantly that this thinness "plays back" upon other nonpolitical spheres.

The force of this criticism is captured by Charles Taylor. He asks, "Why can't we make [modus vivendi] liberalism itself our common purpose?" He concedes that it may work pragmatically such that it may be accepted by enough people "to muffle the potential conflict" (Taylor 1987, 20). However, such a solution has severe problems.

For one thing, it tends to sideline or even undercut a sense of public virtue, or a strong sense of commitment to the well-being and survival of society. Since free societies must live by spontaneous cohesion, the lack of such spells doom. When fear and coercion must take up the slack in the absence of virtue and spontaneous commitment, despotism is not far off (Taylor 1987, 9).

Moreover, Taylor finds "a strange pragmatic contradiction at the core of this position."

> Common purposes are only sustained to the extent that people don't identify themselves exclusively as individuals, but also see themselves at least in part as essentially defined by their adherence to the political community. Common as against merely convergent goods by their very definition must be "ours" as against simply mine and yours and his and hers severally. The common understanding of our way of life as sustaining liberal [i.e., negative] freedom would be in its situation in our lives a common purpose. But what it exalts as valuable is exclusively individual self-

fulfillment, plus relations of fairness between these self-directing individuals. It offers a picture of human life in which common purposes have no valid place, in which they appear more often as potential obstacles to individual self-development.... A kind of philosophical atomism becomes widespread by which all public enterprises are construed as based on merely convergent purposes.

If this were merely a philosophical inconsistency or if it were a problem that could be hermetically sealed off at the political level, it could perhaps be dismissed as relatively unimportant or even irrelevant. But the claim of many communitarians is that this view threatens to undermine notions of community at all levels (e.g., family, neighborhood, church, ethnic group) as well as the political, thus undermining the very sources of liberalism's own strength. Not only is the consensus that arises out of converging differences too thin, but also the commitment to the diverging perspectives themselves becomes fatefully weakened by the very nature of the process. (See also MacIntyre 1988, 342ff. and Hauerwas 1981, 161, 170). Taylor and other "communitarians" fear that a stress on negative liberty and a purely modus vivendi approach will result in what has come to be termed the "naked public square" (Neuhaus 1984).

One of the results of the modus vivendi position is that, given a sufficient plurality of divergent conceptions of the good, the two principle dialects of moral Esperanto win by default. To mix metaphors for a moment, we may say that the public square cannot remain naked—some language must be spoken there. Even if it is recognized that Millian consequentialism and Kantian deontology have no tradition-independent status we are nevertheless tempted to speak those languages not only in the public square, but also in those areas of our lives where they are not appropriate.

As Stout observes, the first tempts us into speaking the language of the marketplace all the time such that all aspects of our lives are reduced to "units of pleasure and pain, satisfaction and dissatisfaction, so that they can be absorbed into the calculus of utility." The Kantian dialect of Esperanto stresses minimal decency rather than the good life. For this reason one can agree with Stout that it is more modest and less harmful than the Millian dialect. But even if Kantians surrender their claim to "occupy the entire moral landscape" through their a priori "exclusion of most assessment of conduct, character and community from view," the language of minimal rights nevertheless wins by default. What Stout says of the Kantian form of moral Esperanto is also true of a modus vivendi position that excludes thicker conceptions of the good from the public square for the sake of public peace.

> It provides no means for surveying the dangers that ensue when its central concepts begin to pervade the entire culture, eroding not only the capacity to acquire virtues that go beyond minimal decency but also the ability to understand a kind of justice that does not consist in procedural fairness. (Stout 1988, 286)

Unlike the Esperantists, who advocate the naked public square as a matter of principle, the modus vivendi argument for religious toleration leaves open the question as to the extent to which religion or any other "thick conception of the good" is to influence so-called temporal or secular affairs. The desire to escape this horn stems not only from the recognition that the public square cannot remain naked, but also from the recognition that once it is conceded that it is merely a matter of degree just how far a particular conception should go in advancing and pursuing its own conception of the good, there seems to be no a priori way of determining just how far a given religion or coalition of religions may go in such influence to include suppression of heresies or false religion(s) for the sake of the common good. The desire to say something permanent and transtemporal makes the Esperantist approach appealing.

The Esperantist Approach as the Other Horn of the Dilemma

The Esperantist approach constitutes the other horn of the dilemma, and it is subject to two fundamental criticisms. First, it seems to rely on a thoroughly discredited epistemology. Secondly, it distorts the history of religious toleration as it developed in the West over the past three centuries, and thus encourages a form of collective false consciousness and self-deception.

A central contention of this work is that an Esperantist defense of religious liberty rests on an enormously popular but now thoroughly discredited epistemology, namely classic foundationalism. According to Alvin Plantinga, foundationalism is the view

> that some of our beliefs are based on others. According to the foundationalist, a rational noetic structure will *have a foundation*—a set of beliefs not accepted on the basis of

> others; in a rational noetic structure some beliefs will be
> basic. Nonbasic beliefs, of course, will be accepted on the
> basis of other beliefs, which may be accepted on the basis
> of other beliefs, and so on until the foundations are
> reached. In a rational noetic structure, therefore, every non-
> basic belief is ultimately accepted on the basis of basic
> beliefs. (1983b, 52)

Thus beliefs, or attitudes toward propositions, come in two mutually exclusive and exhaustive kinds, basic and nonbasic. A "noetic structure" "is the
set of propositions [a person] believes, together with certain epistemic relations that hold among him and these propositions" (48).

Nothing is particularly problematic with this definition of foundationalism. A dispute arises, however, over what is taken to be "properly basic." At
issue is the question over what is proper or correct for us to hold as a basic
belief. And that, of course, involves a normative claim, very much similar to
debates over morality. As one interpreter of Plantinga puts it:

> Just as debates over morality concern, among other things,
> not how human beings do behave but how it is correct and
> proper to behave to *be moral*, so the debates over basic
> beliefs concern not whether people hold certain beliefs as
> basic but which of these beliefs it is correct and proper for
> them to hold to *be rational*. (Hoitenga 1991, 179)

According to the classical foundationalist, not just any proposition can
function as a properly basic belief. Ancient and medieval philosophers typically restricted properly basic beliefs to what is evident to the senses and
what is self-evident. Modern foundationalism agrees with ancient and medieval foundationalism on the self-evident truths of reason, but rejects what is
evident to the senses in favor of incorrigibility or of what *appears* to the
senses. This is an important shift, but because they agree in sharing a restrictive criterion for what constitutes a properly basic belief we can lump them
together with Plantinga under the label "classical foundationalism."

Thus, to put it simply, classical foundationalism holds that:

> a proposition p is properly basic for a person S if and only
> if p is either self-evident to S or incorrigible for S.

Self-evident propositions are necessarily true or false and include simple arithmetical truths such as

(1) 2+1=3;

simple truths of logic, such as

(2) all bachelors are unmarried men;

and certain propositions expressing identity and diversity such as

(3) blueness is distinct from redness.

Incorrigible propositions are those which fall short of logical necessity and yet cannot be doubted. For instance, a statement such as

(4) I see a red book on the table

is not incorrigible. It makes a claim about something outside my consciousness in the external world about which I may be mistaken. Perhaps I am color blind, such that the book on the table is really green. Or perhaps it is not really a book, but something that just looks like a book. Or, I may be dreaming or may have been hypnotized into believing that there is a red book on my table. On the other hand, propositions such as

(5) I seem to see a red book on the table

or

(6) I am appeared to red bookly

as reports about what is immediately present in my consciousness are incorrigible. I may be mistaken about whether or not a red book is on the table, but I can never be mistaken about seeming to perceive a red book on the table. As incorrigible propositions, (5) and (6) are properly basic and I have a right to believe them without support from any other belief. The crucial question is whether a rational person may take other less trivial propositions as properly basic.

Plantinga has leveled two devastating objections to attempts to limit foundational propositions to self-evident or incorrigible propositions. The first criticism is that classic foundationalism is too restrictive in allowing what is to constitute a properly basic belief. He thus offers counterexamples of beliefs that appear to be properly basic but are ruled out from being so by classical foundationalism. If classical foundationalism is true,

> then enormous quantities of what we all in fact believe are irrational.... Relative to propositions that are self-evident and incorrigible, most of the beliefs that form the stock in trade of ordinary everyday life are not probable.... Consider all those propositions that entail, say, that there are enduring physical objects, or that there are persons distinct from myself, or that the world has existed for more than five minutes; none of these propositions, I think, is more probable than not with respect to what is self-evident or incorrigible for me. (Plantinga 1983, 59-60)

The basic strategy here is to argue that any theory that casts doubts on the rationality of memory beliefs, belief in the external world or other minds, all categories of beliefs that we take for granted as veridical, is in some way deficient.

Secondly, and probably more devastating to classical foundationalism and attempts to speak moral Esperanto, is the claim that the foundationalist epistemology is self-referentially incoherent and thus fails its own test of rationality. The proposition "properly basic beliefs must be either self-evident or incorrigible" is itself neither self-evident nor incorrigible. More formally, the proposition,

> a proposition p is properly basic for a person S if and only
> if p is either self-evident to S or incorrigible for S

is neither self-evident nor incorrigible, nor does it seem to follow from propositions that are. The foundationalist therefore accepts at least one belief as properly basic to his noetic structure even though it does not satisfy his own criteria of rationality.

Both criticisms open the door to allowing some beliefs into the foundation of our noetic structure that are neither self-evident nor incorrigible. The crucial question is whether belief in God is among those beliefs. It does not follow that belief in God is properly basic since the class of properly basic beliefs might be larger than what classic foundationalists think it is, but still not broad enough to admit belief in God. But the problem is that atheists or anti-theists have to give a reason for theists to think such is the case.

Here, some theists, most notably Alvin Plantinga, have boldly asserted that the proposition "God exists" is much like other properly basic beliefs such as belief in the existence of the external world, memory beliefs, and the existence of other minds. "Belief in God is properly basic. It is entirely acceptable, desirable, right, proper, and rational to accept belief in God without any argument or evidence whatever" (1983, 39). It is not necessary here to detail exactly how Plantinga considers the proposition "God exists" as analogous to perceptual beliefs, memory beliefs, and beliefs ascribing mental states to other persons (see Plantinga 1982, 270ff.). What is important, however, is to see the implication of this rather bold move. If a theist is entirely within his epistemic rights to believe in God, then it would seem to follow that the atheist (or anti-theist) has no epistemic privilege over that of the theist. At the very least theism is not irrational.

Now, if the status of atheism, or in political-cultural terms, secularism, is not epistemologically privileged (i.e., if the proposition "God exists" is properly basic, and the believer is within her epistemic rights in believing that God exists), it would seem quite difficult for the atheist or secularist to claim moral or political advantage simply on that basis. To put it bluntly, if the assault on the foundationalist project is successful, the claim that the political order ought to govern or legislate from "the presumption of atheism" (see Flew 1976) is no less dogmatic than the claim that it should govern and legislate from the "presumption of theism" or perhaps a particular brand of theism. The naked public square would have no a priori privilege over a thickly clothed public square.

The collapse of classical foundationalism has not only affected the way theists such as Plantinga approach epistemological questions. It is also why many liberals are taking a second look at the so-called existence of self-evident "rights." The existence of such rights, once taken as almost axiomatic among Anglo-American moral philosophers, has become a matter of heated controversy now that the epistemic grounding for these rights has been challenged. Such views are now often seen as embodying simply one among many traditions, thereby subverting claims to universality that all persons must accept, supposedly on the pain of irrationality.

This ultimately accounts for why the attempt to speak moral Esperanto in political philosophy is now increasingly subject to the criticism of contemporary liberals. Michael Sandel (1983) centers his criticism on the claim that what he calls "deontological liberalism" rests on a very specific voluntarist and nominalist conception of the person in which the beliefs held by the self are not constitutive of that self. Priority is given instead to a self that is unencumbered by convictions antecedent to choice. Undue preference is given to what Sandel argues is an internally inconsistent psychological anthropology rather than an ontological one.

Recently John Rawls, partially in response to the criticism of Sandel and others, has argued that when ahistorical Kantian notions of autonomy and Millian notions of individuality serve as the only appropriate foundations for a constitutional regime, "liberalism becomes but another sectarian doctrine" (1985, 246). Larmore charges that those who follow Kant and Mill in coupling their political theory with a corresponding notion of what in general is their personal ideal, "have betrayed in fact the liberal spirit" (1987, 129). Therefore, he argues that liberalism can no longer justify itself by appealing to some particular and controversial view of human flourishing. Rather, "its fundamental justification must be one that foregoes any appeal to the ideals whose controversial character sets the problem, after all, for political liberalism" (1987, 51).

John Horton is representative of a number of moral and political philosophers who have asked whether Mill's concept of harm can provide an Archimedean point for what should what should not be legally tolerated. Horton argues that a conception of what is harmful is at least in part constituted by one's beliefs, and cannot be conceived of as independent of particular moral perspectives. Briefly put, that which is thought to be harmful depends on what is held to be valuable, and insofar as what is thought to be valuable is a matter of disagreement and controversy, so is what is conceived as harmful (1985, 115). Thus,

> When the question of legislation arises, it will often be necessary to prohibit what some see as harmless though others do not, and permit what some see as harmful though others disagree. In any community in which there are significant differences in moral viewpoint there will be no alternative to this. However, in so far as liberalism purports to maintain some kind of neutrality between different moral perspectives it fails to recognize this and attempts the impossible. (132)

Horton then asks rhetorically, "Are we to believe that the real and deep moral differences that divide humanity will not be reflected in different conceptions of what is harmful?" If so, he comments, then "liberalism is in bad trouble" (132–33). This, of course, opens the door to considering that what a theistic society takes to be harmful (blasphemy, heresy, false worship) might be different from what an atheistic or secularist society might take as harmful.

One of the more powerful liberal critics of what we are calling Esperantist liberalism is Richard Rorty. Rorty argues that just as the Enlightenment proposed to bracket many of the standard theological topics that had prior to that time been considered necessary to a well-ordered polity, so we must now for purposes of social theory bracket many standard topics of philosophical inquiry such as "the nature of selfhood, the motive of moral behavior, and the meaning of human life." We should, he urges, "treat these as irrelevant to politics as [Thomas] Jefferson thought questions about the Trinity and transubstantiation" (Rorty 1988, 261–62). Rorty thus urges a pragmatic liberalism in which democracy has priority over philosophy.

Rorty's project leads us to consider the second problem with the Esperantist approach. Suppose that the criticisms of the foundationalist project are correct. If the case for religious liberty has traditionally been made on the assumption that foundationalism was a sound theory of knowledge, would not then our belief in religious liberty, for those reasons and on that basis, create a form of a false consciousness and collective self-deception? Perhaps just as classic foundationalism can be understood as the quest for self-evident and incorrigible truths that would stem the tide of skepticism in knowledge, so Esperantist liberalism can be seen as the search for ahistorical, transtemporal, self-evident, or incorrigible moral first principles—principles that could trump bids for political dominance by a particular religion. And just as epistemic foundationalism gains its strength and plausibility from the fear of skepticism, so Esperantist liberalism gains its strength and plausibility from the fear of religious persecution should a given religion establish cultural hegemony.

A number of contemporary moral philosophers and political historians have called Esperantist liberalism into question on the basis of their study of the rise of the concept of religious liberty in the early modern period. Particularly important in this regard are the writings of Rorty, Quentin Skinner, and Jeffrey Stout, all of whom suggest that Esperantist liberalism was less a contributor toward modern views on religious liberty than it was a result of the factual religious diversity which appeared to make it necessary.

Rorty argued in his highly influential and controversial *Philosophy and the Mirror of Nature* (1979) that the modernist quest for incorrigible foundations to knowledge is the result of an understanding of the mind as a mirror of nature—a repository of world representations—invented under particular circumstances at a particular point in time. It began with the Cartesian quest for certainty in the seventeenth century and was carried into contemporary thought through Kantian and neo-Kantian attempts to provide transcendental groundings for epistemology and morals. Briefly stated, Rorty argues that since historical analysis now reveals the socio/historical contingency of the quest for foundations of knowledge, we should now be liberated from this quest.

Quentin Skinner's historical investigations into *The Foundations of Modern Political Thought* (1978) are also particularly relevant, especially his description and analysis of the sixteenth-century sociopolitical situation of the French Calvinists—the Huguenots. Skinner shows how the Huguenots unintentionally—out of the necessity for survival—secularized political discourse by being forced into making

> the epoch-making move from a purely religious theory of resistance, depending on the idea of a covenant to uphold the laws of God, to a genuinely political theory of revolution, based on the idea of a contract which gives rise to a moral right (and not merely a religious duty) to resist. (Skinner 1978, 2:322; see also Stout 1981, 236)

Particularly instructive is Skinner's analysis of why the Huguenots had good reason to make this "epoch-making move" from a vocabulary of religious duties to one of political rights. The sociopolitical position of the Huguenots stood in sharp contrast to the situation in Scotland, where the Calvinists had broader support among the population and therefore less need to appeal to political rights. Scottish Calvinists tended to argue that they had a religious duty to resist tyranny. By contrast, the French Calvinists, as a beleaguered minority that had just endured the massacres of 1572, needed to perform "the vital ideological task of appealing not merely to their own followers, but to the broadest possible spectrum of Catholic moderates and malcontents" (2:322).

> On the one hand, it was essential for them to construct an ideology capable of defending the lawfulness of resisting on

grounds of conscience, since they needed to be able to reassure their followers about the legitimacy of engaging in a direct revolutionary confrontation with the established government. On the other hand, it was no less essential to produce a more constitutionalist and less purely sectarian ideology of opposition, since they obviously needed to broaden the basis of their support if they were to stand a chance of winning what amounted to a pitched battle with the Valois monarchy. (Skinner 1978 2:310)

The French Calvinists were desperately in need of ideological devices capable of persuading their religious opponents. They did this by bracketing their own specifically religious conceptions of authority. While such religious conceptions of authority were the only available means to legitimate the religious duty to resist, such arguments were bound to work against the Huguenots in that religiously divided situation. Therefore, "they devised tools of legitimation that made religious disagreements inessential, thereby contributing heavily to the secularization of public discourse." They thus helped to "create a point of view from which questions of 'rights' and 'justice' could be considered without allowing religious commitments to enter in" (Stout 1981, 237, emphasis mine).[4]

Out of this conflict rose the modern conception of the state:

> The acceptance of the modern idea of the State presupposes that political society is held to exist solely for political purposes. The endorsement of this secularized viewpoint remained impossible as long as it was assumed that all temporal rulers had a duty to uphold godly as well as peaceable government. The sixteenth-century reformers were entirely at one with their Catholic adversaries on this point: they all insisted that one of the main aims of government must be to maintain "true religion" and the Church of Christ. As we have seen, this in turn means that the religious upheavals of the Reformation made a paradoxical yet vital contribution to the crystallizing of the modern, secularized concept of the State. For as soon as the protagonists of the rival creeds showed that they were willing to fight each other to the death, it began to seem obvious to a number of *politique* theorists that, if there were to be any

> prospect of achieving peace, the powers of the State would
> have to be divorced from the duty to uphold any particular
> faith. (Skinner 1978, 2:352)

This new conception of the state and the new concept of distinctly political
rights came to fruition in the work of the political natural rights theorists of
the sixteenth and seventeenth centuries. Their work can in large measure be
seen as an attempt to minimize the effects of religious disagreement. This
accounts, for instance, for Grotius' attempt to establish a natural law completely independent of the existence of God.[5]

Jeffrey Stout's work can be seen as a critical synthesis of Rorty's insights
into the development of foundationalism in the early modern period and
Skinner's investigations into the rise of the modern state and religious toleration in the same period. Stout leans heavily on the works of Skinner and
Rorty in order to provide a genealogy of the Esperantist position as it applies
specifically on the question of religious toleration. In *The Flight from Authority* Stout fine-tunes Rorty's analysis of the quest for epistemic and moral certainty on the basis of an independent criterion of rationality by focusing on
the breakdown of religious authority brought forth by the Reformation and
the subsequent Wars of Religion. Since there was no longer a single authority to settle equally plausible interpretations of the Christian tradition, and
because the Protestant attempt to reestablish this authority in the doctrine
of *sola scriptura* had failed, recourse was made to a search for self-evident
and incorrigible truths, independent of particular religious truth-claims. The
most notable philosophical figure in this early modern period is, of course,
Descartes (37–61).

Stout argues that the Cartesian and subsequently Kantian vantage point
of rational individuals under constraints of impartiality is an artificial reaction to the collapse of the old authorities and to the breakup of a relatively
homogeneous Christendom. The attempts of the early modern theorists to
ground ethical theory and the "moral point of view" transcendentally or
foundationally are the theoretical culmination of a new tradition that had to
justify the heightened need for cooperation. They were confronted with the
attempt to eliminate the least attractive features of religious disagreement. In
the early modern period, any point of view in which specifically *religious*
considerations or conceptions of the good remained dominant was incapable of providing a basis for the reasonable and peaceful solution of religious
conflict. "Incompatible appeals to authority seemed equally reasonable, and

therefore equally suspect, as well as vehicles of rational persuasion" (Stout 1981, 235).

This had both intellectual and social consequences. The intellectual conflict was reflected in the theological standoff between Catholics and Protestants as well as in the ethical controversies within the respective traditions. However, the social consequences were more telling, since they involved the devastation caused by the religious wars. Quite simply, "the differentiation of the moral point of view was a result of attempts to nullify the effects of religious disagreement" (235). The attempt to demarcate "the moral point of view," and the attempt to speak moral Esperanto, stemmed from the basically correct intuition put in place by particular circumstances that made cooperation and hence toleration seem more important than other values for which one could strive.

Stout argues that the early foundationalists and subsequently their Kantian and neo-Kantian offspring were right to secularize public discourse in the interest of minimizing the ill effects of religious disagreement. Nevertheless there was a cost. If we accept their own understanding of what they were doing we run the risk of collective self-deception.

> We are not bound, however, to accept our ancestors' interpretation of their accomplishment. They did not, by virtue of criticizing authority and theology, raise themselves above history or make themselves autonomous from tradition. In supposing that they did, they instead shielded their own most significant assumptions from sight and thus made the task of contemporary criticism more difficult. *By conflating the moral imperative to contain the effects of religious disagreement with the myth of the completely autonomous man, they made what was in fact a form of self-deception seem the height of virtue.* One effect of this self-deception was a highly misleading picture of the past, a picture which obscured from view just those features of the past that might raise doubts about the myth of autonomous man and the limitations of modern morality. Another was the paradoxical idea that the point of view from which we should appraise and select basic social principles is one in which conceptions of the good are in principle accorded the status of prejudices to be ignored (242, emphasis mine)

Self-deception, then, is the second core criticism of Esperantist liberalism that makes it a horn of the dilemma which needs to be avoided.

It is not surprising then, that we should find Stout in his most recent book, *Ethics after Babel* (1988, 226), advocating a modus vivendi justification for religious liberty and admitting its consequences.

> The right to religious freedom, although real enough, obtain[s] only under particular social-historical conditions. If it could be shown by modes of reasoning commonly recognized that belief in a specific sort of God were both justified and essential for realization of the common good, we ought not to go on showing liberal tolerance to religious dissenters. It is precisely because we fall so short of rational agreement or objective certainty in religious matters that the right to religious freedom obtains in our society. Religious liberty is justified by conditions of discord and uncertainty that might not always obtain.

Stout, as a nontheistic antifoundationalist is thus led to conclude that should the proposition "God exists," or more precisely "A particular kind of God exists," come to be widely accepted as properly basic ("modes of reasoning commonly recognized"), the "right" the religious liberty might not obtain.

The modus vivendi approach to religious toleration is rarely stated so forthrightly. Such frankness, however, causes considerable anxiety among those who want to say something more definitive about the "right" to religious freedom. Therefore I want to outline two broad strategies designed to slip between the horns of the dilemma. Both focus from different angles on the word "know" in the question, "How can tolerance be a virtue when it requires me to do nothing to stop an action which I know to be wrong?" The first strategy is a relativist one. The other is a fallibilist approach.[6]

The Relativist Strategy as an Attempt to Slip between the Horns

It might seem at first glance that someone who took a relativist view of religion and morality would be committed to tolerance as the one virtue he must accept (Harrison 1982, 232). Given the inability of anyone to make a rational choice between alternative religio-moral systems, it would seem that the relativist must necessarily come to the conclusion that we cannot afford the luxury of considering those who disagree with us to be willfully wicked. To insist on backing one's own ultimately unfounded moral or religious belief would be insensitive, self-righteous, and arrogant. An intolerant attitude, the relativist might say, stems from the blind and uncritical, or perhaps even an open-eyed and critical, acceptance of one's own morality/religion as objectively correct. Since the central claim of relativism is that no religious and moral system is morally superior or objectively correct, it seems relativism would yield tolerance as the one virtue the relativist must accept.

"Relativism," according to Geoffrey Harrison, "is a metaethical theory, and its truth or falsity is a question for an outside observer" (239). A moral relativist after examining a number of competing religio-moral systems concludes that when "looked at objectively" one religio-moral system is as good as another (Harrison 1982, 232). The problem comes when we ask what the relativist can mean by "as good as."

"As good as" can be taken in either a moral or nonmoral sense. Suppose we give it a moral interpretation. If one could say that system A is as morally good as system B, then there could be no moral reason to prefer A or B, and hence no reason to prevent anyone from acting in accord with either A or B.

The problem, of course, is that the relativist cannot put such an interpretation on "as good as," simply because, when he does that, he is making a moral judgment. And, when the relativist qua relativist makes such a moral judgment, he ceases to be an outside observer of competing religio-moral systems and becomes a participant within a particular religio-moral system who is thus making judgments from a particular religio-moral standpoint. As Harrison puts it,

> Advocating tolerance or being tolerant are activities which are internal to particular moral systems—the activities of participants. There is nothing the relativist, qua relativist, can say either for or against tolerance from a moral point of view. The moment he does this he ceases to be an observer of morality and becomes the user of a moral system. (239)

Harrison adds that one can give Christian reasons for being tolerant, Kantian reasons for being tolerant, or utilitarian reasons for being tolerant, and we may add Buddhist or Hindu reasons for being tolerant, but one cannot give relativistic reasons for being tolerant.

Now suppose "as good as" is taken in a nonmoral sense such that, for example, B's religio-moral system is "as good as" A's moral system in that it is just as sincerely and conscientiously held, and is as internally consistent and coherent as A's religio-moral system. But a problem arises when we ask how one gets from (1) "Bill's moral system is as internally consistent, coherent, and sincerely held as Mary's moral system" to (2) Mary has no right to prevent Bill from doing anything which accords with Bill's own moral system? (1) certainly does not entail (2). For (1) to entail (2) one would have to insert another premise: (1A) "No one has the right to prevent another person from acting in accord with that person's own moral system, where that system is as sincerely held and is as logically consistent and coherent as his own." But it is quite difficult to see why anyone would adopt (1A) as a moral principle.

But suppose an advocate of a particular religio-moral system did adopt something like (1A). It would seem to be subject to a rather familiar, yet nonetheless devastating paradox. (1A) itself is a moral principle, which subjects it to the same difficulties as the moral interpretation of "as good as." The relativist cannot say that it does hold across all moral systems; empirically that can be shown not to be the case. Nor can he claim that it ought to hold across all moral systems, for that would mean that he would have to surrender his relativism. If (1A) is internal only to a particular moral system, it is hard to understand how those moral systems which denied (1A) could be condemned for being intolerant.

Basically, a relativist argument for toleration, even the one that wants to give a nonmoral definition to the claim that "one religo-moral system is as good as another" can be reduced to the following:

> 1. "Right" or "wrong" can only be coherently understood as meaning "right or wrong" for (or relative to) a given religio-moral system.
> 2. "Right" for a given religio-moral system is to be understood exclusively in the sense that it is sincerely held and internally consistent with other beliefs within that religio-moral system.
> 3. Therefore, it is wrong for holders of a given religio-moral system to condemn, interfere or be intolerant toward the values of another religio-moral system.

This is obviously inconsistent because it uses a nonrelative sense of rightness and wrongness in the third proposition that is not allowed for in the first (see Williams 1982, 171). In short, an argument for toleration from relativism is self-referentially incoherent. The relativist cannot avoid the dilemma.

The Fallibilist Approach as an Attempt to Slip between the Horns

As an alternative to the relativist strategy, a moral realist or objectivist might insist that the relativist got off on the wrong foot by assuming that religious and moral judgments are simply projections of our own attitudes. In contrast to the relativist the moral realist claims:

> (a) there are moral facts and true moral claims and (b) these moral facts or truths are not in any important way constituted by, reducible to, or dependent on our moral beliefs, moral reactions, or attitudes. (Brink 1989, 43)

Since the realist is not compelled to think of all sincere and consistent accounts of the world as equally good, it would seem that he might have better reason to prevent someone from acting in a way that he thinks violates the moral order. It is easy enough to see why. Failure to prevent a wrong that one could have prevented can quite plausibly be seen as contributing to the subversion of that moral order, and perhaps even as conniving with the evil itself. In such a case tolerance becomes a vice.

But we are looking for reasons for keeping tolerance as a virtue. How does the realist attempt to do this? The typical move is to inject a bit of skepticism, or to temper the requirements of realism by an appeal to fallibilism. The realist is not required to say that it is easy to discover the moral order, but simply that our judgments are merely probable or perhaps never more than merely prima facie judgments. For this reason, we should not, the argument goes, insist on their implementation by others since that would require a certainty we do not share. Does this allow the fallibilist to slip between the horns?

Distinguish between moral rules and moral principles. Statements such as "torture for pleasure is wrong," "preventing someone from being punished for what they did not do is right," "killing animals for food is wrong," or "idolatry is wrong" express moral rules. Such statements say that a particular type of action is right or wrong without saying why. Such statements as "one ought always to treat persons as ends in themselves and never merely as means to some end," "one ought always to perform that action which will bring about the greatest surplus of pleasure over pain for the largest number of those affected," "one always ought to act as to realize one's nature" or "one ought always to act in accordance with the revealed will of God" express moral principles. They provide grounds for saying that a type of action is right or wrong.

Take, for example, the propositions "killing animals for food is wrong," "torture for pleasure is wrong," and "false worship (or idolatry, blasphemy, heresy) is wrong." All are analogous in that they express moral rules. All are grounded in more fundamental and contentious moral principles that not everyone shares. (Strictly speaking, even the moral principles cannot be said to be "properly basic" in that they depend upon other more fundamental assumptions, such as "all sentient creatures [and not just humans] should count for one in the utility calculus" or that "all sentient creatures have deontic rights," or "God exists.") None are incorrigible and the truth of each will be defended by appeal to a moral principle that cannot, if the critique of classic foundationalism is correct, be certain.

But why should that concern us? What exactly does the concept of certainty have to do with the concept of tolerance? Why should Mary, a vegetarian, be tolerant of Bill, a meat eater, simply because he is less than certain that the moral principle, say, that "every sentient creature ought to count for one in the utilitarian calculus," is true. Similarly, why should someone who believes that "God wills that only he be worshiped" or "the Catholic Church is the one true church" be tolerant of someone who denies that proposition just because that proposition is less than certain. Or, for that matter, why should a person or society be tolerant of a group of pleasure maximizers who believe that they might get a surplus of pleasure over pain by torturing innocents simply because a moral claim to the contrary fails to reach the heights of apodictic certainty. Viewed in this way, it becomes quite difficult to see exactly what the concept of certainty has to do with the concept of tolerance.

Even if we were to suppose, however, that certainty is a relevant factor, the highly contingent social nature of certainty concerning certain moral propositions tends to undermine its usefulness in the issue. As James Madison observed,

> the strength of opinion in each individual, and its practical influence on his conduct, depend much on the number which he supposes to have entertained the same opinion. The reason of man, like man himself, is timid and cautious when left alone, and acquires firmness and confidence in

proportion to the number with which it is associated. (*Federalist*, 49)

If this observation is correct, and I think it is, the degree of certainty about any relevant moral proposition is going to depend largely on the degree to which it is socially accepted or rejected. To put it in more contemporary terms, the degree of certainty concerning any moral proposition will depend significantly on the existence, strength, and maintenance of "plausibility structures" (see Berger 1967). But that would seem to imply that what one ought to be tolerant of is a highly contingent matter. Tying tolerance to the issue of certainty would thus imply that what one ought to be tolerant about is simply a descriptive matter of tallying up the degree of certainty a given society has concerning a moral proposition at a given period in history. And that looks a lot like the modus vivendi horn of the dilemma.

Of course, a person could say that one ought to be tolerant of all acts whose rightness and wrongness one is less than certain of. But if he was tolerant only of those acts that were ultimately grounded in self-evident or incorrigible propositions he would be tolerant of everything, even torturing innocents for fun. He would probably be an anarchist. Moreover, he would be committed to the proposition that "a person ought to be tolerant of all acts whose rightness and wrongness one is less than certain of." But since that claim is itself neither self-evident nor incorrigible, it is, like the similar claim of the relativist, self-referentially incoherent. The fallibilist strategy is self-defeating.

"Tolerance" as a Conceptual Problem

Thus far we have been treating the problem of religious toleration as a matter of political philosophy and social ethics. But the dilemma of religious toleration lies more profoundly in the very concept of toleration itself. Throughout this book, five key concepts will emerge as particularly relevant to the discussion: tolerance, intolerance, indifference, conviction, and power.

First, the words "tolerance," and "toleration," will refer to an attitude or policy by an individual or group that (a) believes an action to be wrong, but (b) allows it to occur despite that belief. By definition the tolerator must take the action he is tolerating to be significant or nontrivial. The problem is determining what, in fact, is significant or nontrivial.

Suppose Bill advocates the generally held Western position that killing animals for food is a relatively insignificant or trivial matter, and therefore holds that a vegetarian's moral objection to that action, and possibly her intolerance of it as well, are unwarranted. On the other hand, a vegetarian such as Mary takes the killing of an animal for this purpose to be quite significant and nontrivial, and therefore holds that anyone's attitude or disposition toward those performing that action, or supporting that action, becomes a relevant moral consideration. The point is that only one party in the debate needs to take the position that a particular action is significant and nontrivial in a moral sense to make the issue of tolerance relevant.

Now, it might be argued that Mary is, at a given time, tolerant relative to meat eating since she is not willing, for example, to rip the Big Mac sandwich out of Bill's hand and castigate him for being morally insensitive to the plight of innocent animals. She could justifiably be said to be tolerant of Bill's meat eating at this time and in this place. But does this mean we can say she is a tolerant person relative to meat eating, per se? Probably not, if dispositions and intent are included. More than likely, she is simply accepting the fact that the view of Bill and others reigns in the larger society, and she yields to the inevitable. And while acquiescence to the inevitable may be realistic, it is not generally what we would consider tolerance. When Bill calls Mary intolerant, it has little to do with her willingness to let him eat his hamburger now, but rather with her attitude if her views should become dominant.

Thus, two conditions must hold before Mary's attitude can be called "tolerant." Not only must (1) another party (Bill in this case) behave in a manner (X), which the tolerator (Mary) sincerely regards as wrong, but also (2) if she had the power to do so, the tolerator (Mary) must be willing to prevent or hinder the other party (Bill) in this activity. In other words, to be considered tolerant one must answer the following counterfactual question in the negative: Given that a person is now merely acquiescing in a particular state of affairs because she now lacks the necessary power to prevent (X), were she to have the power would she then prevent or hinder behavior or action (X)? If Mary answered affirmatively, she would, for our purposes at least, still be considered an "intolerant person," relative to killing animals for food. If she answered negatively she would be tolerant.

Thus, the popular idea that a person can be both tolerant and indifferent is conceptually confusing. Bill can be said to be neither "tolerant" nor "intolerant" of killing animals for food. Neither Bill nor anyone else is, strictly speaking, tolerant of those actions perceived as indifferent. One is not tolerant of that towards which one is indifferent; one is simply indifferent. The opposite of intolerance is not indifference; it is tolerance.[7]

Now, if tolerance is the antonym, not of indifference, but of intolerance, we might want to know what is the antonym of indifference. I would suggest it is conviction. A conviction is a persistent belief such that if a person or a community has a conviction, it will not be easily relinquished and cannot be surrendered without making that person or community a significantly different person or community than before (McClendon and Smith 1975, 7).

But note how such conviction stands as a presupposition of both tolerance and intolerance. While we might say that tolerance and intolerance compete with indifference such is not the case with conviction. Mary's problem with Bill is not that he is tolerant or intolerant of killing animals for food but rather that he is indifferent. He takes her views to be rather quaint. Moreover, Mary's objection to Bill's position is different from what it might be for one of her fellow animal-rights activists who believes killing animals for food is wrong and yet holds that his convictions concerning "freedom of conscience" prevent him from prohibiting those who do believe animals can be morally killed for food from doing so. What she finds objectionable in Bill's case is not his intolerance but his indifference or lack of commitment to what she takes to be the morally requisite position.

Three positions are possible relative to a given action or behavior: that of being in favor, that of being indifferent, and that of being against it. But we are confronted with a rather strange situation when we realize that having conviction and being tolerant requires behavior (abstinence from action that would prevent that which one is opposed to) of a person that mirrors the behavior of the indifferent person. Since having conviction and being tolerant does not require me to pretend I am in favor of a given action or behavior, one might ask "How can it make sense to require of me that I behave as if I were indifferent on matters on which I am not exactly indifferent" (Dancy 1988, 10)? Or, how can tolerance be considered a virtue when it requires me to do nothing to hinder an action which I know to be wrong?

Here we are confronted with the paradoxical nature of the very concept of tolerance and the source of the larger problem of political neutrality toward conflicting conceptions of the good. Tolerance is the virtue of refraining from exercising one's power to interfere with another person or person's action or behavior even though that action or behavior is believed to be wrong. The problem comes when we try to make sense of this as a virtue, since it seems to require of the tolerator that she act as if she were indifferent toward that which she morally disapproves. That is, it seems to require her to act as if she were indifferent over that to which she is not really indifferent.

The issue is further complicated if we locate the place of the concept of power in our discussion. To be tolerant requires one to refrain from using one's power to prevent an action one considers wrong. Or, given a present absence of power to prevent the action, it requires a disposition to refrain from using that power even if one were to have it. As we have said, mere acquiescence to the inevitable is not tolerance. But even if an individual did have sufficient power to prevent an action or behavior (or had hopes of getting it) she would—unless she was an anarchist—most likely eschew purely personal power in favor of certain legal procedural requirements and protections. That is, even if the non-anarchistic vegetarian did have the personal power to prevent Bill from killing animals for food, she would be unwilling to take the law into her own hands.

Suppose Mary, to continue our example, is not an anarchist. She could be a vegetarian pacifist (rather than a vegetarian just-war theorist) such that she might completely eschew the coercive power of the law solely in favor of moral suasion. She might decry the willingness to use such "power" as a concession to the same type of force, violence, and oppression that leads people to kill animals for food in the first place. For this reason she might urge her fellow vegetarians to simply "witness" to the larger society by their actions and thus rely exclusively on moral suasion. Even if Mary's position on killing animals for food won the day, Mary the pacifist would insist that those who disagreed not be coerced into her position. Mary, in that case, truly would be tolerant.

But suppose Mary, while recognizing the moral force of such a position, never became convinced by what she termed the sectarian, vegetarian, pacifist position. (She called herself a vegetarian realist.) Such a position, she thought, would relegate her and her comrades to the margins of the larger society. She understood quite well, however, that to the extent that she is not an absolute pacifist, that is, to the extent that she is willing to use the coercive power of the law to prevent the killing of animals for food should her views gain hegemony, she would be led out of the realm of purely personal ethics. Once the question of power and coercion is introduced into the discussion, the question of toleration becomes a problem of social ethics and political philosophy.

The analogy between our hypothetical situation and the question of religious toleration should be clear. Given the gravity of the question of religious toleration, one of the most tempting strategies for the person with religious convictions is to renounce entirely the use of force and coercion and become an absolute pacifist. Such a strategy has the advantage of being truly tolerant since the convictions of a religious pacifist do not collapse into indifference. He can consistently maintain that a religious action or behavior is wrong and yet argue that one should be tolerant of that action and behavior since he has renounced a priori all force and coercion that might be applied to prevent such action or behavior from occurring. He thus avoids the type of justification required of the person who believes that force and coercion is morally legitimate in some instances. Unlike the pacifist, the nonpacifist must justify his decision whether or not to use force and coercion in this or that particular instance. And if I am correct, this means that on the question of religious toleration the nonpacifist must give either a modus vivendi or moral Esperantist justification of religious toleration, both of which have their problems.

It should be observed, however, that the pacifist can escape the dilemma only to the extent that he completely renounces all power and coercion. Once he is willing to use power and coercion for any reason, religious or otherwise, he becomes intolerant toward that action which he wants to use power and coercion to prevent. And then, one would expect that the pacifist justify his intolerance of one type of action he considers wrong (say, using coercion to prevent a group of pleasure maximizers from torturing an innocent for fun) and yet remain tolerant of another action or behavior he considers wrong (say, idolatry, blasphemy, etc.). Of course, any number of good reasons could be given for not tolerating the former while tolerating the latter. But the point is that the pacifist must now give justification for the latter, and this forces him to confront the dilemma of religious toleration.

The implication is that only the most consistent pacifist can escape the dilemma. But since all laws involve coercion to some extent, the consistent pacifist would seem to pay a rather high price for his consistency. Not only would he be relegated to the margins of the wider society for taking up such a sectarian stance, but it would seem that he would be committed to the proposition that one should be tolerant of those pleasure maximizers who tortured innocents for fun. Such is the high price the pacifist must pay to escape the dilemma.

Conclusion

Can I solve the dilemma? I don't think so. Can I show that the dilemma extends not only to religious thinkers but also to those without religious convictions? To do that I would need to show how the latter would inevitably be forced into conceding that his own religiously relative stance was actually superior to the more particular religious convictions it transcends. Thus, either secularism itself or some sort of civil religion would be taken as superior to any of the other religious positions it legitimates as worthy of its protection. Of course, if what is claimed to be superior can be said to be a civil religion then the position of the secularist is no longer one of religious relativism but one of holding to the conviction that an individual's particular religion (whether or not it is called that) is, in fact, superior. The secularist may be indifferent to the particular religions within a polity but not indifferent toward what he takes to be the morally superior position of his own civil religion.

While I do indeed think the dilemma extends to those without religious convictions, in this work I will be concerned principally with the dilemma as it confronts a thinker who holds them. To carefully consider every theologian or religious thinker who has written on the subject is obviously impossible. Therefore, I propose to consider carefully the arguments of the man I regard as the best religious thinker on the problem of religious tolerance, John Courtney Murray. If Murray can't solve the dilemma—and I will show that he doesn't—then we may wonder whether the dilemma is soluble.

Of course, any number of contemporary or historical thinkers could be dealt with. I have chosen Murray, first of all, because the problem of religious liberty for him was a central rather than a peripheral concern for much of his adult academic life. Secondly, Murray does not make any of the fairly obvious mistakes of others, and the mistakes he does make are more instructive than those of any other single religious thinker, at least in this century. Finally, Murray is worth considering because of his prominent role in the writing of *Dignitatis humanae*, one of the most important ecclesiastical statements on religious liberty.

In what follows, I will suggest that Murray's work can be mapped onto the structure of the problem as presented in this chapter. In the final chapter, I will survey the positions of three approaches to the question of religious toleration, those of John Rawls, Reinhold Niebuhr, and Stanley Hauerwas, and suggest that their secularist, fallibilist, and pacifist/sectarian approaches respectively cannot escape the dilemma of religious toleration. This, I think, will further support my view that the dilemma is insoluble.

Notes

1. We may call these "worldviews," or conflicting "moralities," "moral paradigms," "visions of life," "*Weltanshauungen*" etc. Any of these terms will suffice as long as they include both religious and nonreligious conceptions so that neither is privileged or ruled out of bounds a priori.

2. What I am calling the Esperantist approach closely parallels what Larmore calls the "expressivist" approach toward political neutrality. Larmore's *The Patterns of Moral Complexity* significantly contributed to my understanding of the differences between a modus vivendi and Esperantist approach toward political neutrality. Larmore rejects the Kantian and Millian liberal conceptions of political neutrality (51ff.) and seems at times sympathetic to a modus vivendi approach (70ff.). In the end, however, he appeals to Hauerwas' notion of an "ideal speech situation" (55ff.), which seems to me to be another form of moral Esperanto.

3. What I am calling the modus vivendi defense of religious toleration John Kilcullen calls the argument from reciprocity in *Sincerity and Truth: Essays on Arnould, Bayle and Toleration* (New York: Oxford, 1988), p. 112.

4. Here, we begin to get some indication of the relation between tolerance and commitment. We will explore the conceptual relation between these two concepts in more detail below.

5. Grotius' concept of natural law was distinctly modern and represents a major shift from the classical and medieval view of Aristotle and Aquinas. For the latter the natural law flowed out from an ordered cosmos which was conceived as the divine world-plan. Whereas for Thomas, positive laws were the outworking of principles of natural law, for Grotius they were grounded instead on human contracts and exclusively in the isolated principle that men should honor their contracts (*pacta sunt servanda*).

6. Perhaps some will prefer to see the dilemma as a stuctured problematic rather than a dilemma. In the text I suggest that Rawls' criticisms of the modus vivendi position as being nonmoral and lacking in the virtue of political stability are not well taken. But I do take the third criticism of the modus vivendi position to be the most serious. Actually, the force of this criticism revolves around the answers to two questions. Both are empirical. The first revolves around whether there is, in fact, some threshold of plurality within a given polity. Just how many divergent conceptions of the good can a polity tolerate? I take it to be obvious that there is such a thing as a limit to diversity, but I am not prepared to say when it is reached or whether, for example, American society is approximating it. Alasdair MacIntyre has referred to modern politics as being "civil war by other means." At what point civil war by other means breaks into just plain old civil war, I am not prepared to say. The second question concerns whether the very process of bargaining does in fact negatively affect more particular subgroups in a liberal society. That is, to what extent does the process of negotiation (out of the concern of avoiding plain old civil war perhaps) in a liberal society tend to corrupt the identity a particular subgroup? Again, this is an open question. Evidence may be presented to suggest that religious subgroups are not adversely affected. If it were shown that there is no threshold to the number of divergent conceptions a polity can tolerate or that the number of competing conceptions

within a polity can be infinite, or that the identities of more particular subgroups within a particular polity are not, in fact, seriously undermined, then the modus vivendi horn of the dilemma would be blunted, but not, I think, eliminated entirely. My own view on the matter is summed up nicely by Francis Canavan.

> [I]t is doubtful whether the typical response of the liberal pluralist society is any longer adequate, that is, to take the dangerously controversial matters out of politics and relegate them to the conscience of individuals, for this way of eliminating controversy in fact does much more. Intentionally or not, it contributes to a reshaping of the moral beliefs of multitudes of individuals beyond those directly concerned. It turns into a process by which one ethos, with its reflection in law and public policy, is replaced by another. Liberal pluralism then becomes a sort of confidence game in which, in the guise of showing respect for individual rights, we are in reality asked to consent to a new kind of society based on a new set of beliefs and values. (1979, 6)

7. Thus G. K. Chesterton's famous quip, "tolerance is the virtue of people who do not believe anything," can only make sense if taken ironically. Tolerance can only be a virtue of people who really believe that what they are tolerant of is wrong. More precisely stated, Chesterton's remark would be "Indifference is the virtue of people who do not believe anything." But there is something odd about saying that "indifference" is a virtue.

Chapter Two

The Thesis-Hypothesis Doctrine
and Murray's First Exploratory Article
on Religious Liberty

MURRAY'S WRITINGS IN GENERAL and his struggle with the dilemma of religious toleration can be understood only if one appreciates the extent to which his work developed "dialectically under the press of counterpropositions" that "set the questions for the discourse" (Wolf 1968, 5). In regard to the religious liberty issue Murray confronted basically two sets of counterpropositions. On the one hand, there was the Esperantist argument for religious liberty as advanced by liberal Protestants and secularists. As we will see in later chapters, Murray would vigorously challenge this approach to religious liberty. On the other hand, he was confronted with the traditional Catholic position, a modus vivendi approach to the question of religious toleration. In this and the following chapter, we will address Murray's attempt to come to grips with the traditional Catholic position.

An Explanation and Summary of the Thesis-Hypothesis Doctrine

The traditional Catholic position on the question of religious liberty had come to be called the thesis-hypothesis doctrine. Basically, it held that the state in principle (thesis) was obliged to recognize the Catholic Church as the true church and to worship God according to the rites of the Catholic Church. This meant that in principle (thesis) the state has the right and duty to suppress the public expression of false religions, although in practice (hypothesis) toleration of false religions is acceptable where legal and consti-

tutional recognition of the true faith is not possible. That is, religious toleration would be accepted as a way of life, but only if necessary. The
"hypothesis" constitutes the modus vivendi horn of the dilemma that
Murray wanted to avoid.

While the term "thesis-hypothesis" was of nineteenth-century origin,
this position was set forth by Thomas Aquinas in the *Summa Theologiæ*
(2a2æ.10.11). After arguing that Jewish rites are to be tolerated because they
foreshadow Christian rites, he says:

> But the rites of other infidels, which bear nothing true or
> useful, are not to be tolerated in the same way except per-
> haps to avoid some evil, to wit, scandal or a division that
> could arise from this or an obstacle to the salvation of those
> who would gradually be converted to the faith if they were
> tolerated. On this account the Church has sometimes toler-
> ated the rites of even heretics and pagans when there was a
> great multitude of infidels.

Pope Leo XIII, who encouraged the recovery of Thomistic philosophy
and urged the reconstruction of the social order on the basis of Thomistic
social thought, set forth this position in *Longingua Oceani* (1895), an encyclical sent to the American Catholic hierarchy in response to the "Americanist
crisis."

> For the Church amongst you, unopposed by the Constitu-
> tion and government of your nation, fettered by no hostile
> legislation, protected against violence by the common laws
> and the impartiality of the tribunals, is free to live and act
> without hindrance. Yet, though all this is true, it would be
> very erroneous to draw the conclusion that in America is to
> be sought the type of the most desirable status of the
> Church, or that it would be universally lawful or expedient
> for State and Church to be, as in America, dissevered and
> divorced. (Leo XIII 1903, 323)

The standard citation that is often quoted to summarize this theory in
the American context is that of Father John Ryan, the most important and
influential American Catholic social ethicist before Murray. In *The State and
the Church* (1922), a book which served for a few decades as a standard

political textbook in Catholic colleges, Ryan put forth the Catholic position with the utmost clarity. Referring to the constitutional provisions for religious liberty in the modern state (including the American one) he says:

> But constitutions can be changed, and non-Catholic sects may decline to such a point that the political proscription of them may become feasible and expedient. What protection would they then have against a Catholic State? The latter could logically tolerate only such religious activities as were confined to the members of the dissenting group. It could not permit them to carry on general propaganda nor accord their organization certain privileges that had formerly been extended to all religious corporations, for example, exemption from taxes.... It is true that some zealots and bigots will continue to attack the Church because they fear that some five thousand years hence the United States may become overwhelmingly Catholic and may then restrict the freedom of non-Catholic denominations. Nevertheless, we cannot yield up the principles of eternal and unchangeable truth in order to avoid the enmity of such unreasonable persons. Moreover, it would be a futile policy; for they would not think us sincere. Therefore, we shall continue to profess the true principles of the relation between Church and State....(38–39)

Ryan hoped that "the great majority of our fellow citizens" would be "sufficiently honorable to respect our devotion to the truth" and not worry about the implications, given the improbability that Catholics would gain hegemony.

It should be understood that the advocates of the thesis-hypothesis doctrine also held that the state could never be called upon to impose the Catholic faith on dissident citizens, a position that grows out of reverence for the individual conscience and the very nature of religion as an act of faith. Catholic doctrine held to a distinction between private belief and public worship.

Thus Leo XIII in *Immortale Dei* (1885) declared, "The Church is wont to take earnest heed that no one shall be forced to embrace the Catholic faith against his will, for, as St. Augustine wisely reminds us, 'Man cannot believe otherwise than of his own free will'" (Leo XIII 1903, 127). This position was also encoded in the Code of Canon Law (can. 752, 1; can. 1351), and was reiterated by Pius XII in his encyclical *Corporis Christi* (1943). But from this one could not conclude that a Catholic state did not have the obligation to restrict sectarian religion in such matters as "the public profession and exercise of their false religion, in their propaganda, [and] in the spread of their heretical doctrines" (Shea 1950, 168).

The thesis-hypothesis doctrine was, of course, defended and articulated by a number of Murray's contemporaries. A concise and articulate defense of the traditional doctrine was set forth by Joseph Fenton. In 1952 Fenton, who by that time had become one of Murray's principal traditional Catholic antagonists, set out to articulate and summarize the principles underlying the thesis-hypothesis position (Fenton 1952). A brief examination of Fenton's exposition and application of the Catholic modus vivendi argument will serve to highlight Murray's dilemma.

The first principle stems from the nature of religion itself. "It is a statement of the fact that objectively religion is nothing more or less than the payment of the debt of acknowledgment which all rational creatures owe to God." From here the argument proceeds analogically. Since it is a moral evil to "withhold from a fellow creature the good which is really due him" it must follow a fortiori that "it is a much more serious moral evil to fail to pay to God the debt of acknowledgment actually due Him because of His supreme goodness and because of our absolute and entire dependence upon Him" (1952, 455). Fenton's view is thoroughly Thomistic in that religion is taken to be a moral virtue being part of that cardinal virtue of justice concerned with what we owe to God in the way of honor, reverence, and worship (MacIntyre 1988, 188). Public acknowledging of God then is to be respected as an aspect of justice and lack of acknowledgment as a deficiency of justice.

The second principle concerns the extent of the obligation of religion or worship. Because man is totally dependent on God

> there is no realm or section of human life which can be exempted from this obligation of acknowledging God's supreme goodness. Thus, not only individual men, but also all societies or groups of men are bound to pay that debt of acknowledgment. If they fail to make that acknowledgment, their conduct is objectively lacking a good which it should include. (455-56)

Fenton alludes to a factor that often obscures this principle: a confused and imperfect notion of religion itself. If people do not come to realize that religion is in the last analysis the payment of a debt or obligation on the part of a creature to his Creator they are likely to look upon its field of operation as in some way circumscribed. That is,

> if they come to imagine that religion has no more meaning than that contained in the basic concept of this reality ordinarily set forth in manuals of comparative religion or history of religion, they will never be able to appreciate the genuine obligation incumbent upon all individuals and upon all groups to worship God. (456)

In other words, if people do not realize that religion is an obligation on the part of a creature to his Creator they are likely to view religion as exclusively a private matter.

Fenton adds that under certain circumstances, groups, states, families and other societies are not in a position to perform corporate acts of worship. This occurs "when the membership of the group is sharply divided in religious belief." Just as a family cannot have its own act of worship when family members have different religions, "it is obvious that the state itself is not in a position to exercise its own act of religion, and to pay its own debt of acknowledgment to God" when the citizens of the state are of different religious persuasions. On such occasions nonperformance of the religious act by the group or community is permissible. However, "even under such circumstances, it is utterly incorrect to say that the condition of the community or group which does not offer social worship to God is, in the strictest sense of the term, a good thing" (456). It remains "objectively deplorable" and is "never *simpliciter* a good thing" (457).

The third principle involves "the truth that God wills that the debt of religion should be paid to Him in a definite and supernatural way." It is God's right to prescribe the method by which he is to be worshiped. He has seen fit to exercise that right: "His message, the divine public and supernatural revelation which comes to us in the Catholic Church, carries with it manifest signs of its own authenticity." And, he adds:

> According to that message, the one acceptable and authorized social worship of God is to be found summed up in the Eucharistic sacrifice of the Catholic Church. It is God's will that men should pay the debt of acknowledgment and

gratitude they owe to Him in the worship and according to
the rite of His own Church. (457)

From these three principles it follows that "the Church and religion are
not in the best or the most desirable position in a land where, even for per-
fectly valid and acceptable reasons, the civil society itself does not worship
God according to the rites of the Church" (457). And, applying the doctrine
to the American situation, Fenton sets forth the hypothesis.

> Our own beloved nation is not in a position to offer its offi-
> cial and corporate worship to God according to the rite of
> the true Catholic Church only because of the fact that
> many of our fellow-citizens have and profess either a false
> religion or no religion at all. Obviously, if we are to think
> and to speak according to the dictates of true faith and
> charity, we cannot, in any way whatsoever, believe that this
> situation is absolutely the best and ultimately satisfactory
> for our fellow-Americans, for our country itself, or for the
> Church.

This, succinctly stated, is the modus vivendi position that Murray set
out to refute, and one that was, in fact, rejected at Vatican II.

Now, what lines of attack were available to Murray? If he was an atheist
or perhaps an acolyte of those "manuals of comparative religion or history of
religion" he most likely would go to the root of the issue and simply reject
the first principle outright. If he was a Protestant who wanted to maintain
some sense of orthodoxy and therefore would not want to deny the first
principle outright, the focus of the attack would most likely be on the third
principle. This would, of course, undercut any case for a Catholic establishment or Catholic intolerance toward religious dissent, although it wouldn't
eliminate the possibility of a Protestant establishment or Protestant intolerance, or perhaps some sort of ecumenical Protestant-Catholic Christian
intolerance.

But what if you are an orthodox Catholic? As an orthodox Christian
theist it is unlikely that you would deny the first principle. And, as a Roman
Catholic you aren't going to deny the third. The focus of the attack that
offers the highest possibility of success seems to be the second principle.
Somehow you will have to negotiate your way around the proposition that
"there is no realm or section of human life which can be exempted from this

obligation of acknowledging God's supreme goodness," and that "not only individual men, but also all societies or groups of men are bound to pay that debt of acknowledgment."

This was Murray's main strategy. We will see that in his first article on religious liberty, Murray seemed to realize that he could not portion off "a section of human life" which was exempted from the obligation of acknowledging God. But then he attempted to finesse his way around the claim that "not only individual men, but also all societies or groups of men are bound to pay that debt of acknowledgment to God." Several commentators on Murray think he succeeded in this. I don't.

Before moving on to an exposition of Murray's first argument we should note one final problem that gives the discussion a distinctively American flavor. Fenton, after mentioning the "reckless and vulgar diatribes" of the anti-Catholic agitators who were "continually charging that Catholics are striving to do away with freedom of religion in the United States," laid down the following challenge:

> In answering these men, some of our less skillful apologists become so confused that they actually give the impression that Catholics are completely and absolutely satisfied with the situation here in America today, that we believe it is to be best that many of our fellow citizens should remain as they are, apart from our Lord, from His Church, and from His true religion.... These writers describe as ultimately good and satisfactory a situation in which the nation itself takes no more cognizance of the true religion than it does of false systems of worship. (460)

Fenton was, in effect, charging those who would oppose the standard thesis-hypothesis doctrine with an ethnocentrism that held religious pluralism to be normative. Murray had to avoid the charge that he made the American religious situation of "free exercise" and "no establishment" a new "thesis" to which the Catholic doctrine of establishment and intolerance were "hypothesis." I am going to suggest that he only partially succeeded in doing so. His success was only partial because in his criticism of liberal Protestant and secularist defenses of religious liberty he took up and advocated a modus vivendi position that he was at the same time trying to avoid in his polemic against those who held the traditional Catholic position.

Murray's First Exploratory Article on Religious Liberty

Murray's first sustained attempt to grapple with the issue of religious liberty appeared in a 1945 article entitled "Freedom of Religion: The Ethical Problem" (1945d). Ironically, he presents there a lucid and succinct case for the position he would later try to refute.

Murray oriented the discussion by insisting that because "Catholic and Protestant theologies of the Church are radically divergent and irreconcilable" (240), a solution to the problem of religious liberty that is conceived in terms of Protestant ecclesiology cannot be accepted by Catholics. Neither could Catholics demand, however, "that the solution of the problem be postponed until Protestants shall have accepted our ecclesiology" (240). He thus thought it important "to be explicit and insistent on the fact that the Church's theory of religious liberty rests initially and fundamentally, not on the dogmatic assertion of a theology of her authority, but on a philosophical explanation of the structure of human conscience and of the State, for whose validity reason itself stands sufficient guarantee" (234).

Murray's hope was that Protestants and Catholics might reach a stable agreement by bracketing contentious theological presuppositions, particularly ecclesiology. As Love states, "Murray tried desperately to maintain a clear distinction between the ethical level of analysis based on reason and natural law and the theological level of analysis based on faith and on the divine law as received in revelation" (Love 1965, 42). As we will see, Murray's deployment of this sharp nature/grace and reason/revelation distinction in the cause of religious liberty could not be sustained.

Murray begins this first discussion of religious liberty with a forthright statement of the fundamental tension within the Catholic position.

> We love God in the truth that He has given us, and we love man in that which is the most divine in him, his conscience. We love God and His truth with a loyalty that forbids compromise of the truth, even at the promptings of what might seem to be a love of man; were it otherwise, our love both of God and man would be a *caritas ficta*. And we love man and his conscience with a loyalty that forbids injury to conscience, even at the promptings of what might seem to be a love of truth; were it otherwise, our love of both God and man would be a *caritas ficta*. (1945d, 232)

Thus, the difficulty that confronts the Catholic on the issue of religious freedom is placed under the rubric of the tension that exists at a more fundamental level of moral theology between the ultimate and objective norm (i.e.,
the Divine law, natural and positive) and the proximate and subjective norm
(conscience). (See Regan 1986, 29–33 and Donagan 1977, 131–38.) Essentially the dilemma of religious liberty is a subset of the broader moral problem that arises from the conflicting demands of autonomy and heteronomy
in Catholic moral theology.

Roughly paralleling this tension is what Murray calls the "architecture of
the problem" (234). He suggests that "the Catholic solution to the problem
of religious liberty must be set forth on three distinct planes, the ethical, the
theological and the political" (234). These distinctions formulated in terms
of law include natural, canon, and civil law (235) and essentially involve an
ethic of conscience, a theology of the church, and a political philosophy of
the state (239). The first is abstract and ethical; the anticipated solution to
the problem is arrived at solely by the light of reason. The second is abstract
and theological; its solution is the light of revelation which completes the
light of reason. The third problem is concrete and political; its solution lies
in the light of revelation as completing the light of reason and in precepts of
political prudence with regard to the common good of the political community (235). The "one supreme theological problem" of "harmonizing the
order of reason with the order of faith" is correspondingly paralleled in the
problem of religious liberty which "consists in harmonizing the solution
reached on the ethical plane in terms of reason and the natural law with the
solution reached on the theological plane in terms of the Church and the
law of the Gospel" (278).

Murray initially intended this article to focus on the ethical problem and
the corresponding question of conscience, while future articles would focus
on the theological and political (or prudential) questions. The discussion in
this article, however, was to be purely philosophical. Murray was seeking a
solution to the problem that would bracket that which was theologically contentious. It was to be confronted

> solely in terms of human reason. We admit into the prob-
> lem only those elements whose existence is certified by
> reason, and we construct our solution out of only those
> conclusions which reason validates…. We prescind from all
> the realities of the present, historic, supernatural order,

which are certified to us only by revelation and known by faith." (242)

Obviously, if Murray could establish a case for freedom of religion here, in the order of pure reason or "nature" he would have established an ahistorical and tradition-independent case for religious freedom. And he would be speaking moral Esperanto at least on the issue of religious freedom. The right to religious liberty would be grounded on the bedrock of philosophical truth. If he can pull it off, the discussion is over. But it will not be that easy.

Before directly addressing the question of conscience, Murray's discussion takes a fateful methodological turn. The issue of religious liberty is broached by an inquiry into the relation between liberty and law. He first discusses the relation between liberty and law in general and then liberty and the two laws to which it is subject, natural law and human law. Murray wants to emphasize the "very intimate relationship between liberty and law," a point that needs to be stressed "against current antinomian theories, consciously or unconsciously held, which tend to conceive liberty as sheer release, total emancipation, and indefinitely expanding spontaneity" (244). Against this perceived antinomian tendency Murray stressed the priority of the reason over the will.

> By virtue of his reason, man is capable of surveying the whole range of truth and goodness, of deliberating about the values that it contains, and of judging that here and now this value is desirable, and to be pursued. Apart from this previous deliberation and judgment, there is no free act. And every free act is an obedience to reason. Precisely in the privilege of being obedient only to reason consists the freedom of the will–its immunity from all less noble determinants [i.e., the passions]. So far, then, from freedom being simply an escape from obedience, the notion of obedience is inherent in the very notion of spiritual freedom: [citing Leo XIII's encyclical "Liberty"] "by its very nature [the will] is an appetite obedient to reason...." [T]he fundamental point is the intimate relation between freedom and reason. But now reason appears, not simply as the power to weigh particular goods and judge them desirable and present them to the will for acceptance as such, but also as the power to discover and understand the "order of reason,"

as an order—*I mean the relation of man to God, his author and last end, and the relation that all free human action has to the attainment or loss of this last end.* (245, emphasis mine)

Confronted with the moral imperative to follow the *ordinatio rationis*, Murray concludes that, by definition, "moral freedom consists in man's deliberate obedience to moral law" (246). In emphasizing the priority of reason over will, then, Murray sets his jaw against the voluntarist-nominalistic tradition in Christian thought and its secular successors. By taking up this realist position Murray excludes an appeal for religious liberty on the basis of what he calls the "liberal concept of freedom."

> If the problem of religious liberty were posited in terms of the so-called liberal concept of freedom, it would be ineffably easy to solve. Or, rather, there would be no problem at all—no ethical problem; for the ethical problem begins only when one perceives the necessary relation between moral liberty and law. (247-48)

This perspective is consistently carried through when Murray goes on to discuss the relation of human liberty to human law. As J. Leon Hooper correctly observes, Murray situated the question of freedom and law against the background of the rational psychological relation of will and reason. For Murray,

> Will and reason are to the "physical order" what freedom and law are to the moral order. Will does not operate as a blind drive independently of reason.... Will always proceeds to act in response to a conceived good. (Hooper 1986, 35)

Murray's intent was not to give a full outline of a philosophy of human law; he is content with quoting from Leo XIII's encyclical *Human Liberty*. Rather, his purpose in this article was to propose in broad outline the Catholic theory as a *tertium quid* between individualism and totalitarianism. The individualistic theory is one in which the individual's freedom of choice is "the supreme freedom, an end in itself; and correlatively it regards the function of the state as simply the protection of the natural freedom of the individual" (252-53). In contrast to Esperantist liberalism, the good, for Murray, is prior to the right. The most tempting strategy that a defender of religious liberty might employ was a rather un-Thomistic nominalist-voluntarist one. It is crucial to understand that Murray declined to take this route.

But Murray's rejection of a liberal minimalist state and the corresponding natural rights theory on which it is grounded will have critical ramifications for his argument for religious liberty. Murray asserted that the State "is *not an amoral entity,* that escapes the control of a higher law—the law of nature and nature's God, which exists before and above all human society." This means "that the State has a moral function as well as purely material, administrative, and police functions" and that in its actions, policies, and legislative code "cannot maintain a position of 'neutrality' or indifference." By nature, "the State, through its laws, is a power singly for the common good, which is not merely material but moral in its scope" (250-51, emphasis mine).

The Catholic theory also avoids, according to Murray, the totalitarian theory of human law and human freedom. The totalitarian view is the flipside of the individualist one. It assigns supreme freedom and absolute sovereignty to the state itself, thus displacing "the absolutely autonomous individual of the individualistic theory as the great god, juridically competent, an end in itself, as sort of *Divina Maiestas,* that claims the divine prerogative of being the source and fount of law" (252). The common error of both views stems from "a complete misunderstanding of the terms of the principle; for both of them fail to situate the idea of liberty and the idea of law in the framework of the eternal *ratio Dei* which is the source of both liberty and law" (253).

Murray then turns to the issue of conscience as a proposed synthesis of the tension that exists between the heteronomous demands of nature and the autonomous demands of conscience.

> On the one hand, the human person is really governed by law—a law that is "given" to it; on the other hand, the human person really governs itself—it gives the law to itself. The doctrine of conscience is the synthesis of these two principles, and resolves their seeming contradiction; in their light the function of conscience appears as essentially mediatorial. (254)

A moral dilemma is created when autonomy must be respected even under the control of a heteronomous regime of law. The dilemma is supposedly resolved when this law becomes somehow interior to man; "he must give it to himself, but as a law it is also given to him" (254). The law as given by conscience is defined as "a practical judgment of reason, whereby in the light of the known law a man judges of the morality of a concrete act, whether it is licit, or prescribed, or prohibited" (254).

Murray quickly adds, however, that conscience, as merely the proximate, subjective norm, is not the norm of its own rightness, since it is regulated by a higher norm not of its own creation. It is not the *legis-lator*, but the *legis-mediator* (254). In its mediatorial function it stands between the objective law and the freely chosen act. This makes the question of the erroneous conscience salient and crucial.

Once again, Murray's distinctions here are thoroughly Thomistic. An erroneous conscience is defined as "a practical judgment with regard to religious belief or moral action, that is formed in ignorance of the full realities of the case, and that, as a matter of fact is wrong" (258). Such an erroneous conscience is of two types. A *vincibly erroneous conscience* involves the case of one "who is in ignorance, but who has a more or less strong suspicion that he is in ignorance" (258). Such a conscience cannot be a right norm of action. Action must be held in abeyance. The single obligation is to be rid of the ignorance by study, consultation, and prayer.

An *invincibly erroneous conscience* is more directly relevant to the issue of religious freedom. It involves "the case of a man who is in ignorance, but who likewise is not in a position to get out of his ignorance, because he does not suspect that he is in it" (259). In contrast to the vincibly erroneous conscience, the invincibly ignorant conscience can be a right norm of moral action. If such a conscience commands or forbids a particular belief or action, one is strictly bound to follow it. This follows from Thomistic realism, which puts reason in a mediatorial position between will and its object:

> In making human nature rational, God made it subject to
> the laws of a rational nature; and one of these laws is the
> general law that *all* laws of human nature must reach man,
> and be imposed upon him, by reason and its practical judg-
> ments. There is no other way, in keeping with the dignity of
> man, whereby his obedience to the laws of his nature may
> be secured, save by these practical dictates of reason, which
> procure obedience, and a rational obedience. It is, there-
> fore, a law of nature that one of the functions of reason is to
> mediate the eternal law of God. Reason may, indeed, per-

form this function badly; it may mistake for law what is not
law, and it may be blind to the law that really is law. (259)

He then, appropriately enough, cites Thomas' statement on the subject (ST
1a2æ.19.5): "When reason erroneously proposes anything as the precept of
God, then to despise the dictate of reason is the same thing as despising the
precept of God." Murray even goes so far as to speak of the presence of "two
wills of God here," which reflects "an eccentricity in the moral order" (260).

But then Murray asks the ultimately crucial question. "If an erroneous
conscience must be followed, just as a true conscience must be followed, is
the status of the erroneous conscience the same as that of the true conscience?" (261) The answer of course is that it is not. Although the person
with the erroneous conscience is bound to respect his conscience even if it is
erroneous, others aren't. This becomes particularly salient when the erroneous conscience is related to legitimate public authority.

> Unlike the right conscience, the erroneous conscience does
> not create any rights that are coactive against legitimate
> authority, or that could prevail in conflict with the rights of
> other men. (261)

The problem of an erroneous conscience is relatively simple if the individual is considered in isolation, standing only before God. But because
human beings are involved in a system of social relationships in which
beliefs and acts have social repercussions, the terms of the discussion are
altered. Thus,

> an erroneous conscience creates no rights as against a legit-
> imate order of law. It is a valid principle of liberty *only in the
> internal forum of private morality,* where the law is simply
> that conscience must be obeyed. But it is not a valid princi-
> ple of liberty in the external forum of the social and juridi-
> cal order, where there is also another law to be considered.
> (262, emphasis mine)

Murray then presents a rather interesting example. A polygamist could
not relevantly claim in court that a law prohibiting polygamy does violation
to his conscience. While the state cannot oblige a man internally to assent to
the truth that polygamy is wrong, it can legitimately forbid a man to marry

more than one wife. The state "does not oblige the polygamist to act against his conscience; it simply asserts its competence in the order of public morality, pronounces a moral judgment opposite to that of the polygamist, and vindicates the order of morality over which it is guardian" (261-62).

Since the "erroneous conscience creates no rights as against a legitimate order of law" we find that Murray's discussion has shifted away from the *rights* of conscience and toward the *duties* or *obligations* of conscience, which is not so surprising considering his insistence that liberty not be discussed except in relation to law. To put it another way, Murray has refused to consider religious liberty as exclusively a negative liberty or as an immunity.

Murray cites five (263-64) obligations of the conscience, the first of which is particularly relevant to our concerns.

> Man has the obligation to search for the truth about God and about God's purposes for man, in all ways in which that truth is ascertainable, and to accept it when found. (263)

What has happened here? The idea of "freedom of conscience," I would suggest, has become more complicated because the supernatural (the theological aspect) cannot help but to affect the natural reason (the ethical aspect) in Murray's schema. Murray is too orthodox to take the deistic option of leaving "natural" obligations unaffected by grace. Moral Esperanto cannot be spoken since even in the realm of nature, "man has a further, hypothetical obligation, which is to accept any higher knowledge of God and any higher law of God which God...may make accessible to him" (264). Because "the obligation of faith in a supernatural revelation has its root in the basic ethical obligation to know God...deliberately to refuse this homage when the fact of revelation is known, would be not merely a refusal of a new divine benefit but a violation of the *law of nature itself*" (264, emphasis mine). Thus, to refuse to pay homage to God and worship him in the particular manner in which he wills is a violation of *natural*, and not simply supernatural, law (see Love 1965, 45).

This will have crucial ramifications for Murray's argument. The initial gap that he wanted to establish between the ethical and theological, nature and grace, and the individual conscience and God's moral law has become significantly blurred. The result is that from a public-juridical perspective there is little, if any, difference between the theological proposition "God exists" and the moral proposition "Polygamy is evil." Therefore, the (moral/

theological) propositions "Man has an obligation to accept the truth about God" and "Man has a moral obligation to avoid polygamy," ought to have a similar juridical or political status, the reasonable conclusion being that if the erroneous conscience that holds polygamy to be morally legitimate should be legally prohibited from acting out its beliefs, so can heresy, idolatry, false worship, or blasphemy even if it is done in invincible ignorance.

Moreover, Murray at this time sees an analogy between the individual and the state. As the individual is hypothetically obligated by natural law to worship God as He [God] wills to be worshiped, so the state as a moral entity is under a *natural* law obligation "to acknowledge God as its author, to worship Him as He wills to be worshipped, and to subject its official life and action to His law" (266). The implications of this personalistic analogy between the individual and the state are far-reaching:

> if the state itself in its public capacity has no right to act as if there were no God, it can hardly agree that any of its citizens has a right to so act, in his public capacity. It is, therefore, morally obliged to assume the position that atheism and actions contrary to the natural law have no rights in the social order and that they can claim no freedom of public advocacy or practice. To this position it is further compelled by its obligation to the common good. Actually the whole social order is founded on the existence of God. Wherefore to spread disbelief in God or immoral practice is to undermine the social order. (268)

While the state has no competence with regard to errors or evils held in one's private life, and while it has no mandate to convert the atheist or secularist, it, on the other hand, has "no juridical obligation to give him free reign in the public life of the community." The mandate to guard the juridical order and the common good "gives the State the right to restrict the propaganda of atheism or secularism and the practice of immorality" (269).

Murray wanted desperately to keep the ethical, theological, and political aspects of the problem distinct. But as we have seen the theological crept into the ethical dimension crucially affecting his argument from "above" as it were, in favor of intolerance. Now we are prepared to see how the political or prudential aspect creeps into his ethical argument from below, only now in favor of religious tolerance.

While the state retains the rights to restrict atheistic propaganda and the practice of immorality, its exercise in particular circumstances is a matter of collective political prudence.

> The right itself derives from the State's obligation to the common good; its use depends on the practical judgment whether or not legislative suppression of this or that evil would, in a given set of circumstances, actually further the common good. In certain social contexts, the attempt to suppress certain errors or evils by legislative action would do more harm than good. It might undermine the authority of the State, if the laws proved impossible to enforce; it might create serious conditions of unrest and resentment, in the country itself or abroad; it might enforce a dangerous trend toward excessive State controls; or, in a word, it might do damage to the very nature of the State as a co-operating unity of free men joined in the bonds of civic friendship; and this damage might not be counteracted by whatever good effect would follow on the suppression of this or that vice. (269)

However, Murray quickly adds that

> a high degree of State tolerance may prove a high degree of "external liberty" as it is called, but it does not prove a high level of moral virtue in the community. When evils have to be tolerated for the common good, it must be that they exist on a large scale and in an institutionalized form. (271)

Once again citing Leo's encyclical "Human Liberty" he notes that "tolerance of evils belongs to the precepts of political prudence" (272).

Religious liberty is, at this time for Murray, purely a question of political prudence and practical reasoning. But that wasn't good enough. As we will see, Murray will attempt to leave this position behind. But what was wrong with it?

Thomas Love was one of the first writers to explore Murray's work in any depth, and his book set the stage for virtually all interpretations of this period of Murray's thought. Love thinks this article expresses Murray's dissatisfaction and confusion. "At this time Murray was confused. He was seeking to clarify his thinking and in so doing to propose an acceptable theory of religious liberty— theologically, ethically, and politically" (Love 1965a, 40). Love is certainly correct in seeing this as a rather exploratory article. But his claim that the article was confusing and that Murray was dissatisfied forces us to ask two questions. To whom is this theory to be acceptable? And, what exactly is "confusing" about this article?

Actually, Murray's article is lucid and logical on its own terms. This leads one to suspect that what Love means by "confusing" is that it didn't provide what he, and perhaps even Murray at this time, wanted—an ahistorical argument for religious liberty that would override Protestant charges of Catholic "intolerance" and, more polemically, Catholic religious bigotry. In any case, it does seem to be a rather clear argument for religious liberty on the grounds of collective political prudence. While Murray never explicitly disavows the tack taken in this article, it is fair to say that he was not satisfied with the conclusions. It is not surprising that Murray's article received no Catholic criticism. In fact, George Shea, one of Murray's more perceptive traditionalist critics, will later appeal to Murray's 1945 argument to criticize his theory as it developed in the late 1940s and early 1950s (Shea 1952, 164).

Murray's subsequent dissatisfaction raises another question, one that is probably more important for a proper interpretation of Murray. To whom must this theory appear acceptable?

One writer who has vigorously tackled the issue of acceptability is the sociologist John Murray Cuddihy. His book *No Offense: Civil Religion and Protestant Taste* (1978) is a study of what happens to European political and religious beliefs when they land in America. He argues that civil religion exercises an unremitting pressure on traditional religions and forces theologians into a defensive, apologetic stance toward the larger culture. Theologians become preoccupied with avoiding offense, or more precisely with avoiding the appearance of religious incivility. American religious pluralism and civil religion convert religious scandal into civil offense. In the process, religious particularism dissolves and theological identity is eclipsed.

Murray serves as one of several case studies of this process. Cuddihy argues that Murray was forced to struggle with how his Roman Catholic Christianity must appear to American Protestants. Murray's aim was to "disembarrass the Church of the appearance of incivility that accrues to it in the Anglo-American environment of the 'civic culture'" (Cuddihy 1978, 67). His church-state theory and his theory of religious liberty "was designed to legitimate Catholic participation in the neutral-secular structures of the national civic-culture" (71).

But what was it exactly that was so offensive about this "prudential" argument? What was so un-American about it? Why would Protestants find it so offensive? What exactly does this say about Murray's subsequent dissatisfaction? If I am correct about the theoretical coherence of Murray's 1945 argument, then it cannot simply be dismissed as being conceptually muddled or confused, as Love implied.

Cuddihy argues that the offensiveness of the traditionalist position involved withholding "interior assent" to the establishment and free exercise clauses of the First Amendment (77). Murray's views in 1945 did not depart from this tradition. But, Cuddihy asks, would not "interior obedience" to the First Amendment, be perceived by the traditionalists as a religious act? Regardless of how he would answer that question, Murray would lose. If he holds that assent to the First Amendment was strictly a prudential and political act, then his Protestant and secularist contemporaries would be offended because he does not really believe in religious freedom per se. They would thus remain suspicious of Catholic loyalties.

On the other hand, his very inoffensiveness would offend the traditionalists. The attempt to avoid this offense, might force him into an attempt to ground religious liberty on moral Esperantist grounds that would avoid the appearance that he was capitulating to the Protestant and secularist *zeitgeist*. Cuddihy says that in 1945 "civil religion was knocking on the door. Murray refused to open it" (72). He seems correct in that judgment. But this, of course, leaves open the question of whether Murray's "dissatisfaction" with this first argument and his subsequent polemic against the traditionalists reflects a temptation to go through the door. Cuddihy seems to think it did, and his interpretation is certainly plausible. Murray's attempt to disembarrass the Catholic position may partially account for his polemic against the traditionalists. Even so, this should not be overemphasized, because it must be balanced against his simultaneous and highly charged polemic against liberal Protestants and secularists. Any claim that Murray was pressed into his position on religious liberty as a result of sociological factors unique to the American situation must be balanced against Murray's own criticism of any moral Esperantist attempt to give "interior obedience" to the First Amendment. If his polemic against the traditionalists would reflect a willingness to go through the door of civil religion, then his polemic against liberal Protestants and secularists would reflect an unwillingness. Murray, in other words, is face-to-face with the dilemma of religious toleration.

Chapter Three

Murray's Polemic
Against the Catholic
Modus Vivendi Position

WHILE MURRAY NEVER EXPLICITLY disavowed his position of 1945, it does seem to be his intent to have written two articles addressing the question from a theological and political perspective. They were never written. Instead, he turned his energies toward an historical investigation of Catholic church-state theory in the hopes of establishing a firmer case for religious liberty, one that would presumably go beyond a merely prudential argument. The fruits of his labor were a number of articles published between 1948 and 1955, articles that were both historical and polemical in nature. The more historical studies can be read as an attempt to construct a narrative of the development of Catholic church-state doctrine that would make the thesis-hypothesis doctrine seem less plausible. The conclusions he drew from his historical studies were challenged by the traditionalists, and this in turn resulted in an instructive polemical exchange between the two positions. My central claim will be that Murray needed to speak moral Esperanto in order decisively to defeat the position of the traditionalists but, for better or worse, he simply could not master the language.

In the course of constructing his narrative of Catholic church- state theory Murray makes three crucial distinctions that he seems to think will defeat the thesis-hypothesis doctrine:

> (1) A distinction between the direct and indirect power of
> the Church in temporal affairs. A subset of this distinction

is a re-statement and re-interpretation of the requirement for *concordia* or harmony between the spiritual and temporal powers.

(2) A distinction between a "lay" and a "laicized" state. More concretely, Murray sought to make a strong distinction between the "laicist" state of Continental liberalism and the "lay" state of Anglo-American liberalism.

(3) A distinction between state and society.

Murray's first academic article published after "Freedom of Religion," was entitled "Governmental Repression of Heresy" (1948f). He opens by insisting that "the discussion must proceed from an historical point of view. Nothing is more unhelpful than an abstract starting point" (1948f, 33). At once one is confronted with a problem which requires brief comment.

One cannot but be somewhat surprised by Murray's strategy here. If the core problem with the thesis-hypothesis position is that it subjects religious liberty too much to the historically contingent, specifically the existence of Catholic societal hegemony, it would seem that grounding this new article in history was a tack that was unlikely to succeed. One would expect him to place less emphasis on history, not more.

Recent commentators on Murray, most notably J. Leon Hooper (1986), have suggested that this methodological turn reflects a turn toward "historical consciousness" and accounts for Murray's willingness to speak of the evolution of doctrine. Whatever truth there may be in this observation, a core problem remains. Interpretations that overemphasize the historical emphasis in his work tend to play down another aspect of the problem also addressed by Murray, one which "presents enormous difficulties" (34). The problem is that "one must have a doctrine that covers all...contingencies and is inspired by none of them; for insofar as it would be inspired by the particularities of a transitory situation it would not be a doctrine of the Church universal, part of her eternal and unchangeable deposit of truth" (35). What makes an exploration of the Catholic tradition in this matter particularly difficult is that "all the theories of Church-state relationships were influenced by the facts of the problem as those facts existed at the time" (35).

On the one hand, Murray would assert that an abstract starting point was unhelpful. He thus sought to steal the thunder from the thesis-hypothesis position by rejecting any "ideal" pattern for church-state relations. Thus, in contrast to his position in 1945, he argued that nothing is more unhelpful than the phrase "error has no rights."

> As it stands the statement is meaningless; for rights are
> predicated only of persons (or of institutions). If it means
> anything, it means that error is error; but this is hardly a
> "principle" from which to draw any conclusions with
> regard to the powers of the state. (1948f, 33)

On the other hand, he needed to find a stable doctrine that would not
leave his own church-state theory completely subject to the relativities of history. He needed some first principle in defense of religious liberty that could
not be compromised or subject to political negotiation.

While Murray has been understood by some as a "progressive" Catholic
because he stressed the "development of doctrine." However, it is important
to notice the full context of his argument on this matter.

> Our whole question then has to be viewed in historical per-
> spective. The doctrine of the two powers has had a long
> history and has seen much development; and there is no
> reason to suppose that the development is entirely ended.
> Apart from a view of this development it is impossible for
> the theologian to succeed at his task, which is to vindicate
> the internal consistency of Catholic doctrine at any given
> moment, and to show forth the fact that the development
> has been truly organic, *in eodem scilicet domate, eodem
> sensu, eademque sentitia.* In a matter in which the relativities
> of the political order have played so large a part it is not the
> theologian's task to defend as necessarily permanent and of
> divine origin every right that the Church or the state has
> asserted or exercised in particular periods of history. His
> task is the formulation of principles in such terms that they
> may be asserted as *constantly valid,* and their organization
> into a coherent system that will *cover all contingencies*
> because it is dependent on none. (1948f, 34, emphasis
> mine)

This requires several comments. First, that which is subject to development
is the doctrine of the two powers. This presupposes that there are, in fact,
"two powers, that of Church and State." That there are "two powers" is not
subject to development. The one principle that is unshaken, is that of the
duo sunt of Pope Gelasius.[1] Two there are, august emperor, by which this

world is ruled on title of original and sovereign right—the consecrated authority of the priesthood and the royal power.

Secondly, the reason this doctrine can be said to be subject to development is simply that the "relativities of the political order" have made it such. Where particular doctrines of the church are not subject to such political relativities, one could easily conclude that "development" is not called for. Thus Murray, commenting on the suspicion, prejudice, and hostility resulting from Fr. Ryan's position on church and state, comments as follows:

> These feelings are indeed widely active, and are a serious obstacle to the work of the Church. Obviously, if this result is simply part of the scandal always provoked in the world by the mystery of the Cross, one can only suffer it. However, one would like to be very sure about the right of a government to repress heresy. More precisely, one would like to be sure that this political empowerment of a secular ruler is somehow an inherently necessary prolongation, as it were, of the dogma that the Catholic Church is the one true Church. If it is a piece of eternal unchangeable truth, blessed be he who is not scandalized at it. But before pronouncing the benediction, one would like, I say, to be sure. It is not a question of adapting the truth to secularist susceptibilities; it is a question of the truth itself—what is it. (1948f, 27)

Among those things not subject to historical contingency is that the Roman Catholic Church is the one true church and that there are, in fact, two "powers" (rather than, say, just one). Murray never deviated from this stance. But this places him in a bind. He has, it seems, set up the problem in an asymmetrical manner. In one sense, he is correct in implying that Ryan and other traditionalists would see the empowerment of a secular ruler with the right to repress heresy as an "inherently necessary prolongation" of the belief that the Roman Catholic Church is the true one. It is for Ryan a "necessary prolongation" in the sense that he would conceive it as rational to advance and pursue the (true) Catholic conception of the good in the public square and that this might require legal structures against heresy.

But in another sense it would not be a "necessary prolongation." This can be seen if we understand that the traditionalists could, in one sense, add the temporal qualifier "given sociocultural hegemony" to the assertion that the government has the right to repress heresy in a way that neither they nor Murray would willingly adopt the proposition "The Catholic Church is the one true church." While the traditionalists could affirm the statement "Government has the right to suppress heresy, given the Catholic sociocultural hegemony of the population," neither they nor Murray would ever affirm the statement "The Catholic Church is the one true church, given the sociocultural hegemony of the population." They believed as Murray did that the proposition, "The Catholic Church is the one true church," was true regardless of who or how many within the nation believed it. Moreover, Ryan and the traditionalists were not saying, in the sense required by Murray, that the "right" to repress heresy was a "necessary" prolongation of that proposition. It was for them also only a "contingent" prolongation. Murray, in other words, seems to be equivocating with the term "right," and ascribing to the traditionalists a conception to which they did not subscribe. This unrecognized equivocation will cause him further difficulties as he develops his narrative and fine-tunes his distinctions.

The Direct-Indirect Distinction

Murray began his historical study by attempting to outline three theories of the power of the church in the temporal order: the theory of direct power and two theories of indirect power. St. Bellarmine and John of Paris were brought forth as two examples of the latter. Through these explorations he sought to determine how the church came to defend the governmental repression of heresy or more generally religious intolerance.

The starting point of the direct power theory was that it took the church's confession of the "primacy of the spiritual" to mean that the temporal power emanates from the spiritual power, the church. The theory asserted that Christ, as both Priest and King, delegated to Peter and his successors a direct jurisdiction not only over spiritual affairs but temporal ones as well. While the Pope, according to this view, ordinarily uses only the spiritual sword and delegates the ordinary use of the temporal sword to the prince, he nevertheless retains dominion over it. If the prince is delinquent in his duty, the Pope recovers the use of the temporal sword for the superior interests of Christendom.

The error of this view, according to Murray, "lies in its violation of the autonomy of the state, in its misconception of the origin, nature, and scope of civil authority" (1948f, 39). Clearly, since the prince is conceived simply as a direct instrument of the church—the Pope, as "head" uses the prince simply as one of his "arms"—it follows that "the right of the prince to repress heresy by penal measures is entirely coherent with this theory, as a necessary consequence of it..." (40).

Murray suggests that here lay "the origins of the theoretical justification of the 'right' of Catholic governments to repress heresy." Before the age of Christendom no theoretical justification was attempted. It grew out of the historical fact that the first Christian emperors simply assumed power for a purely political reason—the unification of the Roman empire. While the Church was unhappy over the idea of an empire sustained by the church, "she gave practical acquiescence to the idea of a Church protected and defended by the Empire" (40). Even St. Augustine, Murray argued, was content to justify coercive measures against the Donatists by an argument that was in effect *ab eventu*.

Murray's aim was to try to turn the tables on the thesis-hypothesis theory. Conceding that one can say that the medieval prince had a right legally to repress heresy, one is not then speaking absolutely (in thesis) but in a hypothesis since this

> governmental right was surrounded at the time by various contingencies of fact that gave rise to a special juridical situation. It would be very risky therefore to generalize from the actions of the early Christian emperors, or the emperors in the "translated" empire, or the kings and princes of medieval Christendom, or of Renaissance and Reformation times for that matter, to absolute, permanent "rights" that are, as it were, in thesi the empowerments of something called "the state." (1948f, 42-43)

When Murray turns his attention toward an analysis of the church-state theory of St. Bellarmine (1542-1621), the polemical thrust of his historical narrative becomes clearer. The first step was to locate historically the doctrine of "direct power." The second step was to suggest that because the right to repress heresy was rooted in an historically contingent and false theory, it must also be historically contingent and false. But for his argument to work, he had to collapse a couple of influential "indirect" power theories—theories that were less than tolerant—into a theory of direct power. Or, he at least had to show how, in reality, they were direct power theories at crucial points.

Murray had two motives for turning his attention toward St. Bellarmine. First, as the Counter-Reformation's greatest defender of the Papacy, he was the favorite theorist of contemporary advocates of the thesis-hypothesis doctrine. If Murray succeeded in contextualizing Bellarmine's Church-State theory, he would succeed also in contextualizing the thesis-hypothesis doctrine of the traditionalists. Second, Bellarmine was not an overt advocate of what Murray had been calling the direct power theory. In fact, some of Bellarmine's contemporaries considered him a heretic because of his advocacy of the indirect power of the papacy and his restrictions on the papal *plenitudo potestatis* (42). So Murray has to show that Bellarmine's indirect theory collapses into the direct theory where, in turn, the right to repress heresy can be historically located. His task is to show how Bellarmine's theory was "transitional," that while it was on the one hand "buttressed by a firm political philosophy of the political power as natural in its origin, end and functions" (44), on the other it was "too much fashioned on a set of facts that had ceased to be facts" (1948f, 43). In short, Murray would try to show that Bellarmine's depiction of the "indirect" power was really "direct."

Bellarmine's primary preoccupation, according to Murray, was "to present a purer notion of the entirely spiritual notion of the Church's power against the 'temporalization' of it by the [hierocratic defenders of the] direct-power theory." At the same time he wanted to preserve the prerogatives of the papacy against Gallican and regalist theories with their "laicist" tendencies. Against these latter two movements he wanted to assert, first, that the spiritual authority of the church does indeed reach into temporal society. Secondly, he wanted to assert that the conscience of the prince as prince, not merely private individual, is subject to the spiritual authority. Against both extremes, claims Murray, "he was impelled to develop, out of the Thomistic tradition, the natural law concept of political power" (44). It was to Bellarmine's merit that he

> revived the Thomistic philosophy of political power as natural in origin, temporal in end and field of competence; thus he clarified afresh the radical distinction of the two powers that was denied or obscured by Reformers, regalists, and hierocrats. (1948g, 503-4)

Bellarmine's theory of the indirect power, Murray argues, is simply a direct power limited to exceptional use" (1948f, 45). Murray finds it flawed partly because of Bellarmine's reliance on St. Thomas, who also lived at a time when he could plausibly say that "kings are vassals of the Church" (1948g, 503) and thus could not work out clearly the implications of the autonomy of the political order. Bellarmine's indirect theory was also flawed because polemical preoccupations did not permit him to go deeply into the idea that "the finality of the temporal power, though inferior, is a genuine finality in its own right" (504).

Murray argues that Bellarmine's "indirect power" is in reality a genuine and immediate jurisdiction over the temporal order. Bellarmine, for example, claims that the Pope can rightfully depose princes and set up others in their place, can make and abrogate civil laws, and can authoritatively summon to his tribunal as a temporal judge the case of two rulers at war (1948f, 44-45). Moreover, Murray cites Bellarmine's criticism of the Diet of Speyer at which Charles V was obliged by the Lutheran princes not to enforce the ban on Luther, to respect his life, and permit Lutheran propaganda. Bellarmine argued that "without doubt Christian princes are obliged not to allow their subjects freedom of belief, but to see to it that faith is kept, which the bishops and particularly the Pope teaches as the one to be believed" (48).

What is the theoretical root of this reduction of the indirect power to the direct power? Bellarmine, according to Murray, started out well enough. In the midst of dealing with the controversy over whether the temporal power could be a judge in religious controversy, Bellarmine appealed to the principle that the secular power "can do nothing beyond the empowerment (*virtutem*) it receives from its causes; now the causes of secular magistracy are human and natural; the efficient cause is the election of the people, the end is the peace and temporal tranquility of the commonwealth; therefore the ruler as such has empowerment and authority only of the human order, such as the people can give and such as is required for the preservation of temporal peace" (cited in 1948g, 505).

Murray called this a "fertile principle," which was nevertheless mitigated because Bellarmine also rested his theory on particular time-conditioned terms (1948g, 508), particularly the unity of the *respublica christiana*, as an operative political reality. It was Bellarmine's historical judgment, according to Murray, that was mistaken. He was still captive to the "dream of Origen" (1948f, 46; 1948g, 506), which in its medieval form amounted to the unity of church and state under one *respublica Christi*. "The same unitary concept of society appears constantly as a first premise" (1948g, 511).

Murray argued that the rise of the modern nation-state had disrupted the essential pattern of the *respublica Christi*. This, coupled with the Protestant revolt, had destroyed the very foundations of the religious unity of Europe. Bellarmine wrongly assumed that "if coercion and punishments are faithfully applied, the result would be the restoration of religious unity"

(1948f, 49; see also 1948g, 509). Murray's main point is that Bellarmine's argument against religious liberty

> rests on appeal to the factual and juridical peculiarities of a special historical situation, which are contingent; but it makes no appeal to the principles of Bellarmine's own political philosophy, which are permanent. He uses his natural-law concept of the state in order to prove that the prince is not a judge in religious controversies, because his is of the human, natural order, possessed for a temporal end, for whose achievement he has limited empowerments given to him by the people. This is the permanent truth. But it plays no part in determining the role that the prince should play as "guardian of the Church." Here Bellarmine switches to an historical, concrete concept of political sovereignty, that rests on an hypothesis. The prince may not declare anyone a heretic, but he may burn him if he is one (1948f, 49-50).

This passage gives some indication of Murray's considerable polemical skills. Through an historical analysis of Bellarmine he has attempted to turn the tables on the advocates of the thesis-hypothesis doctrine by historicizing the state's right to repress heresy. If there was any "thesis" to construct, then the controlling principle must be Bellarmine's principle: The rights of the Prince, or state, or government "derive from natural law, so they are limited by natural law." If such an empowerment exists, it must come from some "hypothetical, contingent source."

> In a word the prince's right to repress heresy will not be in a philosophy of the state or in a theology of the Church, but in a situation of fact. Civil intolerance is not thesis but hypothesis. (1948f, 50)

As an alternative to Bellarmine's pseudo-indirect use of ecclesiastical power, Murray turned toward another Catholic whose reflections on matters of church and state he thought came "closer to a permanently valid systematization of the data of revelation" (1948f, 52) on the issue. The theory of John of Paris, while not above reproach, "contains the seeds of a development" that could more plausibly guide the thought and action of the contemporary church in its relations with the state and society.

Murray presents John of Paris as a theorist who, like Bellarmine, sought to split the difference between hierocratism and regalism. (For the detailed history see 1949e, 180ff.) According to Murray, he sought to form a concept of the state that would grant it sufficient autonomy from the pontifical power while at the same time keeping it subject to papal direction.

Here Murray brings to the foreground the statement of *duo sunt* of Pope Gelasius. Murray reiterated this doctrine repeatedly throughout his writings—the implications of which we will address shortly. Here we are concerned with noting that in Murray's narrative John of Paris is the figure who, despite the Gallican tendencies in his thought, "touched once more, and gave fuller statement to, the original doctrine of Gelasius I, the authentic Christian tradition." This position had been "obscured from sight by political realities and by the theory of 'political Augustinism,'" a somewhat messianic concept of governmental power as a direct agent of supernatural redemption" (1948f, 53).

John's chief originality lay in his application of St. Thomas' concept of the state as a natural institution. Murray points to this as the doctrine that dissipated the "equivocation that lay at the root of 'political Augustinism'" (54). John worked out the concrete political consequences of the doctrine that St. Thomas had worked out in the "remoteness of the School." He is both Gelasian and Thomistic in stressing that both powers are from God—from whom "both originate in different ways and for different ends, as respectively sovereign in their own spheres." Yet

> John takes the step that St. Thomas had not taken; he derives, from principle and not from historical fact or contingent juridical situations, the norms of collaboration between the two powers. (55)

This, of course, is exactly what Murray is looking for.

John adopts St. Thomas' natural law conception of the state as "an exigence of nature, independent of grace or sin, unmodified in its essence by redemption." Nevertheless, as a good Aristotelian he recognized that the legislative, judicial, and coercive authority of the Prince also has a moral function. He directs the people to God but only through "temporal ends that are properly human and to a common temporal welfare that enshrines the human element of morality.... The limits of his *direct* power are set by natural law" (56, emphasis mine).

At the same time, Murray claims that John did a great service in clearly establishing the meaning of the "exclusive spiritual character" of the church's sovereignty. For John:

> The Church too is a *regnum*, but wholly and entirely a *regnum sacerdotale*, whose power extends to nothing that is not necessarily related to the priestly redemptive work of Christ, the dispensation of the sacraments, the preservation of the Church's own unity, etc. (56)

Here the dilemma comes to the fore in Murray's historical narrative. Murray, commenting favorably on the moral responsibilities of the Prince in John's theory, concludes by saying, "His function is high indeed, but not messianic." To which a critic might respond by asking: Granting that the Prince's theory is not messianic, just how high is its moral function? And commenting on the "purely spiritual" function of the church we might ask, How "purely" spiritual? A "high" moral requirement of the Prince calls for a thick garment for the public square and reopens the issue of moral and—unless he grounds morality foundationally or transcendentally, or totally abstracts reason from revelation or nature from grace—religious intolerance. An emphasis on the purely spiritual function of the church implies a naked public square and leaves him susceptible to the charge of advocating what, as we will see, he is also most anxious to avoid—a church restricted to the sacristy. In other words, even if one were to grant that the state is purely a natural institution, he would need to set forth a natural law limit not to the direct but to the *indirect* power which he concedes the church must still maintain.

Murray was anxious to argue that "John's dualism is as radical and unattenuated as was Gelasius's." At the same time, he needed to establish that "in determining the relations between the two powers he does not permit their differentiation to be blurred" (57). But have they not already been blurred when he nevertheless maintains, as a good Aristotelian, that not only the church but also the state has a moral function?

Murray, however, was fully aware that he needed to cover this exposed flank (1948f, 63; 1948g, 219). By emphasizing the "purely" spiritual nature of the church's power, he could plausibly be open to the charge of advocating a naked public square, a view of the polity that views all spiritual influence in public affairs as illegitimate. He would seek to deflect this charge by first insisting that although the spiritual power was indirect, it was still a power. He would then make a further distinction between a state that recognized the legitimate indirect power of the church, a "lay state," and a state that didn't, a "laicized state."

Murray sought to avoid advocating a naked public square and a church restricted to the sacristy by emphasizing the indirectness of the power, which was for John of Paris in contrast to Bellarmine's position, really indirect, and yet really a power. But he gives the notion of power a slightly different nuance. The indirect power of the church is "more properly an influence than a power; it is proper to an advisor, who has no authority beyond that of superior wisdom" (1948f, 60). This power is indirect in that "the action of the Church terminates at conscience and its Christian formation." While purely spiritual in nature, it "*indirectly* may and should have effects in the temporal order" (59, emphasis mine). The jurisdiction of the church's power is "indirect in the purest sense; the temporal is not directly touched...; only the spiritual (conscience) is directly touched" (60).

As we have seen, after disposing of St. Bellarmine and the purported permanent right of the church to intervene directly and use coercive power in the pursuit of spiritual ends, Murray turned to John of Paris' theory of the indirect power hoping to find an argument that would allow him to repudiate the use of power for advancing purely spiritual ends. Murray's working assumption at this time seems to be that a rejection of the direct power theory would lead to a rejection of the use of state coercion for spiritual ends altogether. Thus Murray would say that "the Church has no right to demand of the state what the state is not required by nature to give." Moreover,

> the state itself is a perfect society, with its own finality, outside of which it cannot act (any more than the Church can act outside of hers), and with its own autonomy, that forbids the use of its powers as instruments to ends that are not its own (analogously, the powers of the Church can not be used to ends that are not her own). (1948f, 75)

Hooper is right in saying that Murray assumed that the advocacy of coercive force for spiritual ends could only be accepted "within an image of a unitary, nondualistic society, an image which is not true to modern political and social facts" (Hooper 1986, 57). But it is important to understand that the matter was not simply a question of political and social facts.

Murray was also making a normative claim about the modern democratic states vis-à-vis the medieval state. The former was "mature" while the latter was not.

Thus, in the midst of his case against Bellarmine, Murray found it necessary to justify the church's direct involvement in temporal affairs during the Middle Ages.

> Actually, what the Church did was to step into a political vacuum, created by the absence of a political institution able to constrain the monarch to obedience to law. She found a vague and chaotic Germanic right of popular resistance to unjust authority that was insufficient for its own purposes, and she transformed it into a new system of regular juridical procedure for the restraint, deposition, and punishment of Kings. (1948g, 528)

This, he said, was a necessary response to a "contingent, time conditioned" situation. But not only that, it was a response to a political and social disorder of an "immature" or adolescent state (1948g, 526).

> The adolescent as he grows, differentiates himself from the parent; and though the general parental right of direction and correction remains valid, certain expressions of it are no longer valid, no longer "right." They were rights only in the hypothesis of adolescence. So it was with the civil order. It grew up; it became a State; and as a State it differentiated itself from the Church, as a society in its own right, with its own institutions to direct and correct its action. And its growing self-consciousness inevitably led it to reject the performance of certain offices in its regard that the Church, in default of agents, had performed. One of these was the ecclesiastical intervention against unjust authority, as an institutional procedure that once had political and constitutional status. This status was now denied it by the adult State, come into the consciousness of maturity. (1948g, 530)

Murray goes so far as to call this differentiation an "intention of nature," which has "moved the problem of Church-state relations into a new phase."

> The problem in its new phase is governed by the new
> dyarchy, *Church and Christian citizen*, which has behind it
> all the warrant in theological and political principle, and in
> papal approval, necessary to legitimate the erection on it of
> a genuine Catholic thesis. (1949e, 231, emphasis mine)

In other words, the new problem under the conditions of modernity is not, strictly speaking, one of church and state, but rather one of church-as-mediated-through-the-individual-conscience-of-the-Christian-citizen and state. Hence, its indirectness.

At this point, Murray appropriates and transforms Leo XIII's notion of *concordia* or harmony between the two powers. By employing this concept Murray tries to keep the separation of the two powers from being a strict and absolute separation. The concept of *concordia* also keeps the indirect and spiritual power still a power. Leo had posited the necessity of an "orderly relation" between the two powers of church and state. While questioning whether Leo "fully realized the modern problematic in regard to the exercise of the indirect power" (1949e, 220), Murray argued that he put forth a principle that suggested its solution. Because the power was indirect, the issue no longer involved that of the medieval *sacerdotium* and *imperium*, but rather the *sacerdotium* and *civis idem et christianus* (1949e, 222). If there is conflict and not harmony between the two powers the conflict is felt "in the depths of the *personal* conscience" (1949e, 220, emphasis mine). The "finality of this harmony is not a social but a *personal* unity—the integrity of the human personality" (1949e, 221). In short, Murray has situated the hierarchy of the church one place removed from the civil power and declared the recognition of such as an act of civil maturity.

Murray would later receive substantial criticism on this notion of "mature state." Edward A. Goerner (1965, 169-84) is particularly critical of Murray's claim that the Anglo-Saxon democracies are an exemplar of the mature adult state, and charges Murray with a bit of Anglo-American chauvinism. Murray is quite clear, however, that the reason the issue of religious liberty is better seen against the background of political life in the Anglo-Saxon countries is that "the Anglo- Saxon political tradition suffered only briefly the blight of absolutism" (1949e, 187), roughly from Henry VIII until the Glorious Revolution (see McElroy 1989, 25ff.).

To understand why he resorted to this metaphor, Murray's reference to the "adult state" must be placed within the context of the indirect-direct distinction. By employing the metaphor of adult state, Murray was making a normative claim—that the hierarchy of the church ought to be at least once removed from the civil power. Similarly, it was only when the civil power was immaturely organized in some sort of monarchical form that the temporal power of the church ought not in the first instance to be mediated through the conscience of the Christian citizen, but rather through the monarch.

Now, Murray seems to have believed that this was a powerful argument against the Catholic modus vivendi position. The assumption was that the advocates of the thesis-hypothesis doctrine could only maintain their position by making a counterclaim for the normative status of a monarchical form of government. And indeed, Murray's assumption has some warrant, which can be seen if we consider Murray's article "For the Freedom and Transcendence of the Church" (1952a) and the reaction it occasioned from one of his traditional Catholic opponents, Francis Connell.

Largely in response to Murray's argument Connell, in an article entitled "The Theory of the 'Lay State'" (1951), insisted that the doctrine of the Kingship of Christ (as promulgated in Pius XI's encyclical *Quas primas*) "ascribes to civil rulers the obligation to obey the law of Our Savior in their official acts" (11), and for that reason they are not limited merely to the precepts of natural law. He conceded that the state cannot be bound to all the laws Christ intended for individuals since the state cannot be baptized, receive the Holy Eucharist, or strive for eternal life. Nevertheless,

> the state can be bound by the positive law of Christ in the sense that civil rulers as such can be *directly* (and not merely through consideration for the beliefs and desires of the citizens) bound to acknowledge in the Church of Christ the authority to exercise certain functions which otherwise would belong to the state itself by natural law, and to promote in certain respects the supernatural activities of the Church. (Connell 1951, 12)

As an example of how the positive law of Christ imposes the positive law of Christ on "civil rulers," Connell cited Christ's injunction "to make disciples of all nations" and "to go into the whole world and preach the gospel to every creature." Surely, concluded Connell,

> this implies on the part of civil rulers the obligation to allow the preachers of the Gospel to teach their people the truths of salvation—and this, in turn, implies the obligation

> binding the civil rulers to investigate the credentials of
> those who claim to bear a divine message, to find out
> whether or not their doctrine bears the seal of divinity. It is
> absurd to say that in such a case the civil rulers are bound
> to allow the preaching of Catholic doctrine on the ground
> that the citizens have a right to the practice of their religion,
> because in the case visualized the citizens have not as yet
> accepted the Catholic religion. In other words, the right of
> the Catholic Church to preach the Gospel, *independently of*
> *every civil power*, implies an obligation of the state, imposed
> directly by Jesus Christ, to permit the legitimately dele-
> gated preachers of the Gospel to enter its territory and to
> announce their message to the people without hindrance.
> Surely, this is an obligation over and above the obligations
> prescribed by natural law. (13)

Murray pounced on an almost unconscious assumption of Connell,
which was reflected in his use of the term "civil ruler." This gave Murray, at
least in the American context, a rhetorical if not a substantive edge in the
debate. Perhaps, Murray charged, when Connell speaks of "the state," he
"unwittingly means the unlimited monarch in the tradition of French classical monarchy, who was also 'Father of the People,' possessor of the *ius politi-*
cum, and hence the single source of law and governmental decision"
(Murray 1952a, 37).

Murray challenged Connell's constant identification of "the state" and
"the civil ruler."

> Only one who was, perhaps unconsciously, thinking in
> terms of absolute monarchy would speak of the civil rulers
> and *their* people; the phrase is straight out of the vocabu-
> lary of the eighteenth century, the age of the enlightened
> despot. In this universe of discourse the personal pronoun
> was appropriate.... On the other hand, how silly it would be
> to speak of "the President of the U.S. and *his* people"!
> (1952a, 37)

Murray's tactic is clear. As the title of his rejoinder ("For the Freedom
and Transcendence of the Church") suggests, Murray argued that advocates
of the thesis-hypothesis doctrine had bound the church to a particular form

of civil government, a monarchy, thus denying the church's freedom from all political forms. He then put forth his central contention.

> In a political hypothesis where there is a dispersion of polit-
> ical responsibility and power among a variety of institu-
> tions and men, whose functions of rule are constitutionally
> limited, an obligation to investigate the truth of the Church
> is impossible either to understand or to apply. (38)

In a word, Fr. Connell, according to Murray, "wants the harmony between human law and positive divine law to be conceived in a special way—by the action of a centralized monarchy with unlimited power, acting under the directly exercised jurisdiction of the Church" (39). He is in fact "a crypto-monarchist" (43).

Most commentators on Murray see this, quite rightly, as a brilliant Catholic defense of constitutional democracy. While Goerner is correct in pointing to an important weakness in Murray's project— his failure to analyze and evaluate the nature of political forms (monarchy, aristocracy, and democracy)—this criticism must not be overstated. For one thing, Murray obviously thought that constitutional democracy was the preferable form of government since this was implied in his metaphor of the "mature state."

More importantly, though, the question of political forms is not directly relevant to the central question in the discussion: religious liberty. Murray seems to have assumed that the putative right to suppress the public expression of a false religion is nullified simply by an appeal to a democratic rather than a monarchical form of government. But it is not clear what democracy per se (i.e., the procedural question) has to do with the substantive question concerning religious toleration.

In a response to Murray that is often overlooked in the secondary literature, Connell focused on the problem by putting forth Murray's argument in the following syllogistic form (Connell 1952, 55):

> 1. Christ did not make any absolute laws for civil rulers that
> civil rulers would be incapable of fulfilling in any real, con-
> crete political situation.

> 2. But it is impossible under a government such as we have
> in the United States for the civil officials to investigate the
> truth of the Church (the credentials of Catholicism).

3. Therefore, Our Lord laid down no law that is absolute, binding all civil rulers under the Christian dispensation to investigate the credentials of Catholicism.

Connell centers his sights on the minor premise.

> If what is meant is that certain unfortunate conditions prevailing in our land, particularly the fact that so many of our citizens are not concerned with seeking the one true religion, render it the most feasible policy for our government to show equal favor to all religions (and consequently exempt the civil officials from the obligation of seeking the true religion as far as any governmental policy is concerned) I fully agree.... I firmly believe that for our land *the most practical policy* is to have equal freedom for all religions, and I cannot see any probability of a change of circumstances in future [sic] (even the gaining of an overwhelming majority of votes by Catholics) that would justify a change in our national policy of equal rights for all creeds.
>
> However, if the meaning of this minor is that it is essential to a democratic form of government to show no special favor to the one true religion, so that there need be no attempt on the part of the officials to discover the true religion, I deny the minor. *I cannot see why homage cannot be rendered to Christ the King, and obedience given to His laws, and special favor shown to His Church in a democracy, just because it is a democracy.* (1952, 55, emphasis mine)

This passage is worth quoting at length because it responds to Murray's implied contention, which is central to the direct-indirect distinction, that the Catholic thesis only holds in a monarchy where the power of the church is *direct* and not in a constitutional democracy when it is *indirect*. While Murray was quite perceptive in identifying and criticizing Connell's implicit monarchical bias, his defense of a constitutional democracy as a superior form of government simply does not address the central substantive contention of the thesis-hypothesis doctrine. Connell (1952, 56) put it quite lucidly: "from the undeniable fact that in the United States conditions are such as to preclude governmental favor to the Church of Christ, it does not follow that it is not the obligation per se of the government in a democracy such as ours to find out the true religion and favor it." After setting forth this argument Connell simply points out what we had occasion to do at the beginning of chapter 2—that Leo XIII had said as much in the encyclical *Longingua oceani* in 1895, when he applied the doctrine to the United States.

Murray seemed to think that a defense of liberal constitutional democracy per se could trump the thesis-hypothesis doctrine since the latter, he believed, rested on monarchical assumptions. But not just any form of liberal democracy would do. This accounts for the second major distinction brought forth by Murray.

The Lay-Laicized Distinction

For many Catholics, including Murray, the "laicized state" were fighting words. They represented a view of church-state relations that grew out of the radical Jacobin anticlericalism of revolutionary and postrevolutionary France. The Jacobin doctrine was capsulated in the slogan "The Church in the sacristy." The church, according to Murray, opposed this view by insisting that she had a right to influence the political, legal, social, and economic institutions of the temporal order. That is, she insisted on maintaining power, albeit indirectly, within the temporal sphere.

Over against the democratic "laicized state" which advocated the naked public square as a matter of principle and a clerical state that advocated a direct influence of the church in temporal affairs, Murray proposed a tertium quid: the democratic "lay state." The lay state, in contrast to the laicist state, would recognize the unique juridical personality of the church, the existence of a spiritual authority that has an independent sovereignty over all its subjects. Thus, the separation between church and state would not be absolute (1948f, 80, 89-90; 1949e, 424).

More concretely, the distinction between the lay and laicized state was reflected in the difference between the type of liberalism that grew out of the French Revolution and that of American Anglo-Saxon liberal democracy. Murray's strategy would be to argue that the latter more closely approximated the norm of the "lay state." The church's nineteenth-century condemnation of "liberalism" was valid if restricted to Continental liberalism but less so if applied to the Anglo-American variety.

In an early *America* article entitled "How Liberal is Liberalism" (1946c), Murray tried to explain the church's nineteenth-century condemnation of liberalism. Most Americans, Murray said, have little idea of the nature of the liberalism the church had condemned in the nineteenth century. Insofar as the term means anything to the average American it simply "stands for the sum total of all things that enlightened modern men consider worthwhile." However, nineteenth-century liberalism was not "just a sentimental mood, an inherited persuasion of very vague content." Rather it represented "a highly doctrinaire social theory, resting on premises as dogmatic as any ecclesiastical belief." This variety of liberalism embraced "a militant secularism, a systematic denial of the relevance of religion to social life" (1946c, 6). Proposition 3 of the *Syllabus of Errors* was targeted against the liberal concept of abstract liberty. That proposition condemned the view that "Human reason, having no regard of God, is the sole arbiter of truth and falsity, right and wrong; it is a law unto itself, and of its own natural resources it is adequate to secure the good of men and peoples." Because this was the basic premise upon which the men of the French Revolution proclaimed freedom of religion, Murray believed Pope Gregory XVI correctly condemned it. It is a *deliramentum*, an absurdity, a piece of nonsense because it "contradicts the first principle of ethical reason—the sovereignty of God over the human conscience" (1946c, 7).

Proposition 39 of the *Syllabus*, Murray argued, was directed against the paradoxical results of a freedom of religion grounded in this manner. It condemns the claim that "The republican state, as the origin and source of all rights, possesses a juridical competence that is circumscribed by no limits." At this point Murray will not attempt to show "how the Liberal theory of the atomic individual, with its rationalistic premises, logically led to state socialism." He was simply content to state the paradox.

> When individualistic Liberalism gave every man the "freedom" to make his own little religion, it also let the Leviathan State move in to make the real, big religion—social secularism. Every man could privately be as religious as he pleased. But let him not attempt to make his religion a force in shaping the structure, the institutions, the spirit and tendency of society. Blocking such an attempt was the mighty power of the only divine majesty which Liberalism acknowledged—the state. (7)

For these liberals, the drive for separation of church and state was "only an intermediate objective." Their ultimate aim, inspired by Rousseau, was "a completely secularized society, in which religion would be denied any vital influence on the political, social, economic or educational life" (7).

Murray's thoughts on this subject were deepened and received further articulation seven years later in his article, "The Church and Totalitarian Democracy." He was particularly influenced by several historical studies. From Geoffrey Brunn's *Europe and the French Revolution: 1799–1814* (1938) and Christopher Dawson's *Beyond Politics* (1939), he received further confirmation of his intuitions about the religious nature of Continental Liberalism. He thus cites (1952b, 528) Brunn's observations on the nature of the clash between church and state in the Revolutionary period.

> For the first time in modern annals the *civitas humana* was set forth unequivocally as the ultimate reality in the place of the *civitas Dei*; for the first time the authority of reason was unblushingly acknowledged as superior to the authority of revelation, and the doctrine of human perfectibility (shortly to be reformulated as the doctrine of progress) was substituted for the doctrine of miraculous redemption.

Similarly, he quoted Dawson (531) to support his claim that Jacobin democracy was also "religious" as well as totalitarian. Dawson claimed that the Jacobin solution to the problem of church and state was "the prototype of all our modern revolutionary and communitarian movements."

> Although it finally resulted in the separation of Church and State, this was the very opposite of the ideal which it consciously aimed at. Its intention was to unite rather than separate, to destroy the traditional dualism of the two powers and the two societies to reabsorb the Church in the community. Nevertheless, the community was not a secular community in the strict sense of the word. The new Republic as conceived by Robespierre and St. Just and by their master Rousseau before them was a spiritual community, based on definite moral doctrines and finding direct religious expression in an official civic cult....

However, the most important influence on Murray was J. T. Talmon's *The Rise of Totalitarian Democracy* (1952). Murray points out that Talmon, in situating the roots of totalitarian democracy in the two Rousseauist principles of rationalist individualism and political absolutism was actually reiterating, "with his own accent," the errors which Propositions 3 and 39 of the *Syllabus of Errors* had condemned (1952b, 534).

But even more importantly, Murray found further confirmation of his own developing train of thought in Talmon's desire to clearly distinguish "totalitarian democracy" from what he called "liberal democracy." This would dovetail quite nicely with a distinction Murray had been stressing in his polemic against the traditionalists— the distinction between the laicized state of Continental Liberalism and the lay state of the Anglo-Saxon democracies.

While Murray was sympathetic to Talmon's work, he does make one criticism that deserves special mention, since it serves to illuminate the problem with the distinction between the lay and laicized state in particular and the broader dilemma in general. Murray states that Talmon was in error when he implied that "liberal democracy" emerged from the same eighteenth-century premises as did "totalitarian democracy" (532). Murray wanted to keep the differences even more distinct than did Talmon. But his attempt to make a clear distinction between the philosophical premises upon which the American type of liberal democracy rested and those of "totalitarian democracy" would put him in a bind.

In 1949 Murray had delivered a scathing criticism of an individualistic natural rights reading of the First Amendment, one he identified with its author, James Madison (1949i). Murray had in effect conceded that the most significant figures involved in prohibiting the establishment of religion and guaranteeing free exercise had in fact been influenced by the same individualist premises as those of the Continental Liberals. This had particularly come to the fore in Murray's scathing criticism of Madison's natural rights arguments for religious liberty in the Virginian's famous *Memorial and Remonstrance* (1785). We will examine Murray's criticism of Madison and Locke in more detail in chapter 5. The relevant point to be stressed now is that in 1949 Murray was willing to concede what he was quick to deny to Talmon in 1952, namely that the lay American state had philosophical premises not so different from the Continental laicist state. Why?

Understanding the polemical context helps. Murray wrote his article "The Church and Totalitarian Democracy" as "a background study of Leo XIII" (1952b, 525). Murray needed desperately to show that in his condemnation of liberalism, Leo XIII had in mind the Continental "laicized" version and not the Anglo-Saxon/American "lay" version. At the same time he needed to locate the foundations of the latter in a more acceptable tradition.

Thus, while he could agree with Talmon in distinguishing two types of democracy, he insisted upon adding:

> The essential distinction is between democracies based on the Continental Liberalism of eighteenth-century origin, and those inspired by the liberal tradition, whose antecedents are longer, and importantly *medieval and Christian*. (532)

How could American Catholics oppose *that*?

The full implications of Murray's argument must await further exposition. But if we keep in mind his assertion that the root of all secularist monism is the denial of the Gelasian dualism—"Two there are" versus "one there is"(1952b, 532)—and couple it with his claim that "the preservation of this dualism in some functional form is the distinctive mark of true democracy as over against the totalitarian type" (1952b, 535), then we are prepared to understand why the liberalism of the American republic should not be thrown out with the Continental Liberalist bathwater. Murray wanted to prove that the American understanding of religious freedom as embodied in the First Amendment was distinct from the laicist state of Continental Liberalism in that it admits of a dyarchy of rule over man. The terms of the dyarchy visible in the First Amendment are not state and church (the manner of dyarchy is constitutionally excluded by the provision against "establishment of religion"), but state and the human person, *civis idem et christianus* (to adopt Leo XIII's phrase). The American state does not recognize on the part of any church the right to direct an authoritative intervention in the processes. However, it does recognize in American society a "spiritual power" that stands, as it were, not only over against it—the Christian conscience, whose demands are acknowledged as relevant to the political order, whose right of moral judgment on all the processes of government is likewise acknowledged, guaranteed free expression, and provided with institutional channels for it (1949e, 189).

Not only that, but the First Amendment provides for

> the immunity of conscience from governmental coercion, and the freedom of conscience to impose upon government the moral demands that are permanent exigencies of the human spirit in consequence of its obligation "to obey God rather than man." (189)

Murray was attempting to move in his argument from the free exercise of the religious conscience granted in the First Amendment to a positive constitutional recognition of the spiritual power. For Murray the influence of the spiritual power terminates in the conscience, is manifested in lives of Christian citizens, and then has temporal political effects (see Love 1965, 70). But, as Love perceptively points out, even if one allows that there is an immunity of conscience recognized in the "free exercise clause," this hardly implies any right to impose upon government any religiously inspired "moral demands" (71).

How, we might ask, could Murray make this rather obvious mistake? Again, an understanding the polemical context is crucial. Murray needed to assert that the First Amendment does in fact embody a positive constitutional recognition of the spiritual power in order to keep a clear distinction between a lay and laicized state. A positive recognition of the spiritual power would stand in sharp contrast to any constitutional view that sought to exclude the spiritual power by restricting the church to the sacristy.

Now, the distinction could still be maintained if the laicized state did in fact represent a hostile attitude toward the church while the lay state took neither a positive nor hostile attitude. Not having a negative attitude toward the church is still distinct from having a positive attitude. But that still leaves open the question concerning the extent to which the church through the laity is to have consequences in the temporal world.

This most crucial question was masked to a certain extent by Murray's distinctions between lay and laicized state and the direct and indirect power of the church in the first place. By employing these distinctions, Murray shifted the emphasis away from the extent to which the church would have consequences in the temporal world to the means by which it was to have such. So, for example, he stated:

> The question does not concern the substance of the right of the Church to judge and—in medieval terms—to direct and correct all human affairs under their religious and moral aspects. The question concerns rather the manner of exercise of this right. More exactly, the question is, who shall be the *executor*, so to speak, of the Church's moral judgment? *This has always been the ultimately crucial question.* (1949e, 218, emphasis mine)

The executor of the right to intervene in temporal matters is, for Murray, the Christianly informed conscience of the citizen in a constitutional democracy—not the Christian monarch. But if that is the ultimately crucial question, we might ask what it has to do with the narrower question of governmental repression of heresy and the broader issue of religious freedom and toleration, or the even broader issue of God's will for the state? I ask the question rhetorically at this point, because this passage is a microcosm of his historical-polemical narrative as a whole. Murray's distinctions shift the focus of the debate away from the substantive issue of religious liberty, to the procedural question of "how" and by "whom" that influence is to be effected.[2]

Moreover, Murray shifted the terms of the debate without adequately addressing the possibility of civil intolerance of false religion by the laity—civil intolerance indirectly, from the bottom up, as it were. Murray's historical field of vision was understandably limited to secular intolerance from the bottom up, as represented by totalitarian democracy and religious intolerance from the top down, as represented by the Catholic state. But it did not extend to the issue of lay intolerance from the bottom up. Murray never accounted for the kind of procedurally fair democratic intolerance one might encounter, for instance, in Puritan New England or to a lesser extent in early nineteenth-century America. Lay religious intolerance is still religious intolerance.

Several times during this period he does come close to addressing the issue. At one point Murray even recognizes that there is not, in John of Paris' indirect theory any more than there is in Bellarmine's, "any limitation to the sheer scope of the primacy of the spiritual power; it extends to all that howsoever touches the supernatural end of man" (1948f, 69–70). But to the extent that grace pervades nature, that is, inasmuch as the nature/grace or reason/revelation distinctions are not absolute, everything and anything could plausibly touch "the supernatural end of man" unless one does what Murray does not want to do—restrict the church to the sacristy.

On several occasions, he comes close to addressing the question of democratic religious intolerance but not insignificantly avoids the issue. Addressing the issue of the variety of juridical forms confronted by the church as the "religion of the state," Murray states:

> Its modalities and implications in some future "new Christendom" on the democratic model, spontaneously arisen through the inner transformation of man, would be difficult

to predict. Perhaps the appellation, "religion of the *state*," may fit badly. But one expects that the new wine would hardly tolerate confinement in certain of the old wine skins. (1948f, 84)

And, in a lengthy footnote that directly challenges the view of Ryan, Murray concludes:

> Finally, it should be clear that, when one undertakes to predict what the constitutional provisions for religious liberty would be if the United States ever were to grow into religious unity, one is certainly not interpreting Leo XIII but indulging in some dubious theological and political crystal gazing. No one who knows the history of Church-state relationships and the part that experience has played in them would venture on such predictions. (1948f, 93, note 39)

These responses, I want to suggest, avoid the most crucial question in the debate. The issues posed here touch at the core of the issue and cannot be dismissed as "dubious theological and political crystal gazing." One can certainly appreciate the unwillingness of Murray to be overly speculative, but the crucial issue to be addressed concerns the nature of the argument for the toleration of an act society overwhelmingly considers religiously offensive and immoral, and which that society considers to be a threat to their political unity. Moreover, the question is not entirely speculative, since Murray admitted that given the historically contingent nature of the adolescent state "the medieval prince had a *right* to repress heresy" (1948f, 41). The principle of social dualism was not particularly relevant in this case. However, he then adds:

> one is not then "speaking absolutely," but in a hypothesis— in the hierocratic hypothesis of the origin and end of political power, in the social hypothesis wherein heresy was treason and treason heresy, and in the political hypothesis wherein the unity and good of the state (if one may use the term "state" of Christendom or its units) was identically the unity and good of the Church. The governmental right was surrounded at the time by various contingencies of fact that gave rise to a special juridical situation. It would be very

risky therefore to generalize...to certain absolute, permanent "rights" that are, as it were, *in thesi* the empowerments
of something called "the state." (41–42)

First, it is not clear that the claim to suppress heresy because it was trea-
son requires the hierocratic view of the end and purpose of political power.
One could plausibly make the same claim on the sort of social dualism and
theory of indirect power that Murray says John of Paris advocated.

Secondly, Murray is again equivocating with the term "thesis" here. In a
sense, as we have argued, even Murray's opponents would claim the right to
repress heresy is not "absolute" but "contingent" upon certain conditions of
societal fact. But they were not putting forth a political or social claim as
Murray suggests here. They were putting forth a moral claim based on their
Christian theological convictions which said that society would be better off
if it were united by the one true religion. And they simply argued that the
state as a moral entity and as the guarantor of the common good ought to
preserve and promote that unity. It might be true, as Murray says, that "the
concept of the *Ecclesia universalis* as a religio-political entity long since
ceased to have basis in fact" and that "the *crimen ecclesiasticum* is no longer
also *crimen politicum*" (1948f, 42). But that "fact"—that "is"—simply does not
yield the moral claim that society ought not to be so unified. That "political
unity is now a particular order of unity in its own right" (1948f, 72) does not
imply that it ought to be, especially given Murray's understanding, "Pluralism is against the will of God."

In short, while Murray could challenge the completely secularized
"laicized" state by emphasizing the indirectness of the spiritual power, he
had no analogous point to make against the Catholic modus vivendi position
when the legitimacy of that indirectness was conceded.[3] If we may once
again employ a recent metaphor, Murray agreed with the traditionalists that
the public square could not and should not be naked. But he had to provide
a strong argument for a thin garment over against the thicker one proposed
by the traditionalists. The distinctions between the direct and indirect power
of the church and the lay and laicized state, I have suggested, did not do the
job. He had, however, one more distinction.

The Society-State Distinction

A number of commentators on Murray have taken note of the importance of
the society-state distinction in his thought and have commented on how his

development of the implications of this distinction have served as a Catholic defense of limited constitutional democracy. In the exposition that follows, I will critically examine this distinction along with the correlative Roman Catholic doctrine of subsidiarity and ask whether this doctrine can extricate him from his dilemma, as some have maintained. I will show that it fails to do so, and will suggest that the dilemma that confronts the Catholic social theorist on the issue of religious liberty can be located within the broader tension that exists between the doctrine of subsidiarity and the issue of state's responsibility for the common good.

Thomas Love argued that Murray's carefully distinguished ethical, theological, and political dimensions put forth in his 1945 argument became "hopelessly blurred," because of his failure to distinguish the state from society (1965a, 48), and this was why, by implication, his first argument for religious liberty failed. Similarly, John Coleman argues that Murray's use of the society-state distinction undercut the traditional prohibition of the public expression of non-Catholic religion. He argues that

> By appealing to the distinction between society and the state, Murray shifted the burden of public acknowledgment of the sovereignty of God from the state—which is, in any event, incompetent in religious matters—to the wider society, the people acting through their voluntary mediating structures and corporate groups. (1978, 39)

Coleman is typical of a number of Catholic defenders of Murray's position on religious liberty. He argues that the Catholic case for religious liberty for non-Catholic churches depends upon the distinction between state and society and on the principle of subsidiarity as middle terms in the argument (48). The principle of subsidiarity in Catholic social thought involves the recognition of "intermediate associations" that stand "between" the state and the individual. It is a principle of Catholic social theory that attempts to split the difference between statism and individualism by recognizing the authority of non-state societal structures.

Murray did indeed shift the focus of the argument toward the society-state distinction. And indeed, this was a significant contribution toward a Roman Catholic defense of constitutional government, particularly, as we shall see in the next chapter, of the American democratic experiment. However, by suggesting that we uncouple the issues of democracy (the procedural question) on the one hand and religious liberty (the substantive question) on the other I hope to show why this distinction could not extricate him from the dilemma.

Two immediate factors led Murray to make the distinction between society and state. The first involved the attempt to refute the seemingly logical deductions of his traditional Catholic opponents. The following deductions, Murray claimed (1948f, 28-29), are not legitimate, even though each premise is true:

> 1. *Society* can only be saved by a return to the law of Christ.
>
> Therefore the *state* has the function of promoting this return to faith and therefore *government* must act in this manner, e.g. by "exterminating" heretics.

> 2. The good of *society,* even in the temporal aspects of life, is impossible without the practice of the supernatural virtues—faith, mortification, charity, patience, magnanimity, etc.
>
> Therefore the *state* has an interest in these virtues; and therefore the *government* must concern itself with their observance.

> 3. What is "error" and what is "vice" always has a social reference and tends to the injury of *society.*
>
> Therefore all error and all vice come under the cognizance of the *state*, and must be suppressed by the action of *government.*

The first motive for distinguishing between society and state was to sustain, along with his traditionalist Catholic antagonists, an anti-individualist position (expressed in the premises of each argument). Murray agreed with traditionalists: not only the individual soul, but also society, is responsible to God. At the same time he wanted to deny the seemingly logical implications of political intolerance that the thesis-hypothesis position in church-state theory drew from this. The intent of the distinction would be to stress the importance of non-state, societal structures by stressing that the state is merely one of these structures.

The second motive for emphasizing the distinction grew out of his discussion of "totalitarian democracy." As we have seen, it was crucial that Murray distinguish his concept of the lay state, which permitted the indirect power of the church in temporal affairs, from that of the "laicized" state of revolutionary and postrevolutionary France. In his article, "The Church and Totalitarian Democracy" (1952b), Murray argued that coupled with the "dechristianization of France" (527) was the "politicization of all social life" and the "obliteration of all distinction between state and society" (526).

The first principle of the social monism that grew out of revolutionary France was that the political aspect encompassed all of societal life. Society is absolutely homogeneous in that all political parties, estates, and corporate bodies are disallowed. They are representative of "partial interests" in Rousseau's sense.

> Society therefore is composed directly of individuals, all absolutely equal; there are no social entities intermediate between the individual and the state. (1952b, 536)

With Murray's motives for making this distinction clear, I now intend to examine the philosophical and theological roots of the society-state distinction and the principle of subsidiarity in Aristotelian and Thomistic political theory. My concern will be with determining whether the society-state distinction can do the work Murray wants it to. Can it yield an ahistorical case for religious liberty for non-Catholic churches as Coleman suggests?

Both Love and Coleman give the impression that the society-state distinction was virtually unheard of by Murray's conservative Catholic opponents and by Pope Leo XIII and Pius XI. Love, for instance, recognizes that Murray, if his project is to be successful, must remove the state (though not society) from being "subject to the law of Christ, bound to obey the teachings of Christ, to be ruled by the Gospel, etc." (1965a, 79, citing Murray 1948f, 29). Murray's dilemma is particularly acute, Love realizes, in large part because Murray himself admits that the popes, specifically Pius XI's *Ubi arcano* (1922) and *Quas primas* (1925), do claim that state, society, and government are subject to such.

As already suggested, Murray's strategy here is to dismiss these claims as having grown out of a papal polemic with the "laicized state."

> The meaning of such papal statements is luminous in the light of the false doctrines of laicism that are condemned; but the precise extension of meaning is to be understood by us, as by the Church herself, *ex natura rei*: what is the law of Christ for the state, or government, or society, as

> determined by the action and end proper to each of these
> realities. (1948f; see Love 1965a, 79)

Love takes Murray's basic point to be that in the controversy with the advocates of the laicized state, the popes inadvertently employed the concepts of "society," "state," and "government," in a confused manner. To be consistent, says Love, Murray should have said that the popes simply failed to recognize that they were dealing with two distinct problems, that of "church and society" and that of "church and state." Instead Murray claims that the intention of the popes has always been to emphasize the broader question of church and society and that, unfortunately for polemical reasons, the narrower problem of church and state seems foremost (Love 1965a, 80).

Love is perceptive in pointing to Murray's rather ingenious but misguided move here. But the point needs to be pressed a bit harder. The papal assertions that the state and government (as well as society) were subject to the law of Christ, etc., cannot be dismissed, as Murray claimed at this time, simply as a polemic directed at Continental Liberalism. They did indeed make the distinction between society and state, but their reason for making the distinction was not simply polemical, nor can it be said that the popes were all that confused about the church-society and church-state problem.

The society-state distinction was recognized by Catholic social thinkers long before Murray. But it was recognized within the context of Aristotelian-Thomistic political theory. As such, the distinction could not, in and of itself and without radical surgery, release the state from its obligations to "the law of Christ."

Popes Leo XIII and Pius XI both recognized the society-state distinction, and the latter, particularly in his encyclical *Quadragesimo anno* (1931), even gave definition to the correlative doctrine of subsidiarity, which meant a recognition of "intermediate associations" which stand between the state and the individual. But they both could also consistently adhere to the thesis-hypothesis doctrine and argue for religious intolerance. Why such a view is not inconsistent, contrary to the views of Love, Coleman, and Murray, can be answered by an inquiry into the Aristotelian-Thomistic view of societal differentiation upon which they constructed their social philosophy.[4]

Set against the quasi-totalitarian *polis* of Plato's *Republic*, which recognized no independent structural identity of various societal institutions, it has often been asserted that there is a "kernel" of societal differentiation in Aristotle's thought (Nisbet 1973, 396). As a contemporary Thomist puts it,

Aristotle "maintained the autonomy of lesser social groups in political society" (Schall 1987, 35).

Such an assertion, however, needs to be qualified because, despite their differences, both Plato and Aristotle favored a hierarchical society. In contrast to the Platonic society which consisted simply of a threefold division of society into classes (ruler-philosophers, civilian-military administrators, and the masses—the "community of pigs"), Aristotle's hierarchical society did indeed allow for a greater measure of societal differentiation. Aristotle recognized that the "components which are to make up a unity must differ in kind" (Aristotle, *Politics*, 73), a differentiation that included classes of persons as well a hierarchy of lower and higher levels of communal life. However, the differences of kind were all parts of the *polis* as the original societal whole.

For Aristotle the *polis* is the comprehensive community embracing as its parts domestic communities (*familia*)—including man as head of household, wife, children, and slaves, the kinship community (*sib*), as well as marketing and trade relations (the sphere of retributive justice). Although from a historical (chronological) viewpoint man must exist before the organization of the city-state, nevertheless the individual, the family, and other differentiated societal groups are secondary to the city-state from the moral and ontological perspective. The *polis* represents the ultimate perfection of societal life. The *polis*, says Aristotle, "is by nature clearly prior to the family and the individual, since the whole is of necessity prior to the part...(11). The metaphysical assumptions of Aristotle are not to be seen as radically distinct from Plato, at least as far as their social ontologies are concerned.

> In the Republic of Plato the organic model is employed in characterizing the relation of man to society. Both are conceived as organic unities containing functionally interrelated parts. The virtue of justice becomes basic and is defined in terms of fulfilling one's function. In Aristotle's *Politics* one can find a developmental version of the organic model. The individual is seen as realizing himself in various social entities, starting with the family and culminating in the *polis*. Both Plato's and Aristotle's social philosophies are made possible by a metaphysics which one finds reality in forms. Individuals are only real to the degree to which they participate in these forms or realize the forms within them. (Boonin 1969, 76-77)

As the final two sentences suggests, Aristotle's view of human society, from its smallest unity to the city-state (*polis*) was founded metaphysically in the substantial form of human nature. Since man is unable to realize his essential end in isolation, the disposition toward communal life is implied in his rational nature. This innate social impulse is realized in a hierarchy of lower and higher levels of communal life. Each lower community strives for its perfection in a higher association culminating in the *polis*—the perfect human community—which embraces all other communities and individuals as its parts (Dooyeweerd 1958, 3:201).

According to Aristotle's natural philosophy, all reality moves from potentiality to actuality according to its own nature. Aristotle held that this process required a first cause, the Unmoved Mover, a pure form which draws to itself all things both rational and nonrational through a universal teleological impulse. Thomas Aquinas took over this natural teleology. For Thomas every creature also moves teleologically to its own end, and toward its own natural good and fulfillment. But at the same time each creature serves those hierarchically situated above it so that the whole creation reaches towards its fulfillment (Skillen 1974, 57-58; Leff 1958, 216-18).

While nonrational nature is immediately directed by God to its end, rational nature is directed by means of rational freedom. Man, as a rational creature, shares in the *lex aeterna* through the rationally discerned *lex naturalis*, which according to St. Paul, is written in the heart (*Summa theologia* 1a2æ.91.2; 1a2æ.93.2; 1a2æ.94.6). Of this Copleston comments:

> Although man cannot read off, as it were, the eternal law in
> God's mind, he can discern the fundamental tendencies
> and needs of his nature, and by reflecting on them he can
> come to a knowledge of the moral law. (1955, 213)

This has key implications for Thomistic political theory because Aquinas, following Aristotle, also held that the impulse toward political society is naturally implanted in mankind, who correspondingly strives for this good by nature. Concerning this, Ullman (1965, 179) writes:

> Thomas held that it was man's "natural instinct" which
> brought forth the State, that is, organized human society.
> Consequently, to Thomas, the State was a product of nature
> and therefore followed the laws of nature. It was "natural
> reason which urges" this human association, and for the

> working of the state no divine or supra-natural elements
> were necessary, because it had all the laws of its own opera-
> tion within itself. Since "nature leaves nothing imperfect,"
> Thomas called the state a perfect community. (*Summa theo-
> logia* 1a2æ.90.2)

Thomas thus almost unhesitatingly accepts the Aristotelian social ontology and subordinates all nonpolitical relationships to the state, which is the perfect natural community.

There is a caveat, however, one that recognizes and gives theoretical grounding to the basis for the Gelasian dualism. Thomas recognizes that the state is a *societas perfecta* only in the natural sphere. In those matters pertaining to eternal salvation the state remains subordinate to the sacramental institution of grace, the church, which is the *societas perfecta* in the supernatural sphere (Skillen 1974, 61; Dooyeweerd 1958, 3:218-20).

There is thus a relativizing of the natural order because the teleological order is extended to embrace a final subordination of the natural hierarchy. In recognizing the freedom of the church in its own realm and even granting it supremacy, Thomas thus broke with the absolutist state. "Two there are." There is no monism here. On this Murray was certainly correct. But there is more involved.

Aristotle's thesis was that individuals and lower natural communities were parts of the *polis*. But to that Thomas added "only insofar as they belong to the same order as the *polis*," to which the church did not belong. The latter was supernatural. This manner of relativizing the absolutist pretensions of the state creates two problems relevant to our discussion. The first pertains to the relation of the natural to the supernatural, the second to the place of state within the natural realm.

Copleston observes that Aquinas could not simply say that the state exists to secure man's temporal final end, while the church exists to secure the attainment of man's supernatural final end because, as a Christian, he was convinced that man had only one final end, a supernatural one. So, while he indeed held that the state was a "perfect community," the monarch should facilitate the attainment of man's supernatural end.

> On the one hand, St. Thomas' Aristotelianism rendered any
> complete subordination of the State to the Church or any
> tendency to regard the monarch as no more than a kind of
> employee of the Church quite foreign to his thought. On

the other hand, if man has one final end, a supernatural
end, which is primarily cared for by the Church, it follows
that the Church is a superior society. The State is a natural
institution possessing its own sphere, the common good in
the temporal order; but there cannot be a complete and
absolute separation between the sphere of the state and
that of the Church, since man has been placed in this world
to secure a supernatural end; and his temporal life must be
directed to the attainment of that end. (Copleston 1952,
169-70)

The Dutch philosopher Herman Dooyeweerd presses home the dilemma created by Thomas' social ontology. He recognizes that the supremacy which
Thomas ascribes to the church-institution is effective in denying the state
any competence in internal ecclesiastical affairs. However,

in addition, the final judgment concerning the question
which affairs pertain to the natural and which to the supra-
natural sphere, can only belong to the Church. Since in the
Thomistic view the autonomy of natural reason is only of a
relative character and human nature is in need of supra-
natural perfection, it is the supra-natural ecclesiastical institution which alone can establish the Christian principles of
government. And, as the infallible interpreter of natural ethical law, this Church alone is in a position to pass judgment
concerning the limits of competence of the State.
(Dooyeweerd 1955, 3:220-21)

That's the first problem, one that Murray attempted to diffuse, unconvinc-
ingly I have argued, by emphasizing the indirect power of the church in temporal affairs.

The second problem concerns the nature of the state within the natural
realm. Because other social structures, particularly the family, maintain a certain autonomy, there is, for Thomas (and for Leo XIII), a distinction between
society and state. However, just as for Aristotle, the state still maintains hierarchical supremacy over other units of organized society as the guarantor of
the common good.

Thomas, following Aristotle, held that human reason is capable of discovering that nature requires a differentiated social order. In keeping with

Aristotle, he held that "the light of reason is placed by nature in every man, to guide him in his acts towards his end." However, this inclination could not be accomplished in isolation apart from a group. Humans are inclined by nature to associate with other humans and human reason can recognize a duty to do so. It is "natural for man, more than for any other animal, to be a social and political animal, to live in a group" (*De Regimine Principum*, Bigongiari, ed., 1:175).

Just as the inability of individuals to sustain themselves solely as individuals leads rationally to group activity, the inability of smaller groups to be self-sufficient leads to a differentiated social order where "higher" groups can aid "lower" ones in pursuing their natural purposes. There is in this sense a society-state distinction, one that recognizes the ontological existence of non-state societal structures. But reason can not only discover that nature requires a differentiated social order; it can also discover one that is (consistent with Aristotle here) hierarchically structured.

> Now since man must live in a group, because he is not sufficient unto himself to procure the necessities of life were he to remain solitary, it follows that a society will be the more perfect the more it is sufficient unto itself to procure the necessities of life. There is, to some extent, sufficiency for life in one family of one household, namely, in so far as begetting of offspring and other things of the kind. Self-sufficiency exists, furthermore, in one street with regard to those things which belong to the trade of one guild. In a city, which is the perfect community, it exists with regard to all the necessities of life. Still more self- sufficiency is found in a province because of the need of fighting together and of mutual help against enemies. (*De Regimine Principum*, Bigongiari, 1:178-79)

Richard Regan observes that in an early work, *De Regimine Principum*, Aquinas had argued that social cooperation of family units and a division of labor is necessary simply for human survival and material well-being (Regan 1986, 38). However, in his later works (e.g., *Summa theologia* 1a2æ.72.4), he follows Aristotle more closely and argues that social cooperation is necessary to achieve specifically human goals of intellectual and moral well-being. Neither families nor small groups can adequately provide for either material or nonmaterial well-being.

Applying the Aristotelian principle that "the whole is of necessity prior to the part," Aquinas concluded that in a logical and philosophical sense "every multitude is derived from unity" (*De Regimine Principum*, Bigongiari, 2:180). Because the body politic represents the unity (the whole) of the natural order, the multitude of groups within the body politic are parts within the whole. Man is destined to live in a hierarchy of social groupings with the family at the base and proceeding through a variety of societal groupings to the state at the apex. The purpose of the state is to promote the common good both materially and spiritually. Its hierarchical supremacy over other units of organized society stems from its specific function to care for the common good (Regan 1986, 39-40). But if the state is to care for the spiritual well-being of society and that spiritual well-being is determined to be negatively affected by the propagation of what that society takes to be false religious ideas, would it not seem to follow that false religion could be suppressed, quite consistently, for the sake of the common good? The scholastics obviously believed it did.

Now, what might the Catholic doctrine of subsidiarity imply for this position? Might it, as Coleman and others have suggested, serve as a middle term to defeat the claim that the state has the obligation to suppress false religion for the common good?

Although the term "subsidiarity" was not used or explicitly defined until Pope Pius XI's *Quadragesimo anno* (1931), the concept referred to by the term is assumed by Aquinas and is present in Leo XIII's *Rerum novarum* (1891) and *Immortale Dei* (1885). As Coleman suggests, it is "a subset rule of the larger distinction between society and state" and, broadly speaking, concerns the harmonious relation among persons and groups in a hierarchically ordered society.

The word "subsidiary" derives from the Latin *subsidiarius*, which means "of or belonging to a reserve." John Cox (1943, 117-18) notes that the "reserves" in the Roman army were the auxiliary corps held in waiting on the third line of battle for the possible emergencies or demands. From this original application the Latin word and its derivatives have come to mean "supplementary," "furnishing aid," and "auxiliary." These meanings, according to Cox, bring out both the positive and negative functions of the principle.

> *To be by nature and concept subsidiary* means that every
> social action must be a supplementary help; and that every
> social group must be a *complementary* entity, in the sense
> that its very reason for existence is the supplying of auxil-

iary aid; this aid is summoned forth, like the reserve action of the Roman Legion, not to initiate action, but *to strengthen, reinforce, and perfect that which has already begun.* The negative side of this principle implies that the social objective cannot consist in absorbing, destroying, or replacing its members, for these annihilative tendencies would be incompatible with society's true role, which is help, supplementation, and completion. (117–18)

Regan sums up the implication of the negative side of subsidiarity by saying that "the state should do for its citizens, families, and voluntary associations only what these individuals and groups cannot or will not do for themselves." What about the positive side? Regan immediately adds, "the freedom of citizens and their associations to act as they wish should be restricted only as much as the common good requires" (1986, 42).

In order to understand how civil intolerance of religion is not *prima facie* inconsistent with the society-state distinction and the doctrine of subsidiarity, and thus cannot do the work Murray wants it to do, it must be realized that the notion of the "common good" serves as a wild card in the theory. Murray, as we shall see, will come to see this later.

Remember that all Catholic parties in the debate agree with the mature Aquinas in maintaining that social cooperation is required to attain not merely material well-being but spiritual and moral well-being as well. In this sense, Thomistic political theory is basically Aristotelian. Because humans cannot adequately achieve material, intellectual, moral, or spiritual well-being apart from their fellows, they form a body politic to promote this common good. However, Thomas' political theory differs from Aristotle's in that Aquinas relates human law to a natural law implicit in divine law. Hence, as Regan summarizes it, "For Aquinas, rightly ordered political power should be exercised within the framework of *both* a divinely ordained natural law *and* a humanly established constitutional law" (1986, 43, emphasis mine). Now, since some "religious" actions conducted by lesser associations could plausibly be seen by the Catholic state as a violation of the natural law (e.g., heresy, idolatry, blasphemy, false worship) and hence a violation of the common good, there would seem to be no a priori reason to rule out the possibility of suppression of such for the sake of the common good, if that society was predominantly Catholic.

In a sense, Murray's dilemma is part of a larger dilemma that arises when we consider the question of hierarchy along with the matter of a plurality of groups (or associations, or societal structures). The relation between the various groups and the higher-level institutions can be seen in two distinct ways. On the one hand, the state can be seen as merely a coordinating device and thus not as a "community" in its own right. An objection to viewing the state in this way is that the very weakness of the state makes it difficult to resolve conflict that erupts among lower "communities." Without an appeal to a higher level of community consensus the lower-level group is tempted to retreat into "a solipsistic moral universe, caught in the trap of subjective value" (Unger 1975, 286). Viewing the state in this manner implies that the state is not to be seen as a "moral entity," if for no other reason than because the state is not an entity at all.

This difficulty might lead one to insist on seeing the state as "a community of communities" responsible for the common good (Unger 1975, 286). It would thus retain its nature as a moral entity. But then the question of which group among the plurality of groups is to have moral hegemony in this community of communities once again arises.

I have gone into this considerable digression to make a point crucial to properly interpreting Murray. The society-state distinction in itself simply cannot do the work Murray wants it to. And the reason for this is that the dilemma with which Murray is confronted as a Catholic lies in a tension deep in the heart of the Aristotelian-Thomistic political philosophy. The state within this social ontology remains at the apex of a differentiated but nevertheless hierarchically ordered society. As such it has responsibility as the guarantor of the common good which can be acquired by reason in accord with natural law. While for Aristotle the natural law was entirely immanent, in the Thomistic synthesis it must ultimately be rooted in the divine law. For a Thomist such as Murray, this would create a problem, because a substantive notion of the common good could not be abstracted from the requirements of the divine law.

Thus, if Coleman (1978, 40) is correct when he says that Murray, by bringing forth the distinction between society and state, shifted the burden of public acknowledgment of the sovereignty of God from the state to the wider society, it must also be admitted that Murray was shifting his argument away from the Thomistic claim that the state must acknowledge responsibility for the morally and spiritually good society and toward a purely functional view of the state. At most this would leave it only responsible for the material good—if that—and thus raise the specter of the naked public square and the religio-moral "indifferentism," which Murray also wanted to avoid.

But that's not all. The entire issue of church-state relations is further complicated by the fact that the church is the one institution that stands outside the whole-part relationship because of its supernatural origin. One of the crucial implications of this is that a separate argument must be made for freedom of the Roman Catholic Church as a supernatural institution, on the one hand, and freedom for non-Catholic and non-Christian religious institutions as mere "voluntary associations," on the other. The institution of the Roman Catholic Church, because of its supernatural origin, is not and cannot be a "mediating structure" within this social ontology, while supposedly other religious institutions, as natural "voluntary associations" would be. And of course, in a Catholic society that would leave open the question as to whether the mere existence of such "voluntary associations" might be a hindrance to the common good, thus legitimizing their proscription. Since this is the case, we might expect to find two distinct arguments for religious liberty—one for the Catholic Church as a supernatural institution and another for those other religious institutions which exist as "voluntary societies," and can thus properly be labeled "intermediate structures." And that, as we shall see, is exactly what we will find in the mature Murray (see Murray 1967f, 280 and chapter 7, 188ff).

Notes

1. "Letter to Anastasius I" in *The Crisis of Church and State, 1050–1300,* ed. Brien Tierney (Englewood Cliffs, N.J.: Prentice, 1964), 13–14. The letter was to the Byzantine emperor in 494. Murray would repeatedly appeal to the Gelasian formula as a bulwark against state authoritarianism and totalitarianism. His slogan was "Two there are, not one there is." What is not clear is whether his appeal to this formula was effective in his polemic with the traditionalists who, as far as I can tell, did not deny the Gelasian dualism but simply applied it in a less liberal way. In a recent article Gerard Bradley argues that while the basic differentiation of society into two orders is common Christian property, there are very different conceptions of it. "Luther's 'Two Kingdoms' is not Calvin's two spheres, and they both differ from Roger William's 'Garden in the Wilderness.' All of them are different from the Gelasian 'Two Swords,' which itself is different from Augustine's nearly contemporaneous conception of 'Two Cities.'" And Bradley adds, significantly enough, that "the liberal secularist entertains his own dyarchy. It is a most peculiar construction, in which, seemingly, all 'value' judgments are private, where the public sphere consists of 'policy goals' served by rational technique" (Bradley 1992, 202-3). That different sorts of Protestants, secular liberals, and traditionalist Catholics might agree that there exist two orders tends to suggest that Murray's appeal to the Gelasian dualism will not, in the end, serve its polemical purpose.

2. I am inclined to believe that this shift to procedural matters serves to further

illuminate Murray's dilemma. Social cohesion can be justified in two basic ways. One model seeks consensus not through a common commitment to procedures, but through allegiance to a common substantive goal or purpose. In such a teleological or end-directed state, dissent from certain constitutive values is regarded as an attack on society itself. Michael Oakeshott has termed this understanding of the state *universitas* in contrast to *societas* (Oakeshott 1975, 199ff.). A state understood in terms of the former is

> an association of intelligent agents who recognize themselves to be engaged upon the joint enterprise of seeking the satisfaction of some common substantive want; a many become one on account of their common engagement and jointly seized of complete control over the manner in which it is pursued.... Government here may be said to be teleocratic, the management of a purposive concern. (Oakeshott 1975, 205-6)

The other main way to speak of social cohesion is to focus loyalty on the institutions and practices which are designed to moderate and conciliate differences of interest or disputes over ethical or religious principles. This latter, which can be termed "liberal," emphasizes formal and procedural, rather than constitutive values, and is similar to what Oakeshott calls a nomocratic state, or a *societas*.

> The idea of *societas* is that of agents who, by choice or circumstance, are related to one another so as to compose an identifiable association of a certain sort. The tie which joins them...is not that of an engagement in an enterprise to pursue a common substantive purpose or to promote a common interest.... It [denotes] a formal relationship in terms of rules, not a substantive relationship in terms of common action.... [T]his constitutive pact [denotes] the description of an outcome: *socii*, each pursuing his own interests or even joined with some others in seeking common satisfactions, but related to one another in the continuous acknowledgment of the authority of rules of conduct indifferent to the pursuit of any purpose. (Oakeshott 1975, 201)

A ruler in this sort of state, he adds, is more a guardian or administrator "of the conditions which constitute the relationship of the *socii*."

> This ruler is a master of ceremonies, not an arbiter of fashion. His concern is with the "manners" of convives, and his office is to keep the conversation going, not to determine what is said. (202-3)

Oakeshott thinks that the modern state is characterized by a tension between these two models. Part of Murray's dilemma may be the problem that his ethics and religious commitments are teleological and substantive to such an extent that he can even concede that "pluralism is against the will of God," while his political theory is compelled to become more procedurally oriented. He must maintain the notion of the state as a moral entity without abstracting his understanding of morality from supernaturally grounded truth claims and, at the same time, he must defend a view of social solidarity, based on procedural rights, which is, at best, indifferent to that religio-ethical understanding. Stressing matters of procedure allows him to advocate what the traditionalists were calling "indifferentism" without actually saying so.

3. Actually, as Love (1965, 85 n. 31) observes, Murray's notion of the indirect power is quite similar to that of Ryan (cf. Ryan and Boland 1940, 324-30). But this makes us wonder just how different, when all is said and done, Murray's position is from that of the thesis-hypothesis doctrine. We will discuss this in more detail below.

4. The importance of the following discussion for Murray's mature religious liberty argument will be explained in detail in chapter 7. It should be remembered throughout that, as Robert McElroy has recently observed, "Thomas Aquinas remains far and away the most important source for Murray's sustained reflections on the nature of politics" (1989, 194 n. 12). We may say that the dilemma confronting Murray would be particularly acute to the extent to which Murray was to remain true to his Thomism. For the exposition in the remainder of this chapter I am deeply indebted to Rockne McCarthy and James Skillen's analysis in *Political Order and the Plural Structure of Society,* particularly the chapter "Subsidiarity, Natural Law, and the Common Good."

Chapter Four

Murray's Polemic
Against Liberal Protestant Defenses
of Religious Liberty

I ARGUED IN THE LAST CHAPTER that the three distinctions employed by Murray—the distinction between the indirect and direct power of the church in temporal affairs, the distinction between the lay and laicized state, and the society-state distinction—could not disarm the modus vivendi position of the traditionalist Catholics. The most powerful argument that could be launched against the traditionalists would have been a moral Esperantist one. But that was a tack that Murray never took.

But that's not all. For while he was trying to overcome the traditional Catholic thesis-hypothesis doctrine, he was also criticizing those positions most likely to succeed in that task. While his polemic against his fellow Catholics seemed to require the establishment of an Archimedean point to justify religious liberty on firmer grounds than collective political prudence, his polemic against liberal Protestants and secularists called for a more contextual, historically sensitive approach to the problem of religious liberty. He would appeal to the latter in the hope that it would undercut Esperantist defenses of the free exercise of religion grounded on ahistorical rationalistic grounds (natural rights) as well Protestant ones based on particularistic ecclesiological appeals (i.e., to the free church tradition). Let us now turn to Murray's polemic against these positions.

The immediate context of Murray's polemic against liberal Protestantism and secularism revolved around a discussion of the meaning and interpretation of the religion clauses of the First Amendment to the U.S.

Constitution: "Congress shall make no law respecting the establishment of religion or prohibiting the free exercise thereof." In short, if liberal Protestants defended the free exercise and no establishment clauses by arguing that they rested on the assumption that churches are voluntary associations with equal sanction by God, Murray would reject it since such a view incorporated into the Constitution a Protestant ecclesiology and hence a theology. By showing how the liberal Protestant position on religious liberty was dependent on a particular, historically grounded ecclesiology, Murray sought to embarrass their claim that religious liberty was a universal ahistorical right.

Murray deploys a similar argument against a more secular natural rights position. If the secularist claims that religion is exclusively a private affair and that all religions are equally true or equally false and therefore none should be privileged, then that particular view of religion, namely, that religion is merely private opinion, is in fact established. Such a conception, Murray will insist, is no less dogmatic than the Catholic view.

In short, Murray argued that any substantive content put into the free exercise clause, and hence any substantive defense of religious liberty, violated the establishment clause. This argument would also strike at any implicit Protestant claim that the religion clauses were the secular analog to the Protestant conception of the church as well as any secular natural rights argument that claimed all religions are equal because religions are a matter of mere opinion. In his view, the religion clauses of the First Amendment did not reflect any theological or philosophical position but were simply "articles of peace." If we borrow a phrase from John Rawls, we may say that Murray viewed the concept of justice embodied in the religion clauses of the First Amendment as political not metaphysical (Rawls 1985). In short, in his argument against liberal Protestants and secularists, Murray would set forth a modus vivendi interpretation, justification, and defense of religious freedom hardly distinguishable from the traditional modus vivendi position he also wants to reject. Thus when arguing against conservative Catholics he had stressed the need for a "principled" justification of religious liberty, one that was not merely political; when arguing against liberal Protestants and secularists he would stress a justification that was purely political.

At this point one may wonder if Murray could be charged with duplicity, since his own reading and interpretation of the free exercise clause as a modus vivendi seems to be the kind of interpretation most amenable to traditionalist Catholics. I don't think so. Murray was not opposing the secularists and liberal Protestants simply to appease traditionalist Catholics.

Murray believed that the Protestant and secularist interpretations of the First Amendment were flawed both conceptually and in their historical analysis. More importantly, the strict separatist doctrine emerging in liberal Protestant literature and in the decisions of the Supreme Court clashed with Leo XIII's doctrine of *concordia* as he understood it.

Murray insisted on maintaining Leo's doctrine of *concordia*, the principle of harmony and cooperation between church and state as required by natural law. However, he put forth this doctrine in a form more in accordance with the notion of the indirect power of the church through the conscience of the Christian citizen. He was intent on explaining to Fenton, Shea, Connell, and church officials in Rome the difference between the aggressive antireligious nature of Continental liberalism and that of the American system which encouraged cooperation between government and religion. However, he clearly felt himself handicapped in this domestic ecclesiastical task by two contemporary events: the rise of what he termed the "New Nativism," and the recent secularist and liberal Protestant interpretations of the U.S. Constitution, particularly the religion clauses of the First Amendment (see Elwyn Smith 1972, 237). Murray feared that the collapse of an accommodationist stance toward religion by the government would eventually lead to an undermining of the notion of *concordia*. He was intent on opposing this trend.

Two articles from the late 1940s give a good summary of Murray's overriding concern at the time. One summarizes his concern with the liberal Protestant perspective on religious freedom and the other with the rising tide of secularism.

In "Religious Liberty: The Concern of All" (1948a), Murray analyzes a manifesto issued by the newly formed organization, "Protestants and Other Americans United for Separation of Church and State." According to the document, the Catholic Church "holds and maintains a theory of the relation between church and state that is incompatible with the American ideal." It is thus "plainly subversive of religious liberty as guaranteed by the Constitution." The design of the Catholic Church, according to the manifesto, was "to fracture the constitutional principle at one point after another where the action can be minimized as trivial or disguised as falling within some other category than that of its ultimate intent," which ultimately included the "nullification" of the First Amendment by securing for the church "a position of special privilege in relation to the State," from which it will be able "to deny or to curtail the religious liberty of all other churches and to vitiate democracy." Murray called this the "camel's nose" argument. Finally, the manifesto charged that two dangerously long steps toward this ultimate goal had been taken. First, the church had achieved privileged access to the ear of the state" through the appointment of an ambassador to the Vatican. Second, as a result of the Supreme Court case of *Everson v. Board of Education* decision, the Catholic school has achieved a position of privilege because they shared with public school children free bus transportation and free textbooks.

Murray placed the manifesto within the history of American anti-Catholic nativism. A glance at American history, he said, shows that "the scare-technique, the nightmare-theory of constitutional defense" are not new. Nor have they lost their power. However, he does find encouraging the fact that

> the ancient spectral threat is now made to walk the night in much more civilized garb. To change the metaphor, the cry through the palace windows is not a horse-shout, edged with frenzy, the articulation of something elemental in the mob. The voice indeed still carries to the Governor, but its tone is quiet, its accents cultured, its rhetoric restrained. (1948a 515)

This could be seen as an improvement, said Murray, since the old Protestant symbols—the Man of Sin, Babylon the Great, the Scarlet Whore, the Arch-Servant of the Dragon—are no longer current in contemporary anti-Catholicism. While we are still "enemies of the Republic," says Murray, these "lurid images of the Apocalypse have vanished, leaving only the pale metaphor of a camel's nose" (515). But even such a slight change in rhetoric might be conducive to dialog.

> Perhaps the thing to do is to go through the City and, where one finds these knots of men, talk to them. There is no agreement between us and them in religious faith: but is this a reason why there should be no lines of communication between them and us in matters where religious faith touches the structures and processes of civil society—their society as well as ours? (515-16)

Murray suggests that Protestants and Catholics read and discuss together the views of Leo XIII, Msgr. Ryan, and Fr. Connell's views of religious liberty, the issue of Spain, the constitutional history of the First

Amendment, as well as the history of American education and the aid to religious schools. If this could be done,

> perhaps we could first measure together the real threat to
> the common American tradition and our democratic institutions—the secularism that bears within itself the seeds of
> future tyrannies. Then perhaps we might form another
> organization with a lengthier but more meaningful title
> "Catholics and Protestants and Jews and Other Americans
> United for cooperative Relations between Church and State
> in View of the Peril of Secularism, Especially in Education."
> (515)

Murray concluded by saying that "it is high time for Protestants to wake up—return to reality—see an analyst—at all events, give up the scare technique, the appeal to fear" (515). While the main technique is effective, "its main effect has been simply the progressive secularization of American society, especially education." On the other hand, "it is time that Catholics, too, woke up."

> We need to go down into the City and prove by more deeds
> than we have hitherto shown that we are the friends of its
> liberties, that our progress is its progress, that our power is
> in its service, that no man has to fear from us infringement
> of any of his rights. (515)

A brief look at another article by Murray gives further insight into Murray's strategy at the time. In "Reversing the Secularist Drift" (1949b), an article published in the Catholic journal *Thought*, Murray addresses the task of the Catholic university in the context of secularism. He opens his article with a quotation from the Catholic theologian Henri de Lubac:

> Underneath the countless currents that are bearing in all
> directions the thought of our contemporaries, there is, it
> seems, a deeper current that long ago set in—one might
> perhaps better call it an enveloping drift: by the action of a
> considerable portion of its elite of thinkers Western
> humanity is denying its Christian origins and turning away
> from God. (1949b, 36)

Murray concurs and later adds that "at the moment almost the whole weight of learning in the United States is being thrown against all we mean by Catholic intellectualism and Catholic faith" (42). Against this secularism Murray insisted that the church not succumb to a ghetto mentality—what he called the "temptation of Thabor." He thus asks rhetorically:

> Is the Catholic scholar a self-enclosed spiritual monad in a secularist world: And is the Catholic institution of learning simply a citadel, a fortress of defense, or an asylum of escape? Does it exist on the periphery or at the center of the present cultural crisis? Has it an orientation rather sectarian in the adequate sense? [Is it] the focus of purely centripetal movements, all its currents incoming, none outgoing? (40)

The rhetorical questions were thinly veiled barbs aimed at what he took to be the siege mentality of conservative Catholics such as Fenton, Shea, and Connell. Murray's underlying objection to their position was that their sort of mentality would not be effective in stemming the tide of secularism. "It is not enough to stand firm against the drift; for after one has stood firm, the drift itself still continues to sweep other minds and souls off into the shallows and onto the rocks" (41). Instead, the "Catholic college and university today ought to be the point of departure for a missionary effort out into the thickening secularist intellectual and spiritual milieu" (40–41). To the question, "Can the drift be reversed, the climate altered?" Murray answered with a confident "yes." This "yes," he added, was not a blind confidence, but a "coldly intelligent, fervently faithful confident—'yes'."

These two articles tell us something about Murray's thinking at this time. His polemic against the traditional Catholics was based partially in the belief that simply standing athwart history yelling "stop" was not enough to stem the onslaught of secularism. But his polemic against liberal Protestants was premised on the belief that not only weren't they standing against the drift—at least the conservative Catholics were doing that—but they were caught up in it and thus aiding and abetting secularism outright.

These articles set the stage for a more detailed examination of Murray's line of attack against the liberal Protestant and secularist understandings of religious liberty. We now turn to examine exactly how Murray tried to split the difference between the liberal Protestants and secularists on the one hand and the traditionalist Catholics on the other.

In "Current Theology: Freedom of Religion" (1945b), Murray tackled the liberal Protestant case for religious liberty for the first time. The immediate occasion for comment was a pamphlet, "Religious Liberty, Its Meaning and Significance for Our Day," published by the Joint Committee on Religious Liberty of the Federal Council of Churches and the Foreign Missions Conference of North America. The work of the committee would eventually result in a book titled *Religious Liberty: An Inquiry*, the actual writing of which was done by M. Searle Bates. Murray had a number of criticisms to make of Bates' work in 1946 (1946b, 1946e). But in "Current Theology: Freedom of Religion," he addressed at greater length the pamphlet along with two related articles in a book titled *Religion and the World Order*, edited by F. Ernest Johnson.

Religious liberty, according to Murray, occupies a unique position among the problems relating to a new world order simply because "no other problem so directly and immediately raises an ultimate issue." At the very outset, the question arises, "What is religion?" How one answers this question,

> will condition the very manner in which one posits the problem of the freedom of religion, and will therefore condition its whole solution, even in the political order. Moreover, the question, what is religion? cannot be fully answered in terms of reason and natural law alone. The decisive answer comes from revelation; and revelation resolves the question, what is religion? into a more concrete form—what is the Church of Christ?

For this reason, he adds, "The influence of ultimate views is inescapable" (88).

While the problem is particularly difficult to discuss, the practical urgency of the problem makes discussion of the topic urgent. On the one hand, Catholics "cannot admit the validity of solutions based on ever more self-assertive theories of the 'autonomy of conscience,' 'religious pluralism,' 'democratic ideals,' 'cultural equilibrium through diversity,' etc.—theories that we must consider false or inadequate" (88-89). On the other hand, attacks on the church's position as being purely opportunistic, and incoherent with ethical principle "will not be successfully met simply by the strenuous defense of the position that the Catholic Church is the one true

Church." However, Murray is quick to add, it is a position that must be guarded at every point (90).

Still, Murray hopes that the controversy could be made intelligent, a task that is hindered by the introduction of confused and false issues.

> I think that we may, without wounding anybody, be quite skeptical about the widespread contemporary fiction that, when Protestantism organizes for political action, it is nobly engaged simply in defending "conscience and the rights of man," whereas, if Catholics similarly organize, they are ignobly occupied with pushing "the worldly, institutional interests of the Roman Catholic Church," as an objective at variance with the welfare of mankind. (89)

In this spirit, Murray addressed the *Statement on Religious Liberty.* An attempt is made, he observed, to consider the idea of freedom of religion in its relation to governmental authority. A corresponding attempt was made to state its content in terms of "civic rights." But he finds the use of the phrase confusing since "it is not entirely clear whether the rights enumerated are to be considered civic in the strict sense (as having their first source in positive law), or also as natural (as rooted in the law of nature)" (91). The latter term seems to be the intended one since it is implied that government is simply to recognize and be the guarantor of these rights. The problem is that within the *Statement* "only one premise is adduced as the basis—the fact that the human person is the image of God" (92).

> Appeal, therefore, is made to a philosophical principle, in itself accessible to reason, though historically it has been mediated by the Christian revelation. The *Statement* considers the problem of religious liberty apart from the hypothesis of a divine revelation whereby God, through Christ, may have determined the existence of a spiritual and juridically perfect society whose rights and freedoms are not simply the projection of the jus naturalist rights and freedoms of its members. The *Statement* moves simply in the hypothesis of natural law. (92)

Murray claims that we cannot get behind the statement to know whether the framers believe that the problem can be solved adequately on a purely ethical basis, or solely on the basis of natural law. In any case, his criticism is that the *Statement* "does not adhere to its own professed standpoint; implicitly it assumes the Protestant religious standpoint" (92).

Protestant thought, he argued, "has a tendency to lay down at the outset a concept of 'the right to religious liberty,' usually conceived in the typically Protestant atomistic way, and then to bring into immediate relation with it all sorts of demands" (94). As an example, Murray points to the logic of the *Statement*. It seems to conclude, from the right to religious liberty based on the fact that man is the image of God, the juridical principle that political, economic, or social disabilities should not be imposed by government on the grounds of religion. "The case," declared Murray, "is ineptly put" (92). "What," he asked, "is the logical sequence between 'man as the image of God' and 'equal subsidies for Catholic and Protestant schools in the Belgian Congo'? Surely, it does not leap to the eye" (99).

Murray thought that the confusion in all this stems from the tendency to regard religious liberty as somehow a *sui generis* category of liberty. This tendency, in turn, is "apparently the product of the Protestant dogma on the absolutism of the individual conscience" (95). Catholic uneasiness arises, said Murray,

> when we are asked at the outset to subscribe to a definition
> of religious liberty, conceived as a category apart, and in the
> perspective of what we consider a sectarian theological
> dogma of "conscience." Such a definition cannot help look-
> ing to us like the platform of a campaign to further, not
> simply respect for human rights in the political order, but
> the institutional interests of organized Protestantism in the
> religious order. (98)

In contrast, Murray argues that the freedom of religious propaganda and the freedom of association listed in the *Statement*

> are simply aspects of the general human rights of free asso-
> ciation and of free discussion. They have *no natural founda-
> tion* separate from these more general rights, nor have they
> any privileged absolutism. *The natural law grants no more
> privileged right to organize for religious purposes than to orga-
> nize for economic purposes.* (96, emphasis mine)

As such, argued Murray, "from the standpoint of ethical principle,"

> the rights of religious organization and of religious propa-
> ganda are subject to the same general standard of social
> control as the general rights of free association and free
> speech—the interests of the common good, as reasonably
> conceived by the collective conscience of the community,
> and as implemented by the authority of the state. (96)

No argument, Murray insists at this time, "can be constructed that does not
lean heavily on an appeal to the common good" (96).

> The old individualist argument ("My mind is free—so,
> therefore, should be my tongue") does not work. As soon as
> one begins to spread ideas, one moves in a new ethical
> dimension—that of the social good; and one comes under a
> new ethical principle of control—the interests of the
> common good. (96-97)

The implications of Murray's stress on the relevance of the common
good become clear in his criticism of Luther Weigle's essay "Religious Liberty in the Postwar World." Weigle claimed that in the name of reason and
conscience the individual has the right to believe, to worship, to live and act
out his belief, to express his belief, to persuade others, to educate his children in religious faith, to organize with others to change his belief and orga-
nizational allegiance, and finally "to disbelieve in God, to deny religion, and
to act, speak, persuade, educate, and affiliate with others in ways appropriate
to this disbelief or atheism" (Murray 1945b, 101).

Murray finds this catalogue of rights to be flawed "to the point of sheer
chaos." Weigle's mistake was primarily due to a "complete failure to make
the slightest suggestion of a theory in whose name these 'rights' can be
asserted" (102). Murray finds it quite incredible that Weigle would imply
that

> belief and unbelief, atheistic propaganda and religious pro-
> paganda are equally legitimate responses to divine revela-
> tion, equally valid dictates of reason and conscience. To
> assert that man, confronted by God and the moral law, has
> a 'right' to disbelieve and to refuse obedience is to deny that

there is a God and a moral law, and consequently to make
the whole question of human rights meaningless. (103)

Of course, the atheist has a right to privately practice his atheism and enjoys
immunity from intrusion by political authority in the internal forum of his
conscience but this right, added Murray, is "based solely on the law that
limits State authority to the sphere of the common good" (104). But does the
atheist have the "right," Murray asked,

> "to carry his atheism into social life by propaganda, educa-
> tion, and organized activity, in such wise that the State
> would have a moral duty to refrain from all repressive mea-
> sures in this regard?" This would be an intolerable position.
> It would amount to a denial that the state has a moral, as
> well as a material, function. To assert that the state has a
> moral duty to regard with equal complacence public activ-
> ity in support of religion and morality and public activity
> toward their destruction would be to imply that religion
> and morality are in no way related to the common good of
> the community, and are therefore matters of indifference to
> the State. (103)

Since disbelief in God and the moral law "tend to destroy the virtue of the
citizenry, in which the common good of society chiefly consists," it cannot
be maintained that the state "would be exceeding the limits of its ethical
mandate, if it were to suppress—not with arbitrary violence, of course, but
by due process of law—public propaganda or education designed to spread
disbelief in God and the moral law" (103). One can justify atheistic propaganda only on the grounds of "legitimate expediency" but never as a "moral
right" (104). Murray is quick to add that in "modern mixed societies" the
evils of repression are greater than the evils repressed and therefore governments should normally choose not to exercise their rights to repress atheistic propaganda. The defense of religion and morality must largely be left to
"the pressure of the common conscience and of public opinion. "But the
motive of the decision is not any moral duty to respect the 'rights of atheism'" (104).

Murray's central criticism has thus far been that the Protestant defenses
of religious liberty "succumb[s] to the abstractionism of individualistic
thought" (107). Such views tend to "isolate religion from culture, to single

out religious freedom as a separate item of national policy, and to judge it by abstract, individualist standards" (108). But an even more fundamental error of such views

> often lies in the fact that they postulate their own type of relationship between religion and culture. They tend to assume that culture is "rich" in proportion to its religious heterogeneity, and that it is somehow impoverished by religious unity; this is an altogether unwarranted assumption.... In its extreme form, this opinion would identify freedom of religion with religion itself; in any form, it fails to consider that, in the concrete, a large "quantity" of religious freedom may be simply the product of irreligion or religious indifference, and, as such, an index of society's religious poverty. (108)

In this context Murray takes up the view of F. Ernest Johnson. Murray finds Johnson's articulation of the problem to be a bit less superficial than most Protestant views, largely because he is less willing to advance an abstract individualist defense of religious liberty and partly because he puts forth what Murray takes to be a valid contention, to wit: "specific guarantees [concerning religious liberty] cannot be secured without reference to the existing cultural situation and a variety of social and historical factors" (cited in Murray 1945b, 108). Moreover, he endorses the following statement made by Johnson:

> If faithful adherence to a national religion is deemed to be an important element in national unity it is difficult to see how a government can be expected to regard with complacence efforts to deracinate its nationals. However this may be, the further contention, so frequently put forward, that no political or civil disabilities are to attach to persons on account of their religious affiliation or non-affiliation, is clearly questionable.

Murray calls this a very honest admission (109). But he then added that when Catholics argued in this way it often and injuriously was called Catholic "opportunism." He also wondered whether or not Johnson's coreligionists would follow him in this matter.

Still, there was enough in Johnson's article for Murray to criticize. He found Johnson difficult to follow when he discussed the ultimate grounds of religious liberty. Johnson offered two fundamental principles. The first is "the spiritual obligation on the part of every person or group of persons to allow every other person a maximum of authentic religious experience." This principle, he says, "stands completely apart from the notion of individual rights. It is highly questionable if religious liberty can be based on the concept of rights.... Rather, its imperatives are found in *agape*–in the constraint of divine love impregnating the community." The conclusion of the matter is, "Practically, therefore, religious liberty is a juridical matter, but ultimately it is not a child of law, but a child of love" (cited in Murray 1945b, 109).

Murray would pounce on the antinomian implications inherent in this sort of appeal to *agape*.

> Liberty to me...means the empowerment from a moral source outside myself–a law whose imperatives are mediated to me by conscience–to act or to refrain from acting; an empowerment which, by reason of its source outside of me, guarantees that my action or omission will be reasonable, conformed to the order of things. But this is what I substantially mean by a "right." I cannot understand, therefore, when I read that religious liberty is to be taken out of the juridical order–the order of rights and obligations–and solved in a superior sphere of its own, the sphere of "love". (110)

"If liberty is not born of law," adds Murray (110), "it would take an obstetrical miracle to bring it forth." And, "To say that religious liberty is a child of love is a nice phrase; but what does it mean?"

Murray suspects Johnson's theory ultimately rests on a theory of religious truth as somehow a truth *sui generis*, "in that the ultimate index of its validity is the sincerity with which it is held" (110). Murray adapts Johnson's metaphor to illuminate the difficulty. Religious truth, under this conception, "is not the child of the object, but the child of the subject" (110-11).

> This would be a correlative of the position that religious liberty is *sui generis*–not the child of law (outside of me), but the child of love (inside of me). Obviously, in the theory

> that sincerity is the measure of truth, I shall have an obliga-
> tion to recognize truth-in-the-experience-of-others as
> authentic, because sincerely experienced. I must feel an
> "inner necessity" to love the truth that others experience,
> equally as I do my own, since both have equal validation.
> (And I suppose that to love truth means to accept it as
> true.) This love gives birth to "religious freedom."

Murray's criticism of Johnson's principles was quite simple: "[T]he matter of intellectual sincerity has really very little to do with the intimate problem of religious freedom" (111).

This article is important because it shows Murray's early resistance to a natural rights argument for religious liberty. Murray would not speak moral Esperanto and he would challenge any attempt to do so. But he went a step further. He realized that Johnson did not want to be impaled on the Esperantist horn of the dilemma with his "coreligionists," and he compliments him for it. But he suspects Johnson will try to slip between the horns of the dilemma by adopting a position of either indifference or skepticism.

Now, it might be argued that all this simply reflected an early polemic of Murray and that his opinions radically changed over the years. But, in fact, his opinion of Protestant defenses of religious liberty remained quite constant throughout his life. It would be expressed in more concrete form in his polemic against the liberal Protestant interpretation of the religion clauses of the First Amendment.

In "Separation of Church and State" (1946e) Murray continued his criticism of the liberal Protestant view of religious liberty and the relation of church and state, applied it to their understanding of the religion clauses of the First Amendment, and outlined in rudimentary form his own interpretation of those clauses. Eight years later, Murray would make essentially the same argument in the article "The Problem of Pluralism in America" (1954c), which would eventually be included without substantial revision in his book *We Hold These Truths* (1960). We must assume, then, that Murray's argument against the liberal Protestant interpretation of the religion clauses remained fairly constant at least until 1960. Moreover, nothing in his writings after 1960 evidences a radical change in attitude.

Responding to the charge that Catholics are the cause of confusion and dismay in their stand on religious liberty, Murray turned the tables and claimed the opposite was the case, adding that "as a matter of fact, the Protestant mind is itself natively confused, endemically unclear in this whole matter" (261). As an example Murray cites M. Searle Bates' *Religious Liberty: An Inquiry* (1945).

Confusion pervades the entire book, says Murray, but it becomes particularly "riotous" when the nature and grounds for religious liberty are discussed.

> He [Bates] does indeed make it obvious that Protestants are most terrifically in earnest over the so-called "principle of separation of Church and State" but he fails rather signally to explain what kind of "principle" it is, and what it rests on, demands, implies, or excludes. (261)

Murray then turns to what he perceives to be the main liberal Protestant confusion: It is first claimed that they embody the "principle of separation of Church and State." Then the confusion begins.

> Imperceptibly it is assumed that the First Amendment is a theological document—a sort of dogmatic decree that lays down a rule of faith. Thereafter it suddenly appears that the First Amendment implicitly "establishes" as the obligatory belief of the American people the doctrine that all churches are simply voluntary societies, of equally human origin and of equal value in the sight of God, each of these offering to man an equally good way to eternal salvation. In other words, it appears that the First Amendment canonizes liberal Protestant ecclesiology to an extreme form and anathematizes as un-American all dissenters from this premise. (261)

Murray adds that Protestants have their own polemical agenda in advancing such an interpretation, since it is possible

> to accuse Catholics of supporting the First Amendment only "in practice" (on grounds of expediency) and not "in principle" (on grounds of conviction); the reason, of course, is that Catholics deny in principle the ecclesiology supposedly contained in the First Amendment. (261)

Rather than dismiss this type of argumentation against Protestantism as "rather disappointing" (Love 1965, 54) or in some sense "immoral" (Hooper 1978, 100), I would suggest that he is making a rather substantial point.[1] He is particularizing—indeed, deconstructing—a claim to universality. He is, in effect, claiming that the liberal Protestant interpretation of the First Amendment reflects a religio-ethnocentric bias in favor of religious pluralism that is, in fact, rooted in the twentieth-century American sociohistorical context.

What was Murray's proposed alternative to this liberal Protestant reading? An "advance toward clarity" would be possible if "we could all agree to take the First Amendment exactly for what it is—not a theological, but a political document. It does not define a concept of the Church but a concept of the State" (261). Against the liberal Protestant interpretation that "makes the First Amendment do the very thing that Congress is forbidden by the First Amendment to do, namely, to play the theologian and promulgate articles of faith," Murray insisted:

> The religious liberty proclaimed by the First Amendment is not a piece of religious mysticism, but a *practical political principle*, ethically grounded on the obligations of the State to the consciences of its citizens and to its own end—social harmony, prosperity and peace. (261)

According to Murray, the First Amendment had a factual premise, the pluralistic religio-social situation in the nascent republic (261). Historical experience, both in Europe and in the Colonies, had demonstrated the political folly of attempting to create or restore religious unity by governmental repression of dissenters, thus defeating its own goal of social unity. The only way to social peace was through disestablishment, free exercise, and the separation of church and state (262).

From 1946 to 1954 Murray was involved in a number of debates with Protestants over the meaning and interpretation of the First Amendment. He exchanged blows with Charles Clayton Morrison (1948b), for thirty-nine years the editor of the *Christian Century*, and with W. Russell Bowie (1949), Dean of Union Theological Seminary. In both exchanges Murray's skills as a master polemicist were evident. The substantive issues at the root of these debates, however, were developed less polemically in a 1954 article entitled "The Problem of Pluralism in America," a work that eventually served as the first and second chapters of *We Hold These Truths*. The first chapter was retitled "E Pluribus Unum: The American Consensus" and the second appropri-

ately enough, "Civil Unity and Religious Integrity: The Articles of Peace."
The "articles of peace" refer to the religion clauses of the First Amendment.

Murray opened his discussion of the "articles of peace" by citing
Edmund Burke's defense of English institutions: "an established Church,
and established monarchy, an established aristocracy, and established
democracy." In *Reflections on the Revolution in France* (1791), from which this
passage is taken, Burke referred to the Church Establishment as "the first of
our prejudices—not a prejudice destitute of reason, but involving in it profound and extensive wisdom." That same year, Murray reminds his readers,
Americans were debating and ratifying the Bill of Rights, including the First
Amendment creating the legal rule that prohibited any establishment of religion. That legal rule against establishment became "the first of our prejudices" (1960, 46; references are to *We Hold These Truths*).

A prejudice, Murray quickly points out, "is not necessarily an error; to
be prejudiced is not to be unreasonable." Prejudices are rather "concrete
judgments of value, not abstract judgments of truth. They are not destitute
of reason, but their chief corroboration is from experience." This allows the
American Catholic to accept the American constitutional concept of freedom
of religion while at the same time it allows him "to admit that other prejudices may obtain elsewhere—in England, in Sweden, in Spain" (47). He adds
that the Catholic community has historically consented to this "political and
legal solution to the problem created by the plurality of religious beliefs in
American society" since it "is by no means destitute of reason" and because
it "involves profound and extensive wisdom." Because American Catholics
share this prejudice, that, claims Murray, "should be the end of the matter"
(48).

But it's not the end of the matter, because there are those who see in
these articles not only law, but also dogma. As such, they fail to see that the
articles "are not invested with the sanctity that attaches to dogma, but only
with the rationality that attaches to law." In short, over against those who
properly view them not as "articles of faith but articles of peace" (49), stand
those who read into them certain "ultimate beliefs, certain specifically sectarian tenets with regard to the nature of religion, religious truth, the church,
faith, conscience, divine revelation, human freedom, etc." (48). For those
who regard them as such, the religion clauses are "invested with a genuine
sanctity" and are "norms of orthodoxy, to which one must conform on pain
of some manner of excommunication" (49).

Of those who dogmatize about these articles, Murray cites three groups.
The main difference is between the first two groups, "between those who see

in these articles certain Protestant religious tenets and those who see in them certain ultimate suppositions of secular liberalism" (49). The first has its historical roots in the modified Puritanism of the free church variety, while the second is rooted in early American deism and rationalism. The third group consists of those more radically secularizing Protestants who see "American democratic institutions [as] the necessary secular reflection of Protestant anti-authoritarian religious individualism and its concept of the 'gathered' church" (50).

Murray asks about a page full of rhetorical questions (50-51) which reduce to two. "Is the no-establishment clause a piece of ecclesiology, and is the free-exercise clause a piece of religious philosophy?" (51). The general Protestant tendency, particularly noticeable in its free-church extreme (especially Baptist), is to answer affirmatively. "Their substance is to be conceived in terms of sectarian Protestant doctrine. They are therefore articles of faith; not to give them religious assent is to fall into heterodoxy" (51).

The secularists dissent from the Protestant theological and philosophical exegesis of the articles in that they refuse to read the writings and views of Roger Williams into the clauses, as do the Protestants. Nevertheless, to the secularists they are also an article of faith, although Murray adds parenthetically that they might prefer to discard the word "faith" in order to speak of "ultimate presuppositions" (51). Against both liberal Protestants and secularists, Murray presses home his central point.

> If these clauses are made articles of faith in either of the described senses, there are immediately in this country some 35,000,000 dissenters, the Catholic Community. Not being either a Protestant or a secularist, the Catholic rejects the religious position of Protestants with regard to the nature of the church, the meaning of faith, the absolute primacy of conscience, etc; just as he rejects secularist views with regard to the nature of truth, freedom, and civil society as man's last end. He rejects these positions as demonstrably erroneous in themselves. What is more to the point here, he rejects the notion that any of these sectarian theses enter into the content or implications of the First Amendment in such wise as to demand the assent of all American citizens. If this were the case the very article that bars any establishment of religion would somehow establish one. (53-54)

Reiterating a point he had made in 1946, Murray argued that to give a "theological interpretation" to the First Amendment or to make it an "object of religious faith" which must be "believed," would be to thrust a religious test into the constitution. The Republic would suddenly become either a "voluntary fellowship of believers either in some sort of free church Protestantism or in the tenets of a naturalistic humanism" (54). Such a notion is, Murray notes, preposterous.

> The United States is a good place to live in; many have found it even a sort of secular sanctuary. But it is not a church, whether high, low, or broad. It is simply a *civil community* whose unity is *purely political.* (54, emphasis mine)

Borrowing once again from Rawls, we may say that the justice of the First Amendment is political not metaphysical or theological. In this article, Murray is clearly setting forth a modus vivendi interpretation, justification, and defense of the religious freedom.

Murray speaks of the "theologians of the First Amendment"—both Protestant and secularist—who stress the importance of ideological factors in the genesis of the American concept of freedom and the separation of church and state. But these, Murray claims, are never entirely convincing. More important than ideological factors are the historical factors: the simple existence of the great mass of the unchurched on the American frontier (who were, fortunately for the Republic, not militantly laicist, anticlerical, or fundamentally antireligious, but rather easygoing, the product more of a naive materialism than of any conscious conviction); the multiplicity of Protestant denominations; the economy (persecution is bad for business); and finally, of lesser importance, the pressure exerted by the widening of religious freedom in England (58-59).

From this Murray concluded, once again, that the only tenable position is that the religion clauses of the First Amendment are not articles of faith but rather articles of peace. The Constitution generally and the First Amendment specifically are not the work of theologians or even of political theorists, but simply of lawyers (56). Murray cited Daniel Boorstin (1953) to suggest the historical inevitability of the clauses:

> It is almost inconceivable that it should not have worked itself out as it did. One suspects that this would have been true even if there had been no Williamses and Penns, no

> Calverts and Madisons and Jeffersons.... The theories of
> these men, whatever their defects, actually made history
> because they exerted their pressure, such as it was, in the
> direction in which historical factors were already moving in
> the new American society. (57)

Murray thus played down the political philosophies of the founders in favor
of their more pragmatic side.

> The artisans of the American Republic and its Constitution
> were not radical theorists intent on constructing a society
> in accord with the a priori demands of a doctrinaire blue-
> print, under disregard for what was actually "given" in his-
> tory. (57)

As we will see, Murray had good reason to play down the political theories of founders such as Jefferson and Madison, since they grounded their
argument for religious liberty to a significant extent on a doctrine of natural
rights. While one can agree with Murray that the American founders were
not dogmatic secularists in the way the French revolutionaries were, it is
nevertheless also true that Murray overstated his case. The American
founders indeed were not, with rare exceptions, "radical theorists" of the
Jacobin French-laicist variety. But that did not mean that some of them did
not bring to the Constitution in general and the issue of religious freedom in
particular the "a priori demands of a doctrinaire blueprint." In fact, as we
will see, Murray himself admitted as much in 1949 when arguing against the
Supreme Court's *Everson* (330 US 1, 1947) and *McCollum* (333 US 203,
1948) opinions. The author of the Amendment, the lawyer James Madison,
and his supporter Thomas Jefferson, both in different degrees had an a priori
blueprint. They both defended religious liberty at least partly on the basis of
John Locke's philosophy of natural rights, a position that evoked Murray's
criticism.

Before we proceed further we would do well to pause and take stock of
Murray's polemic to this point. First, if liberal Protestants justified the no-
establishment and free-exercise clauses by arguing that these followed from
the fact that churches are voluntary associations with equal sanction by
God, Murray would reject them since such a view incorporated into the
Constitution a Protestant ecclesiology and hence a theology. Thus, their
attempt to defend religious liberty as a universal, ahistorical, natural right is

subverted since it is, despite claims to the contrary, dependent on a particular ecclesiology not shared by Catholics. Secondly, if they completely bracketed their religious claims and sought to ground their argument for religious liberty on nonreligious natural rights grounds he would claim that they were capitulating to the secularist drift by ignoring the importance of Christian truth claims for modern society. Moreover, his criticism of liberal Protestantism was buttressed further by an attack on secularist natural rights claims, based as they were upon a highly contentious philosophy that belies its claim to universality. It is to Murray's criticism of this secularistic natural rights claim to universality that we now turn.

Notes

1. Failure to account for the substantive points made by Murray's early polemics against the liberal Protestant defenses of religious liberty has skewed most interpretations of Murray. Even if Murray's polemics were a bit heavy-handed at times, and even if it is true that Murray did not do justice to different Protestant conceptions of the problem, the substantive points of his critique remain relevant. In any case, his arguments are worthy of more consideration than Love has given them and they hardly warrant J. Leon Hooper's claim that his polemics were "immoral" (1986). Only if Murray's polemic against liberal Protestantism and secularism is taken as seriously as is his polemic against the Catholic traditionalists can justice be done to his work.

Chapter Five

Murray's Polemic
Against Secularist Defenses
of Religious Liberty

THE "SYMBOLIC REFERENCE POINT" (Weigel 1989, 89) for Murray's battle with secularism was the publication of an anti-Catholic broadside. When Paul Blanshard's infamous *American Freedom and Catholic Power* appeared in 1949, Murray wrote a brief review saying it was the best statement to date of what he called the "new nativism" (1949d). Two years later, as the book was reaching its fifteenth printing, he published a longer review article entitled "Paul Blanshard and the New Nativism" (1951b).

Murray located Blanshard's anti-Catholicism within a long history of "nativism" in America. The movement peaked in the 1840s and 1850s, its most obvious political manifestation being the famous Know-Nothing Party. The main point in the antebellum and early postbellum period, according to Murray, was that America was free, white, and Protestant. This made the Catholic an alien and menace, not the least because of his subjection to a "foreign power," the Pope. Behind such sentiments, Murray commented, was a long history of anti-Roman bias in the American republic. The *New England Primer* (1688), for instance, taught school children to "Abhor that arrant Whore of Rome, And all her blasphemies; And Drink not of her cursed cup, Obey not her decrees." This sentiment was revived, with a slightly different justification, in the post-Civil War era and was reflected in the American Protective Association. The charge was that the church "would destroy our free institutions and prove the grave of civil and religious liberty" (Murray 1951b, 215; citing Orestes Brownson).

Murray admits that Blanshard "rejects and deplores the religious bigotry of the old Nativist attack." But Blanshard's indictment rests on a different, and for Murray a more pernicious set of premises, which are most visible in Blanshard's constant use of the adjectives "American" and "un-American" as ultimate categories of value. The newness of his nativism is that it is no longer Protestant, which for the Catholic is bad enough, but naturalist, which for Murray is even worse.

> The primary accusation is that Catholicism is anti-American because America is a democracy, and democracy is necessarily based on a naturalist or secularist philosophy, and Catholicism is anti-naturalist. (216)

Murray presents a long list of indictments made by Blanshard against the church (217) that in sum amount to a view of "freedom" that "forbids anyone to introduce, or seek to make operative, in public life any absolute standard of morality." Thus, when an argument is made by a church that presumes to speak authoritatively, it is taken as a direct threat to democracy. Murray adds parenthetically that "all that democracy means, it seems, is 'freedom' in the rather outworn nineteenth-century sense" (218).

Blanshard's indictment of the church is ultimately grounded however, on a particular theory of religion and society. "To state the theory," Murray charges, "is to identify the Enemy." The enemy is not only Catholicism "but all religion worthy of the name" (218). Any religion which claims absolute moral values as relevant to public life can expect to be attacked as being anti-democratic.

Murray identifies four essential ideas that make up Blanshard's theory. The first is that "the sole area of the Church's competence is that of the "devotional life." The Church "belongs in the sacristy." The second and correlative idea is that of the supreme power of the democratic social welfare state over all aspects of secular life, which includes, for Blanshard, the fields of politics, economics, law, medicine, science, social welfare, education, the media, marriage, family community mores. "In all these areas of life," Murray adds, "the power of the democratic community is sovereign; no other authority stands outside it, beside it, much less above it" (219).

Although this appears similar to the French laicism of the Third Republic, Murray noted a difference. What makes Blanshard's secularism distinctly American is the third idea, the claim for "the universal validity of the democratic process for the settlement of all issues arising in the secular sphere, as defined" (219). This idea, one that Blanshard holds with "great passion and sincerity," even leads to the concession that the church may indeed have a social voice. But it may raise that voice only if it is willing to submit to what Murray thought were two fatal conditions.

First, the church must consider itself as merely one agency within the state. Secondly, "it must itself be democratically organized, and its purposes and programmes must be determined, not by a hierarchy empowered to speak authoritatively, but by the membership itself acting through democratic channels." The church may be admitted into public debate on these conditions, provided of course that the church is willing to cede its positions in the presence of the broader prevailing majority. If it maintains a hierarchical structure, however, it must be labeled by critics such as Blanshard as "alien to democratic society." The church is heretical since it does not subscribe to the creedal orthodoxy of majoritarianism, and therefore must be excommunicated from social life.

The fourth idea is that "the singly valid guide of the individual or the collectivity in forming opinions is scientific method." While Blanshard as a nonphilosopher fails to achieve the theoretical clarity of a Hans Meyerhoff, his theory is nonetheless similar to that of Meyerhoff when he writes: "The method of the democratic tradition consists essentially in recognizing the rational criteria of argument and proof derived from the natural sciences as the only authority for judging the validity of a social theory" (from the *American Perspective* cited p. 220). This comes to expression in what is in effect a jurisprudential positivism in which "all law is simply sociological dictate [sic] that the majority is at the moment prepared to enforce" (220).

All this adds up to Murray's conclusion: Blanshard's indictment of the church rests on a new kind of monism.

> He is, to give him a name, a social monist, who wears his monism with the twentieth-century difference. It is not so much a monism of the political *order* (raising the problem of order before such thinkers only draws a bland stare), as a monism of the political *process*. Mr. Blanshard's idol is not so much the democratic state as the democratic process. (220)

Such a monism denies the social dualism as originally put forth by Pope Gelasius. Moreover, it places before the liberal tradition a momentous question. The question takes two forms.

Is there a sacred element in the secular life of man which
escapes from the undivided control of the supreme power
of the State, even the democratic State, and more particularly the democratic majority? Or is the secular life of man
completely secular, enclosed within the State as the highest
social organism, and subject ultimately to the political
power (actually, whether the political power operates
through democratic forms does not, for the purposes of the
question, matter greatly)? (222)

If the answer to the first question is negative and the latter affirmative, then
the experiment in democratic liberalism is doomed, for it will have "relinquished the essential basis of any structural dualism, the concept of the *res
sacra in temporalibus*" in favor of the primacy of the political. By subverting
the "indirect power of the Church," the "liberal tradition will have perished
in the triumph of social monism" (222-23).

Murray's polemic against Blanshard could perhaps be dismissed as a
scholarly case of overreaction against the journalistic excesses of an anti-
Catholic and antireligious bigot. But Murray recognized a similarity between
Blanshard's theory and the direction the United States Supreme Court was
taking in its understanding of the relation between church and state. Most
notable were the written opinions of the Court in the infamous *Everson* (330
US 1, 1947) and *McCollum* (333, US 203, 1948) decisions. The opinions and
decisions expressed by the Court in these cases were the legal manifestation
of what Murray called secularistic "theologies" of the religion clauses of the
First Amendment. An examination of Murray's criticism of what he took to
be the secularist trend of the court reveals how critical Murray was of a
moral Esperantist defense of religious liberty on the grounds of natural
rights. His own view reflects an interpretation of the First Amendment that
is a modus vivendi approach to the question, one that barely separates him
from his Catholic brethren.

Everson v. Board of Education (1947) is the single most important case in
the field of American church-state jurisprudence, particularly in its interpretation of the religion clauses of the First Amendment. The facts of the case
are simple. In 1941 the New Jersey legislature passed a statute authorizing
"local school districts to make rules and contracts for the transportation of
children to and from school." Pursuant to this law, the Board of Education of
Ewing Township, New Jersey, passed a resolution authorizing reimburse-
ment to parents for money spent sending their children to public or Catholic

parochial schools on regular busses operated by the public transportation system (Cord, 1982, 109-10). Everson, as a taxpayer in the school district, challenged the constitutionality of both the school board resolution and the state law as violations of the New Jersey and Federal Constitutions. There were two grounds to his challenge: first, because the state in using public funds for a private purpose, was depriving him of his property without due process of law; second, the "statute and the [school board] resolution forced inhabitants to pay taxes to help support and maintain schools which are dedicated to, and which regularly teach, the Catholic faith," thus violating the due process clause of the Fourteenth Amendment and the establishment clause of the First Amendment, respectively. After losing on appeal in New Jersey's highest court, Everson pursued the First and Fourteenth Amendments to the U.S. Supreme Court.

After quickly disposing of the claim that the resolution and statute violated the "equal protection" clause of the Fourteenth Amendment, Justice Hugo Black writing for the Court delivered the following interpretation of the establishment clause:

> The "establishment of religion" clause of the First Amendment means at least this: Neither a state nor the Federal Government can set up a church. Neither can pass laws which aid one religion, aid all religions, or prefer one religion over another.... No tax in any amount, large or small, can be levied to support any religious activities or institutions, whatever they may be called, or whatever form they may adopt to teach or practice religion. Neither a state not the Federal Government can, openly or secretly, participate in the affairs of any religious organizations or groups and vice versa. In the words of Jefferson, the clause against establishment of religion was intended to erect a "wall of separation between church and State." (330 US 1 at 15-16)

Nevertheless, quite remarkably, Justice Black ruled that the New Jersey law was not unconstitutional.

> The First Amendment has erected a wall between church and State. That wall must be kept high and impregnable. We could not approve the slightest breach. New Jersey has not breached it here. (330 US 1 at 18)

The expenditure of public funds for the busing of parochial school children was thus, despite the "high and impregnable wall" metaphor, declared constitutional. This in turn prompted the famous response of Justice Jackson, who in dissent amusingly remarked:

> The undertones of the opinion, advocating complete and uncompromising separation of Church from State, seem utterly discordant with its conclusion yielding support to their commingling in educational matters. The case which irresistibly comes to mind as the most fitting precedent is that of Julia who, according to Byron's reports, "whispering 'I will ne'er consent,' consented." (330 US 1 at 19)

While Justice Black advocated a "complete and uncompromising separation of church from state, Justice Rutledge, another dissenter, went even further. As did the majority, Rutledge referred to the struggle to disestablish Anglicanism in Virginia during the 1770s and 1780s, and quoted at length from James Madison's famous *Memorial and Remonstrance*. From this history Rutledge argued that:

> Not simply an established church, but any law respecting an establishment of religion is forbidden. The Amendment was broadly but not loosely phrased. It is the compact and exact summation of its author's views formed during his long struggles for religious freedom. (330 US 1 at 31)

But even more sweepingly, Rutledge claimed:

> The Amendment's purpose was not to strike merely at the official establishment of a single sect, creed or religion, outlawing only a formal relation such as had prevailed in England in some of the colonies. Necessarily *it was to uproot all such relationships*. But the object was broader than separating church and state in this narrow sense. It was to create a complete and permanent separation of the spheres of religious activity and civil authority by comprehensively forbidding every form of public aid for religion.... (330 U.S 1 at 31–32, emphasis mine)

Murray, as we shall see, will take aim at this interpretation, charging that it embodies the same sort of unwarranted secularistic reading of the First Amendment and hence of religious freedom as he found in Blanshard. But the worst, from Murray's perspective, was yet to come. One year after *Everson*, in *McCollum v. Board of Education of Champaign, Illinois* (1948), the Supreme Court in an 8-1 decision ruled for the first time that an action by a local school board was unconstitutional under the Establishment Clause of the First Amendment.

The *McCollum* case was different from *Everson* in that no monetary expenditures were involved. In 1940, members of Jewish, Catholic, and some Protestant denominations formed a voluntary association called the Champaign Council on Religious Education. This council asked the board of education to allow public school pupils in grades four through nine to be permitted to attend weekly religious instruction, on a voluntary basis, without having to leave the public school premises. Pursuant to its authority under Illinois law, the Champaign Board of Education instituted a "released time" program whereby students, whose parents gave them permission to attend religious instruction classes, could do so as a substitute "for secular education provided under the [State's] compulsory education law" for not more than forty-five minutes a week. Students who did not attend religious instruction classes were not released from their secular educational obligations. The council provided, at no expense to the public school authorities, teachers of the Protestant, Catholic, and Jewish faiths. The instructors were subject to the approval of the superintendent of the schools.

Mrs. Vashti McCollum, a taxpayer in the Champaign school district and the mother of a Champaign schoolboy, challenged the constitutionality of the "released time" program and asked the Illinois courts to order the board of education to adopt rules and regulations prohibiting all instruction in and teaching of religious education in all public schools. After losing in the Illinois courts she appealed to the U.S. Supreme Court, where her case was heard in December 1947, with a decision handed down four months later.

In reversing the Illinois courts and finding the "released time" program unconstitutional, Justice Black, again writing for the court, held that two points could not be reconciled with the concept of separation of church and state:

> Here not only are the State's tax-supported public school
> buildings used for the dissemination of religious doctrines.
> The State also affords sectarian groups an invaluable aid in

that it helps to provide pupils for their religious classes through use of the State's compulsory public school machinery. This is not separation of Church and State. (333 U.S. 203 at 212)

The released time program was in Justice Black's opinion "beyond all question a utilization of the tax-established and tax-supported public school system to aid religious groups to spread their faith." It thus falls squarely under the ban of the First Amendment...as we interpreted it in *Everson v. Board of Education*" (333 U.S. 203 at 210).

With this background, we are now prepared to take a closer look at Murray's criticism of these landmark decisions. I will argue that at a deeper level, his criticisms reflect a serious challenge to an Esperantist defense of religious liberty.

In an earlier article in *America* (1947c), Murray had praised the *Everson* decision to allow funds to be used in the transportation of parochial school children. However, this praise was clearly focused on the fact that aid for bus transportation was allowed, and not on the argument of the Court. After the *McCollum* decision, however, Murray took a closer look, the results of which appeared in Duke University's law journal *Law and Contemporary Problems* (1949i).

Murray didn't like what he saw and his contempt for the decision was reflected in his opening sentence: "The constitutional law written in the *Everson* and *McCollum* cases is obviously not what is called learned law; consequently one who is not a lawyer, learned in the law, may speak his mind on it." Murray argued that even the favorable majority decision in the *Everson* case put forth a new conception of the problem of the separation of church and state. Despite the favorable outcome of *Everson*, the positions presented in both *Everson* and *McCollum* represented "the first formal efforts of the Court to work out an official contemporary philosophy of the political principle enshrined in the 'establishment' clause of the First Amendment" (1949i, 23).

Because Murray held that "the original American philosophy that inspired the First Amendment was fundamentally sound," he thought it "important to see that it is not corrupted, under the pretext, for instance, of 'development'" (23). One of his main objections to the Court's reasoning was its absoluteness, the irony of which was not lost on Murray.

> I have been given to understand that the present Court has
> a certain horror of absolutes, and is disinclined to give
> room for them in its jurisprudence; if this is so, it is some-
> what ironical that the Court should suddenly have come up
> with one: 'absolute separation of church and state, as an
> absolute principle'. (23)

Given the Court's acceptance of the particularly "rigid, radical, and absolute doctrine laid down in the *Everson* and *McCollum* cases," Murray delved into their justification. Murray's case against what he called the *Everson* line of argumentation is most relevant for our purposes because it is here that he aims his polemical sights on the separation of church and state and a defense of religious liberty based on an Esperantist appeal to natural rights.

Before proceeding to Murray's discussion we would do well to set the context by outlining the main interpretive options before Murray. Three broad historical factors all have been appealed to in interpreting the religion clauses of the First Amendment. First, appeal is often made to the views of James Madison and Thomas Jefferson, who led the fight against the levying of taxes to support teachers of the Christian religion in Virginia. Their political philosophies, as expressed in Madison's *Memorial and Remonstrance* and Jefferson's *Bill Concerning Religious Liberty*, are taken to express a Lockean natural rights view of religious liberty, which in turn is seen to be embodied in the First Amendment. This was Justice Rutledge's view. Another historical factor that is claimed as a genesis of the religion clauses was the Baptist tradition as represented by Roger Williams and other sectarian religious groups. One appeals to this tradition in order to maintain that the religious liberty and disestablishment enshrined in the First Amendment was an outgrowth of voluntarism as a basic ecclesiological principle. Finally, the religion clauses are seen by some as simply a practical necessity arising from the diversity of sects which existed in the early republic.

Murray would argue that James Madison's philosophy of natural rights, with its corresponding view of religion as a "wholly private matter," could not and should not be read into the First Amendment, even though Madison was the primary author of that Amendment. Murray would argue, quite simply, that if this is indeed the way in which religion clauses should be read, then the Court would have ironically established a particular religion–James Madison's religion (see Miller 1987, 134-35). Murray would also reject the Anabaptist line of interpretation as illegitimate because it rests on a controversial theological premise–voluntarism. Rather, he would resort to the practical necessity of the religion clauses given the diversity of sects. He would argue, in other words, for a modus vivendi interpretation of the religion clauses.

The essence of the court's decisions, argued Murray, "is that James Madison's concept of the relations between religion and government, together with the philosophy on which this concept rests, became in 1791 the fundamental law of the land by act of the states ratifying the First Amendment" (27). Murray objected to the historical accuracy of that judgment, and correctly pointed out that the First Amendment was a group effort, not simply the work of one man. But he agreed with Justice Rutledge's observation concerning the essence of the Madisonian concept. Rutledge, according to Murray, was correct when he said:

> As the [Memorial and] Remonstrance discloses throughout,
> Madison opposed every form and degree of official relation
> between religion and civil authority. For him religion was a
> wholly private matter beyond the scope of civil power
> either to restrain or support. (cited in 1949i, 28)

The reference to Madison's *Memorial and Remonstrance* is crucial for two reasons. First, it fairly reflects Madison's views on religious liberty and the separation of church and state. And secondly, it ushers John Locke's natural rights argument for religious liberty into the American discussion. Murray found this objectionable.

Murray's objections to Lockean natural rights theory pretty much reflected the standard Catholic natural law polemic against natural rights theory in general and Locke in particular. His criticisms appeared in an article written in 1950, which later formed the final chapter of *We Hold These Truths*.

As typical of the advocates of a natural law ethic Murray focused in on the thinness of man's duty in the state of nature. In Locke's system, Murray reminds us, the state of nature had the function of establishing the inalienability of the rights of man, as conceived by Locke. He critically cites Locke's statement in his *Second Essay* that man in the state of nature is "absolute lord of his own person and possessions, equal to the greatest and subject to nobody" (1960a, 303). On this free individual rests a single law—the law of nature—its only precept being that of self-preservation, the preservation of his life, liberty, and property.

Murray was also critical of the artifice of the social contract. He cites Locke's statement that men enter society only by their free act: "Men being, as has been said, by nature all free, equal, and independent, no one can be put out of this estate and subjected to the political power of another without his consent" (304-5). Because organized society reflects nothing real, Locke is "that most decadent of philosophical things, a nominalist" (309). The three things that Murray finds most odious in Locke's political philosophy are its "narrow individualism, thin rationalism, and empty nominalism" (314). To adopt this "old Liberal individualism," would imply:

> "Natural rights" are simply individual material interests (be they of individuals or social groups or nations), so furnished with an armature by positive law as to be enforceable by the power of government. In this view one would be consenting to a basically atomistic concept of society, to its organization in terms of power relationships, to a concept of the state as simply an apparatus or compulsion without the *moral function of realizing an order of justice*.... (321, emphasis mine)

It is not surprising, then, that Murray would reject Madison's philosophical defense of religious liberty in his *Memorial and Remonstrance* inasmuch as it is introduced and concluded on the note of natural rights closely related to and probably dependent upon the thought of John Locke.

The immediate historical occasion for the document was a proposed assessment to aid teachers of the Christian religion, an assessment opposed by both Jefferson and Madison. Madison argued in his opening point that religion was essentially a private affair which depended upon the direction of the conscience of the individual. Man's right to direct his own conscience and his right to judge was a natural right. Because the most fundamental of these natural rights was that of conscience, Madison reasoned, one's religion depended entirely upon personal opinion. As such, it should not be coerced or directed by any other man, nor could it be handed over to another human being, since on a more basic level its direction belonged to God.

Madison's argument for religious liberty was largely dependent upon the Lockean view of the state of nature. All men in the state of nature are equal, such that when a person enters into civil society he only gives up the same powers as do his fellows. From this Madison argued that both religious believers and atheists exercised this right. In addition, throughout his *Memo-*

rial, Madison assumed that the church was a purely voluntary organization outside the concern of civil government. The limit of the church-state relation was that the state had the obligation to protect every citizen in the exercise of his religion, allowing all groups to operate freely and preventing any group from injuring or invading the rights of others.

Sandwiched between the natural rights arguments that began and concluded the *Memorial*, however, were a number of other arguments that Madison hoped would persuade those "sectarians" who did not find such a natural rights perspective persuasive. Thus he appealed to those who would see the proposed assessment as an attack on their own conception of Christianity, particularly their voluntarist ecclesiology. He also brought forth a number of other arguments: that to employ the assistance of the state would be "an unhallowed perversion of the means of salvation," that compulsion was not needed in the cause of Christ, and that to imply that it was would cast doubt on the divine origin and efficacy of the Gospel, that it would harm Christianity by hindering the cooperation of the churches, and that it would obstruct the missionary work of the churches by encouraging them to leave or remain out of a state where religion had been established. Finally, he was not above appealing to a slippery slope argument, what Murray referred to as the "camel's nose" argument, that the proposed assessment which would establish Christianity now might well lead to the attempt to establish this or that particular sect "in exclusion of all other sects" in the future. Madison, with a rhetorical flourish, even went so far as to argue that the assessment was different from the inquisition only in degree.

Murray's strategy was to argue that the absolute conclusion reached by Rutledge in dissent in *Everson* and agreed to in principle by the majority could only rest on Madison's own "particular sectarian concept of 'religion'" as expressed in his *Memorial*.

> For Madison, as for John Locke, his master, religion could not by law be made a concern of the commonwealth as such, deserving in any degree of public recognition or aid, for the essentially theological reason that religion is of its nature a personal, private, interior matter of the individual conscience, having no relevance to the public concerns of the state. (1949, 29)

According to Murray, only Madison's theological premise that religion is purely a private affair, coupled with his ecclesiological assumption that the church was simply a voluntary society, could support the absolute conclusion as expressed by Rutledge: No form or degree of official relations between religion and government, and no aid to religion.

Murray pointed to a paradox that points to the folly of reading this particular philosophy into the First Amendment. Such a reading is unacceptable simply because

> it is an irredeemable piece of sectarian dogmatism. And if there is one thing that the First Amendment forbids with resounding force it is the intrusion of a sectarian philosophy of religion into the fundamental law of the land. (30)

The paradox exists when, in order to make separation of church and state absolute it unites the state to a "religion without a church—a deistic version of fundamentalist Protestantism." Referring to Justice Jackson's quip about Byron's Julia, Murray noted that Jackson

> thought up an apt allusion, but he got its reference wrong; actually, it is the philosophizing of the whole Court that reminds one of Byron's Julia, who, in momentary disregard of her original lines and the exigencies of metre, "screaming, 'I will ne'er consent to an establishment of religion'," imposed one on the American people. (31)

Murray, never one to avoid a polemical dig, also adds a highly suggestive comment.

> If today the Court were to take as a premise of argument Madison's particular theory of "natural rights" as deriving from a pre-social "state of nature" (a theory borrowed from Locke), there would be legal howlings. It is not more legitimate to adopt Madison's particular theory of religion in its relation to organized society. (31)

Against this "prejudicial and dogmatic" reading of the First Amendment, Murray argued that if there was to be a sort of official American philosophy in the matter, one promulgated by the Supreme Court, "it must be constructed in the absence of all appeal to sectarian dogmas—Madison's as well

as anybody else's (31). Then, shortly later, he adds that if you take away
Madison's theological premise you can still

> combine Madison's other arguments into a satisfactory
> theory of separation of church and state—a satisfactory
> theory because it will not make separation an absolute, and
> its reasons will be such as to command consensus. (32)

What were these other arguments? According to Murray,

> he appeals to the common law tradition of the distinction
> between ecclesiastical and civil authority; to natural rights,
> as he understood the term, after the fashion of John Locke;
> to the principle of political equality, which is violated by
> civic distinctions on religious grounds; to the exigencies of
> civic unity, "moderation and harmony," in a religiously
> divided society. He also argues from expediency: establish-
> ment is not necessary for religion nor good for it; it is not
> necessary for political society nor good for it. Finally he
> uses the famous emotional argument, the entering-wedge
> argument (nowadays, the camel's nose, or the crack-in-the-
> wall, argument). All of these persuaded Madison of the
> necessity of a constitutional separation of church and state.
> (28-29)

Murray is quite correct. If you eliminate Madison's natural rights argument as grounded in Lockean natural rights theory, separation of church
and state will no longer be an absolute. But what remains to be said is that
this also eliminates a defense of the free exercise of religion on the claim that
it is grounded in a "natural right" to religious freedom. What remains is a
modus vivendi argument for religious liberty, the type one finds sandwiched
between Madison's natural rights arguments in the *Memorial and Remonstrance*. But that makes Murray's position remarkably similar to that of his
traditionalist opponents after all.

Murray's criticism of the liberal Protestant and secularist readings of the
First Amendment and their corresponding defense of religious freedom was
ingenious. He, in effect, showed their understandings of the separation of
church and state to be as tradition-dependent as that of the Catholics. As we
have seen, Murray argued that if there was to be an official American philos-

ophy on the matter of religious freedom and the relation of church and state "it must be constructed *in the absence of all appeal to sectarian dogmas*" (1949, 31). Murray's argument against the liberal Protestants and secularists was that their appeals for religious liberty were, in fact, sectarian dogmas, all disclaimers to the contrary. Murray simply showed their attempts to speak moral Esperanto to be flawed.

But conceding the brilliance of Murray's polemic, we now want to turn the criticism toward Murray himself. Did Murray himself completely avoid a "theological reading" of the First Amendment? We have already noted that Murray claimed that the First Amendment was distinct from the monism that characterized the modern laicized state in that it supposedly recognizes that a dyarchy of life governs the life of man and society. As such, it recognizes a spiritual power that stands not only over against it, but above it (1949e, 189). But that in itself, it would seem, is also a "theological" reading of the First Amendment.

The claim that the First Amendment admits a dyarchy of rule over man is just as much a particular "theological-philosophical" reading as is the liberal Protestant and secularist readings. One could easily enough imagine a secularist charging that the proposition "The First Amendment recognizes a spiritual power" or "The First Amendment admits a dyarchy of rule over man and society" to be "theological." Would not a Marxist who saw the "Two there are, not one there is" doctrine as a threat to secular unity, consider these to be theological assertions?

The problem, once again, is that Murray must appeal to a purely modus vivendi reading of the First Amendment to defeat the Esperantist readings of the liberal Protestants. But he needs just a little substantive philosophical and theological content—the transtemporal papal assertion "Two there are"— to defeat a radically secularist reading of the documents. When he confronts a reading of the First Amendment or, more generally, an argument for religious liberty that incorporates a contentious theological or philosophical premise he historicizes that premise. But when he confronts a more pragmatic approach he appeals to a transtemporal principle that itself could be labeled as an expression of a particular theological tradition.

The implications of this type of approach to church-state matters was addressed by one of Murray's traditionalist critics, George Shea. Shea suggested that Murray's position, consistently carried out, would require radical surgery on Thomistic political theory. He had confronted Murray directly in the *American Ecclesiastical Review* in an article entitled "Catholic Doctrine and 'The Religion of the State.'" He challenged Murray's views by appealing

to the arguments of the early Murray of 1945 against the "new Murray" of
the late 1940s who had been criticizing the thesis-hypothesis doctrine (Shea
1950, 165). The following year in an article entitled "Catholic Orientations
on Church and State" (1951) he took a more indirect tack against Murray,
not mentioning him by name, even in the footnotes while referring to his
articles (1951, 407, n. 8; 409, n. 15). Instead Shea sketched a review of a
book on political theory by Oswald von Nell-Breuning (405) and used it as a
foil against what he called the "new school" of Catholic political theory.

Shea quickly got to the crux of the matter by pointing to the rather novel
definition of the state advocated by the new school, noting that "one may no
longer, with the scholastic writers, define the state as *societas naturalis, perfecta, completa*, as *societas civilis (-politica) perfecta*, or identify them with the
body politic, political society" (Shea 1951, 406-7). Unlike Nell-Breuning,
who still, properly for Shea, insists on formulating the question as "What is
the supra-temporal essence of the state?" rather than "What is the character
of the modern state?" Shea cites the opinion of Jacques Leclerq, a "European
leader of the new school," who is clearly standing in for Murray here.
According to Leclerq:

> The modern state is something essentially—and therewith
> also conceptually—different from the ancient state, from
> the medieval state or that of the 17th century.... Democracy
> and state are sociological, not philosophical categories, that
> is, they stand in the stream of time, not in the world of
> ideas! ...[T]he state is no longer what the Scholastics viewed
> it to be, the highest and most thorough (*intensivste*, i.e.,
> complete) natural community, the *societas completa*; it is
> instead, pre-eminently a *technical apparatus* used by a mul-
> titude of human individuals and communities, societies, to
> realize their ends.... (cited in Shea 1951, 408)

Shea immediately sees the implications of this purely functional conception of the state for the question of church-state relations in general and religious liberty in particular. If the state is purely a "technical apparatus,"

> then obviously it is not within the competence of the state
> to choose between the churches, or to support the truth
> and moral values—to judge as to these things no more
> belongs to the state than it does to any other technical

administration or administrative apparatus. (Shea 1951, 409)

Moreover, whatever material assistance the state might owe the true church would not stem from its being the true church but simply from the fact that its members "constitute a notable group of citizens who, as such, have some claim upon the services of the technical apparatus, the state, toward the realization of their ends" (Shea 1951, 409-10). Although he doesn't use the term, Shea, in effect, is accusing Murray and the new school of promoting what has come to be called "interest group liberalism," or more recently a purely "procedural republic" (e.g., Sandel 1984). In such a procedural state the church is just one among many competing interests.

Now, despite Murray's talk about a purely political reading of the religion clauses, he would not settle for that. He certainly was not an interest group liberal and he was deeply critical of those who advocated a purely procedural democracy. But an understanding of how Murray sought to deflect this charge helps further to illuminate the broader dilemma. For when confronted with a purely procedural or pragmatic state, Murray almost instinctively made recourse to natural law. While in 1945 Murray had come to the conclusion that an argument for religious liberty on the basis of natural law would not work, he nevertheless brought it in through the back door in order to avoid a pure modus vivendi position and therefore avoid the type of criticism leveled by Shea.

Murray's problem was that while he never learned to speak moral Esperanto on the subject of religious liberty, he would not be content with a pure modus vivendi approach. In fact, in order to avoid the ill effects of pragmatism in American politics, he argued in *We Hold These Truths* that the American experiment could only survive by a return to natural law doctrine. The church, he insisted, must have influence in temporal affairs not simply as one more interest group among others, but because she was the one institution in modern America that still held to the doctrine of natural law. Just as Murray's understanding of the state as a moral entity and as the guarantor of the common good would undercut any Esperantist case for religious liberty, so would his appeal to "natural law" undercut a pure modus vivendi position. In the remainder of this chapter I intend to show that while Murray had given up on an argument for religious liberty from natural law in 1945, he nevertheless brought it in the back door in order to pull up short of a pure modus vivendi position.

Murray considered his *We Hold These Truths* to be a "primer on pluralism" (Pelotte 1976). By pluralism he meant

> the coexistence within the one political community of
> groups who hold divergent and incompatible views with
> regard to religious questions—those ultimate questions that
> concern the nature and destiny of man within a universe
> that stands under the reign of God. Pluralism therefore
> implies disagreement and dissension within the commu-
> nity. But it also implies a community within which there
> must be agreement and consensus. (1960a, x)

In his book, Murray addressed what he perceived to be the growing loss of a
moral consensus. Charles Curran accurately summarizes Murray's "auda-
cious proposal" in *We Hold These Truths*.

> Our governmental system is based on the American con-
> sensus—the truths we hold. Catholics can readily accept
> the American political consensus including the First
> Amendment guarantee of religious freedom and the separa-
> tion of church and state because it is based on natural law.
> Unfortunately, today, when it is most needed, the consen-
> sus no longer exists. The only solution is to rebuild the
> consensus on the basis of natural law. Not only can Catho-
> lics accept the principle of the founding fathers of our
> nation, but today Catholics are the only ones with the abil-
> ity to rebuild and to rearticulate the consensus. (Curran
> 1982, 219)

Murray believed that the rise of pragmatism among the American intellectual elite was a primary reason for the loss of a public consensus, and that
this in turn had resulted in a moral vacuum in American domestic and foreign policy. The pragmatic claim, as understood by Murray, was that America
is a new kind of open society in which the consensus is and can be "purely
procedural." It thus "involves no agreement on the premises and purposes of
political life and legal institutions." Our democratic institutions are conceived as purely formal categories; "they are simply channels through which
any kind of content may flow" (1960a, 84).

In opposition to this pragmatic trend, Murray attempted to ground a "public philosophy" in an appeal to "natural law." He argued that "only the theory of natural law...can give an account of the moral experience which is the public consensus and thus lift it from the level of sheer experience to the higher level of intelligibility..." (1960a, 114).

Murray recognized that technically the contents of the consensus are 'remote precepts of natural law' which are "'removed' from the primary common precepts and from the immediately derivative [i.e. proximate] precepts as particular conclusions are 'removed' from the generality of the premises that engender them" (117-18). Consequently, they are not self-evident, as are the primary precepts of natural law, and thus suppose a thorough analysis "of the existent reality in its full complexity in a given historical moment" (1960a, 118). As such, the application and articulation of the consensus is the task of the wise and intelligent (118-19).

Murray cited St. Thomas' statement, "Since the rational soul is the proper form of man, there is in every man a natural inclination to act according to reason, that is, according to virtue." Murray held that this dynamism is more fully released in the wise and honest and then adds that "this quality of being in accord with reason is the *non-contingent element in the body of thought that constitutes the consensus.* Brute fact or sheer experience have no virtue to elaborate themselves into controlling rules of public conduct" (1960a, 119, emphasis mine). Murray desperately wanted to avoid brute fact and sheer experience as the ultimate authority for a public consensus arising out of the convergence of separate interests.

The crucial question is whether he can do it on a purely "natural" basis, abstracted from other, deeper, theological commitments and, if not, whether those deeper theological commitments can legitimately be brought forth in the public square. If, as Murray recognized in 1945, man has not only the obligation to seek God in the order of nature but also the further hypothetical obligation to accept any other knowledge God may make accessible, it would seem that deeper theological commitments could not be ruled out of the public square, at least not a priori. In fact, such theological commitments could arguably be obligatory on the basis of natural law.

Murray, it seems, resorted to the doctrine of natural law in order to avoid impaling himself on the modus vivendi horn of the dilemma. Yet, his appeal to the remote precepts of natural law cannot do the job. To decisively trump claims for religious intolerance, he would have to appeal to the purportedly primary principles of practical reason which, unlike secondary principles, are not subject to historical contingency. Grounding the "right" to religious liberty in the remote precepts of natural law is not enough to defeat Murray's traditionalist opponents simply because the content of the remote precepts is itself dependent upon particular historical and sociological factors. It is, for this reason, the task of the wise to make a prudential judgment. It is true that any judgment must constantly refer to the self-evident and constant first principles of practical reasoning. However, as Murray's 1945 arguments imply, appeal to such first principles of practical reason as a basis for freedom of religion is futile. For one thing, any discussion of liberty must be made within the context of each type of law, divine as well as natural and positive. For another, the constancy of any claimed first principles of practical reasoning is due to their being so formal and abstract that they simply cannot provide the concrete principle necessary to override societal claims for religious intolerance should the proper conditions hold. In short, Murray's appeal to natural law undermines the concrete degree of freedom that each person should have in matters religious. Such an appeal cannot rule out the affirmation of religious intolerance. To put it bluntly, Murray is overconfident about the value of remote secondary precepts of natural law.

According to scholastic natural law doctrine, the absolute first principle of practical reason is that good is to be done and pursued and evil avoided (ST 1a2æ.94.2). Such a principle is self-evident and immediately perspicuous (Finnis 1980, 33ff.). Once the terms are understood, all humans with the use of reason must assent to this principle. With the aid of experience, human beings come to recognize that their good includes preservation of one's life, sexual union, family life, and the need to seek after truth in society with other humans. Humans can supposedly assent to these primary precepts of practical reason without any inductive or deductive reasoning.

Reason is also able to draw conclusions about particular types of human acts from these first principles. These "conclusions" constitute the secondary precepts of the natural law. Secondary precepts are of two types: proximate and remote (ST 1a2æ.100.1). Proximate secondary precepts flow so readily from primary precepts that most persons recognize their validity in most cases although they can be distorted by passions or bad habits (ST 1a2æ.94.4). Remote secondary precepts on the other hand require considerable reflection. Thus many will fail to recognize the remote precepts. Discovering the remote precepts is thus the province of what Murray, following Aquinas, referred to as the "wise."

The secondary remote precepts are the most difficult to discover for two reasons. First, they involve a certain distance from the so-called evident certainty of the primary precepts. Since an axiom is always more certain than the conclusion deduced from it there is bound to be some diminution of certainty. Secondly, they are more difficult to discover because individual cases are bound to concrete and contingent circumstances. Now, it seems rather odd that Murray would find in the remote precepts of natural law, that is, in contingent and uncertain precepts, the most *"non-contingent element in the body of thought that constitutes the consensus."* That is a fairly thin thread on which to hang one's argument for religious liberty.

But, more importantly, it is difficult to see how this could have any force against the modus vivendi position of the traditionalist Catholics. Murray's opposition had already reached the conclusion that the remote precepts of natural law required religious tolerance on the basis of the concrete and contingent circumstances that held in American society. If this indeed is the case, we are forced to ask a few probing questions: What exactly is the difference between Murray and the traditionalists? How will he distance himself from the traditional modus vivendi position? Or, perhaps more accurately, how will he come to perceive the difference between his position and theirs? These questions will be addressed in the next two chapters.

Chapter Six

Murray on Religious Toleration Before, During, and After Vatican II

THUS FAR WE HAVE EXAMINED Murray's arguments for religious liberty prior to his being censored in 1955. The image that perhaps best captures Murray's project during those years is one which sees him as tracking in two opposite directions, largely depending upon the stance taken by his polemical opponents. When he argued against the modus vivendi position of the traditionalists he tracked towards an Esperantist defense of religious liberty. On the other hand, when he argued against the Esperantist position of liberal Protestants and secularists he tracked back toward a modus vivendi defense. In this and the following chapter, I examine his mature thought on the subject leading up to, during, and following the Vatican Council's "Declaration on Religious Freedom" (*Dignitatis humanae*). During this period, the imagery which best captures his approach to the subject of religious toleration is different. He is best seen, not as tracking in one direction or another, but as standing between the horns of the dilemma, refuting arguments as they come from each side.

My understanding of Murray's writings during this period differs from a more conventional interpretation. This more standard interpretation is summarized nicely by John Rohr, who finds Murray's early efforts "somewhat muddled and confused if judged in the light of the sharp clarity that characterized his later works" (1978, 11). I hope to show that there is nothing particularly lucid about Murray's mature argument for religious liberty. Despite his intent to construct a "unitary theory," his own constructive position is seriously ambiguous. Ironically enough, what is clear in Murray's mature writings are the arguments he gives against a number of arguments in favor of religious liberty. The ambiguity of Murray's own final argument results, I suggest, because there is, in fact, no firm place to stand between the horns of the dilemma.

Murray on Religious Liberty Immediately Prior to Vatican II

Murray's mature thinking on the matter of religious liberty cannot be understood outside the context of his participation in the evolution of "The Declaration on Religious Freedom." Thus, our exposition of Murray's mature position primarily will explore his writings within the context of his contribution to that document as well as his comments on final text. First, however, we will examine two important unpublished articles written in the late 1950s. These articles give us some insight into Murray's thinking immediately prior to Pope John XXIII's call for a Second Vatican Council.

Murray's censure at the hands of the traditionalist defenders of the thesis-hypothesis position should not cloud the fact that his polemic against the secularist and liberal Protestant defenses of the "free exercise of religion," was not too different than one might expect from his traditionalist opponents. His more traditionalist Catholic brethren would fully agree with Murray that, because of the particular conditions which held in the early American republic, "any other course [than religious freedom] would have been disruptive, imprudent, impractical, indeed impossible." Nor were they likely to deny that "the demands of social necessity were overwhelming" (1960a, 59-60). In fact, if one only reads those articles in which Murray argued against liberal Protestants and secularists, one might wonder just what complaint the traditionalist Catholics could have against Murray. This leads one to ask: Just exactly what was the difference?

Two unpublished articles written in the late 1950s, "Church and State: The Structure of the Argument" (1958a) and "*Unica Status Religio*" (1959a) reveal that Murray attempted to distance himself from the traditionalists in two ways. First, he tried to suggest, as much as possible given the sensitive nature of the church politics involved, that the thesis-hypothesis position was sub-moral and based on mere expediency. In this sense, Murray's attack of the thesis-hypothesis doctrine was similar to John Rawls' criticism of modus vivendi liberalism as being sub-moral (see chap. 1). Secondly, Murray's understanding of the "common good" and of a "Catholic society" was more nuanced and developed than that of the traditional opposition. The first argument was more rhetorically effective than substantive. The second makes a good point. But since Murray's own position ultimately rested on the grounds of collective prudence he still could not place sufficient distance between himself and the traditionalists, at least not to the satisfaction of his liberal critics. In short, prior to the call for Vatican II, Murray was still caught between the horns of the dilemma.

In "Civil Unity and Religious Integrity: The Articles of Peace," an article originally published in 1954 and which served as the second chapter of *We Hold These Truths*, one finds Murray hinting at a problem that would be addressed explicitly in the two unpublished articles under discussion. Immediately following his claim that the First Amendment is best read as a practical political principle that grew out of social necessity, Murray, somewhat defensively, makes the following comment:

> It remains only to insist that in regarding the religion clauses of the First Amendment as articles of peace and in placing the case for them on the primary grounds of their social necessity, *one is not taking the low ground.* Such a case does not appeal to *mean-spirited expediency* nor does it imply a reluctant concession to *force majeure*. In the science of law and the art of jurisprudence the appeal to social peace is an appeal to a high moral value. Behind the will to social peace is an appeal to a high moral value. Behind the will to social peace there stands a divine and Christian imperative. This is the classic Christian tradition. (1960a, 60, emphasis mine)

The emphasized phrases are revealing. Murray, I would suggest, was responding to the frequent charge that the American Catholic position on matters relating to the church and state was based on mere expediency and was hence opportunistic. Although he does not explicitly mention the thesis-hypothesis position, clearly implicit in this statement was Murray's attempt to challenge the common perception among many Americans that American Catholics did in fact take the low ground on the matter of religious liberty.

But what Murray denied in his 1954 article, he assumed to be the case in the two unpublished articles written in 1958 and 1959. In these articles Murray claimed that the thesis-hypothesis doctrine did in fact consider a constitutional situation from which the legal institutions of establishment and intolerance were absent as "evil in itself." In other words, Murray seemed to concede that the American perception of the Catholic position was correct. As he now defined the traditional thesis-hypothesis doctrine, disestablishment and legal tolerance could "only be defended on the ground of fact, as a lesser evil in the concrete circumstances" (1958a, 11). According to Murray,

> the thesis is based on one duty of government and law— their ultimate duty to the truth. The hypothesis is based on another duty of government and law—their more proximate duty to the public peace. The latter duty is of a lower order than the former.... The fulfillment of the former duty is a positive good; the fulfillment of the latter duty is a lesser evil. (1958a, 12-13)

Thus, if the legal institutions of establishment and intolerance are introduced into a polity it is "not the fact, estimated by a prudential judgment, that they are practically necessary or useful for the common good with a special set of circumstances." Rather, according to the logic of the thesis-hypothesis doctrine, "the question of the practical necessity or utility of these institutions may be postponed, or even disregarded" (1958a, 13-14). According to Murray, the traditional position held that "whenever the twin legal institutions of establishment and intolerance are lacking, the constitutional situation is evil *in se* and *per se*, since it represents a violation of principle" (1958a, 16). Thus, from the traditionalist perspective,

> it may not be said that the First Amendment to the constitution of the United States is a good law within the unique American circumstances. The American constitutional situation is evil, in univocally the same sense, for instance, in which the constitutional situation of the Third French Republic was evil. (1958a, 16)

The proposition that Murray seems to foist on the traditionalists is: "Because the Constitution tolerates non-Catholics, it's an evil Constitution." And if it's an evil Constitution, it would seem that acceptance of it could have reasonably been seen as expedient and "a reluctant concession to *force majeure*."

Secondly, Murray distinguished his position from the traditionalists by setting forth a more nuanced and developed understanding of a "Catholic society" and the "common good." According to Murray, when advocates of the thesis-hypothesis doctrine decide the crucial issue of whether establishment or intolerance is concretely possible,

> the quality of the Catholic population does not enter into
> the argument. That is, it is not necessary to reckon with the
> prevailing level of religious knowledge and practice, with
> the general cultural level, with the level of political aware-
> ness, with the existent capacity for self-government, with
> the possibility that the dangers from heretical doctrines,
> etc., might be obviated in other ways than by the force of
> law, etc..... It does not matter whether this religious legisla-
> tion is framed for an ignorant, apathetic, nominally Catho-
> lic multitude, or for a Catholic body politic that is
> reasonably literate—religiously, politically, culturally.
> (1958a, 14-15)

This was not an entirely new emphasis for Murray. He had already made a similar point in his exchange with Shea in the early 1950s. In a response to the criticisms of Shea, Murray asserted that the advocates of the thesis-hypothesis position were not entirely clear about what they meant by a "Catholic society." But to the extent that they were clear, they tended to assume that the advocates of the thesis-hypothesis doctrine simply meant "a territory with a Catholic population."

> This statistical concept is in fact the social term of reference
> that apologists of the state-church have in mind when they
> speak of its theological necessity in a situation where
> "Catholics are in the majority," or "in an overwhelming
> majority," or a "quasi-totality." (1951, 349)

Murray rejected this statistical concept of a Catholic population as a "pseudo-abstraction." In contrast to a statistical concept, which cannot be taken as "a valid term of reference for any human law," he argued for a more nuanced notion of "'the people,' which is not a statistical concept but a truly socio-ethical-historical concept, concrete, living, and dynamic" (350). Therefore when we

> seek the social term of reference for the positive law
> whereby a state-religion is established, we shall not find it

> in the pseudo-abstract statistical concept of "the popula-
> tion" (even as qualified by the term "Catholic") but in the
> concrete concept of "the people." This concept includes
> both rulers and ruled and their political relationship, the
> whole contingent, historically conditioned order of orga-
> nized human associations, the total institutionalization,
> similarly contingent, of public, private, and group life, and
> the individual genius that in the course of history always
> comes to be stamped upon every genuine people. (1951,
> 351)

Factors other than a simple factual majority of Catholics are relevant when
the issues of church establishment and religious intolerance are to be considered as matters of public policy.

In his 1958 and 1959 articles Murray developed this theme further by
placing it within the context of a developing notion of the "common good."
Murray was still claiming that a central task of the state is "to organize and
direct the social cooperation toward the common good" (1959a, 6). However,
he now nuanced that assertion by saying that *Publica utilitas* or *bonum com-
mune*, is a complex and organic concept (1959a, 37, also 1958a, 27-8). The
state is "to do that which is useful, or more useful, for the common good of
the member-persons of society." Nevertheless, it "does not undertake to do
everything that is possible, or everything that might be desirable. The state is
not the champion of every good cause, simply because it is a good cause"
(1959a, 39). The answer to the question of which of the two alternatives,
intolerance or tolerance, will be more useful to the public advantage is not,
says Murray, "necessarily simple." The statesman cannot

> be myopic, as if only immediate or short-term effects were
> in question; he must also take the longer view. Will a vin-
> dictive "anti-clericalism" be the outcome of legal intoler-
> ance, to the detriment both of religion and of the unity of
> peace? Or will the absence of intolerance generate a reli-
> gious indifferentism and a political incoherence that will
> undermine the vitality of the social consensus? (1959a, 46)

Particularly important is Murray's understanding of the scope of the
common good. Murray advocated a "unitary theory" in which the problem
of tolerance and intolerance is placed in the wider context of the interna-

tional community. "[T]he good of this community of peoples and states," Murray argued, "is a higher good than that of any particular people or state, as the good of the universal Church is likewise the higher good" (1958a, 20–21).

> There is the good of the particular political society and the good of the Church there located. There is also the good of international society and the good of the universal Church, everywhere located. These latter goods are, by definition, the higher goods; and their requirements exercise a due measure of control over more local decisions. (1958a, 31)

What are we to make of these criticisms of the thesis-hypothesis position? First, it is not clear that the advocates of the thesis-hypothesis position understood the absence of intolerance or Catholic Church establishment in the way Murray claimed they did. Leo XIII's letter *Longingua oceani* certainly had some good things to say about the church-state situation in the United States. He did suggest that it was better than other situations. Of course, Leo did say it was not the best situation, but there is little evidence to suggest that he took the American situation to be a lesser evil, let alone an evil per se. Perhaps the American situation was not so much a lesser evil as a lesser good.

The same can be said for Murray's contemporaries. Recall, for instance, Fenton's reference to "our beloved nation" as not being in a position to offer its official and corporate worship to God according to the rites of the Catholic church. Is Fenton's "beloved nation" a nation that is evil *in se* and *per se*? Is there really any indication that Fenton would not recognize the difference between an aggressively anticlerical Jacobin state and the American state?

Consider also the following statement in which instruction is given to Catholic teachers in the public school:

> Neither in the classroom nor in her associations with teachers of other creeds may the Catholic use expressions savoring of indifferentism. She may, indeed, explain and uphold the American system granting equal rights to all religions, but in lauding this system she should make it clear that she is limiting her praise to our own country, because of particular conditions prevailing here, and that she has no intention of condemning other lands in which a different

> procedure prevails. She must not speak in such wise as to
> give the impression that all forms of religious belief possess
> a natural right to exist and to propagate. Only the true reli-
> gion possesses such a natural right. (Cited in Blanshard
> 1951, 84)

This statement could have been written by Murray. At the very least, there is hardly a proposition that Murray would deny. It was written in fact by Francis Connell, one of the principle American defenders of the thesis-hypothesis doctrine. One suspects that the difference on this first point was more rhetorical than substantive.

More plausible is Murray's claim that the traditionalist advocates of the thesis-hypothesis position had too simplistic and underdeveloped a notion of the common good, and of conditions necessary for the instantiation of the institutions of establishment and intolerance. Particularly important were his claims that the scope of the common good extends to "the international society and the good of the universal Church, everywhere located" (1958a, 31). By expanding the notion of the common good, Murray—and the church, should she adopt Murray's position—would be in a position to override national claims to intolerance by appealing to the damage it might cause to the international common good.

One could conceive of an advocate of Murray's new position, arguing against the traditionalists in a given nation as follows: We know that in your country you have a Catholic population, even a Catholic "people" in the more pregnant sense advocated by Fr. Murray, and that you think a policy of intolerance would be for the common good of your nation. However, as the church universal, we have determined that when the international situation is taken into consideration, this would not be prudent. If you are intolerant toward Protestants, this will hinder our evangelization efforts in countries that are predominately Protestant. After all, we live in an increasingly shrinking globe, and national considerations should take a backseat to international concerns. Besides, three hundred years of experience have taught us that religious freedom is a better bet than religious intolerance.

Now, this certainly seems to be a plausible argument. Unfortunately, Murray never develops this notion further. After 1959 this argument drops from sight. Why?

The most satisfactory answer is that this is a modus vivendi argument which could not be advanced in the polemical context in which Murray found himself in the 1960s. Donald Pelotte, in his intellectual biography of

Murray, notes that during the first session of Vatican II in 1962, the attitude of the Americans on the topic of religious freedom was of pastoral and pragmatic interest. But in private correspondence Murray insisted on "the need for more than a pragmatic solution to this complex problem."

> I think this is a mistaken view of the problem as it exists in the concrete. The practical question is, what is Catholic theory—theological, political, ethical—in the matter. This is what intelligent people want to know, inside and outside the Church.
>
> If the council refuses this question, and is content simply to say that "in today's circumstances everybody ought to have a full right to religious liberty," we shall be exactly where we are at the moment, in the very predicament from which we want to escape.
>
> This is easy to see. Ottaviani's "two standard" theory (what I call the disjunctive theory) will remain on the books, untouched, as the essential and pure Catholic doctrine (he holds that it is *proxima fidei*, and Ruffini agrees). And the Council's "practical" statements will look like sheer concessions to "today's circumstances"—a matter of expediency, or, in a word, the thing called "hypothesis," again affirmed to the joy of the curial Right, who will have triumphed in what will have been in effect no more than affirmed by the Council of their own doctrine. Not to be misunderstood, one point. I do not say that the American constitutional situation is "thesis." My point is that the whole disjunction, thesis-hypothesis, is invalid in sound and pure Catholic principles, and ought to be discarded. Like its supportive concept, the "Catholic state," it is a time-conditioned disjunction, involved in the realities of history....
>
> All this is part of my first difficulty with the document—its unwillingness to face the issue in the full concreteness of its amplitude, which includes the vital practical importance of its theoretical aspects.
>
> We have a heaven-sent opportunity to effect a genuine development of doctrine in this matter—an absolutely necessary development, and one that can quite readily be

effected. The opportunity should not be missed by a too
distant flight into the "practical," which is really a flight
from the practical problem. (Letter of August 2, 1962; cited
in Pelotte, 1976, 79-80)

Pelotte comments on this by saying that Murray was seeking to erect a
unitary theory which would be "limited to principles, with no admixture of
the historically conditioned. It could then be applied in various circumstances with equal validity" (1976, 80).

But that certainly was not the unitary theory Murray set forth in 1958
and 1959 where he was quite willing to ask about the historical "usefulness"
of religious tolerance or intolerance for a given people. Then, Murray
claimed that his own view "asserts that, with men, as with God, the problem
of both tolerance and intolerance is a problem in wisdom and virtue"
(1958a, 20). The final norm of judgment on the issue of tolerance or intolerance is "the juristic norm of usefulness for the public advantage." This
"single norm of judgment is likewise concrete and practical. The public
advantage is to be considered *in situ*, in a complex context of manifold fact,
as it is invested with particular exigencies" (1958a, 30).

Whether the legitimate application of Catholic principles is to be intolerant in practice, he continued, "will depend on the utility or necessity of
intolerance in practice. The judgment is practical, to be made in the light of
the practical juristic norm" (1958a, 36). "In the final instance, it is the
answer to the *quaestio facti* that determines the decisions of the state—
whether to command, prohibit, permit, tolerate, abstain from legal action, or
conclude that the very right of legal action does not exist in the given circumstances" (1959a, 44).

The decision of the statesman to support either tolerance or intolerance,
Murray had claimed,

> will be an act of civil prudence. It will be an act of the
> virtue proper to the statesman. If the decision is for the
> legal institution of intolerance, it will be an act of civil pru-
> dence. Contrariwise, if the decision is for the legal institu-
> tion of tolerance, it will also be an act of civil prudence. In
> either case, the law that is made will be a good law. (1959a,
> 48-49)

He later added that what is required is a "wise prognosis of the diverse
socio-religious effects of establishment versus non-establishment" (1959a,

55). "The law that better serves the public advantage in the given circumstances," he continued, "is the good law in the given circumstances" (1959a, 57).

All this hardly seems to be a theory void of the historically conditioned. If Pelotte were correct, we would expect Murray to put forth some sort of Esperantist defense of religious liberty in order to defeat the "pragmatists" at Vatican II. But Murray can't do that as long as he sets forth an argument from prudence that finds its validity *in situ*, even within an international context.

Here again we catch a glimpse of Murray caught in the dilemma. His seemingly derogatory mention of the term "practical" in 1962 stands in sharp contrast to his commendatory use of the word "prudence" in the 1958 and 1959 articles. It also stands in sharp contrast to his claim that the First Amendment is good law because it is, in fact, a *practical* political principle. Murray was no doubt correct that any "practical" statements coming out of the Council would look like mere concessions to contemporary circumstances, especially to certain Protestant and Esperantist natural rights theorists. But so would his earlier arguments from prudence and public utility. Murray could hardly distance himself from his traditionalist opponents as long as he was willing to subject the question at hand to judgments of prudence and public utility.

On the other hand, the crux of Murray's strategy against the traditionalists is emerging with increasing clarity. He will try to make the modus vivendi position of the traditionalists appear less than moral and thus distinguish their "pragmatic" argument from his "prudential" argument. But this will create a problem for Murray, one that can be illuminated by a brief examination of the virtue of prudence (*phronesis*) and the vice of cunning (*astutia*) within the Catholic tradition of moral reflection.

In order to distance himself from the traditional Catholic position, Murray would have to make the thesis-hypothesis doctrine appear to be what his secularist and Protestant opposition said it was: an opportunistic position based on "mean-spirited expediency." In the language of the Thomistic tradition, this would mean that Murray would have to argue, and probably could only have been taken as arguing, that the traditionalists could only arrive at a position of tolerance, not on the grounds of the virtue of prudence, but rather on the basis of the most characteristic type of false prudence, cunning (*astutia*) (ST 2a2æ.47.8). By this is meant "the insidious and unobjective temperament of the intriguer who has regard only for 'tactics,' who can neither face things squarely nor act straightforwardly" (Pieper 1966, 19–20).

Josef Pieper tells us that in traditional Catholic teaching, "the virtue of prudence is the mold and mother of all the other cardinal virtues" (1966, 3). To the modern mind, however, it appears more as an evasion of goodness than a prerequisite. While "modern man cannot conceive of a good act which might not be imprudent, nor of a bad act which might not be prudent" (5), "Classical Christian Ethics...maintains that prudence is part and parcel of the definition of goodness" (5).

Aquinas, for example, followed Aristotle in holding that the exercise of *prudentia* is required for the exercise of other virtues and as the one virtue in which the intellectual virtues cannot be exercised (MacIntyre 1988, 196). Aquinas also followed Aristotle in classifying types of prudence into that which is concerned with one's own good, that which is concerned with the goods of the household and that which is concerned with the good of the political and social community. But there is a difference. While it is true that for Aquinas as well as for Aristotle, the good legislator needs to exercise *phronesis* in legislating for a *polis*, the difference is that for Aquinas

> *prudentia* is exercised so that human law accords with the divine law, more especially in respect of the divinely ordained precepts of natural law. Thus, *prudentia* always has for Aquinas a theological dimension. Even when it is exercised as an acquired virtue rather than a supernatural virtue. (MacIntyre 1988, 197)

St. Thomas' discussion of prudence is unlike Aristotle's in that for the former it is to be exercised with a view to the ultimate end of human beings (ST 2a2æ.47.4).

To put it differently, the theological dimension is always present for Aquinas because perfected obedience to the natural law requires the virtue of justice in full measure (ST 2a2æ.79.1). But it is not the virtue of justice as such with which he is concerned, since in Aquinas' view religion is a moral virtue, being part of that cardinal virtue of justice concerned with what we owe God in terms of honor, reverence, devotion, adoration, prayer, sacrifice, and worship. In short, the Thomistic stance relative to the notions of practical knowledge, practical reasoning, and prudence always presupposes "the type of rational knowledge of God exemplified in the conclusions of the *Prima pars*" (MacIntyre 1988, 188).

As we have already seen, Murray wanted to minimize the historically conditioned nature of an argument for religious liberty by an appeal to the classical notion of the "wise man" in whom the transhistorical is embedded and ordered. What Aristotle's wise man, the *spoudaios*, actually does will be particular to a certain time and place but, in principle, will be an expression of abiding truth. This is true also for Aquinas. But for him, prudence must be understood within the context of a recognition of the ultimate true end of human beings which is outside and beyond every finite state achieved in the present life (ST 1a2æ.5.4), namely in the state of perfect happiness which is the contemplation of God in the beatific vision (ST 1a2æ.3.7). *Prudentia* is the human analog to that ordering of creatures to their ultimate end which is God's providence. As God creates and orders particulars, we act rightly if we reproduce that ordering, presumably also in our social systems. As Alasdair MacIntyre points out, the virtue of justice as a moral virtue (ST 2a2æ.81.4) means that a society in which the truth of the Christian religion has been recognized also requires political acknowledgment, a position, MacIntyre adds, that is "strikingly at odds with that of liberal, secular modernity" (1988, 201).

Now, from an Esperantist "moral point of view," one that abstracts from all theological context, the virtue of prudence cannot help but be perceived as less-than-moral, opportunistic, or "merely" expedient. As John Langan observes, when the traditional Western framework of divinely established teleology was replaced and "the moral life came to be seen as based either on altruistic feelings or on universal norms of reason, prudence came to be regarded as interested calculation, not as moral virtue" (1986, 514). What the modern mind finds objectionable is that the classical and Christian view posits a single ultimate end to which prudence should be directed. That accounts for Pieper's observation that it is incomprehensible to the modern mind that it would be the "mold and mother" of the other virtues.

One can easily understand how a Kantian or a utilitarian might see the "hypothesis" of the traditional Catholics as less than moral, merely expedient, or opportunistic. But it is less obvious how a natural law theorist might make the same charge. However, one way for a Christian natural law theorist to make this charge stick would be to drive a wedge between the natural and theological virtues and take Aquinas' distinction between the two more seriously than he would have allowed. When Catholic moral theologians forget that Aquinas insists as strongly as Augustine that natural virtues are but "a false likeness to virtue" (2a2æ.23.7), they tend to construct a natural law theory that all too closely resembles those "thin" and overly rationalistic natural rights theories that Murray found so objectionable.

For reasons that will become obvious in the next chapter, it would be unfair to say that Murray really wanted to speak moral Esperanto. Nevertheless he was tempted to move in that direction. Despite his "deconstruction" of natural rights theory, he was still sensitive to secularist and liberal Protestant charges of opportunism, the contemporary label for the false virtue of cunning. Therefore he had to sufficiently distance his position from his fellow Catholics' by claiming his was not subject to the same difficulty. He had to paint the traditionalists as being crudely pragmatic (*astutia*) while his own position rested on the moral high ground—in the virtue of prudence.

Failure to see this, I think, has contributed to a number of misunderstandings of Murray's mature writings on religious liberty. Pelotte mistakenly took Murray's attempt to appear less crudely pragmatic as necessarily implying its opposite—an ahistorical argument for religious liberty. On the other hand, Goerner (1965, 169-84) mistakenly takes Murray's argument to reflect a "historicism." Hooper goes even further, suggesting that Murray eventually outgrew his old Thomistic natural law doctrines and came to recognize "the contingency of the theological propositions that guided church thought and action" (Hooper 1986, 200). Murray, according to Hooper, eventually came to realize that "the Church's understanding of itself as a timeless embodiment of Christian truth...must give way to a recognition of itself as principally and primarily a community of ongoing historical inquiry and transforming love" (201). Murray thus ends up looking remarkably similar to a nineteenth-century liberal Protestant.

Although these divergent interpretations are overly simplistic, they are understandable. Murray's position was, in fact, becoming increasingly ambiguous. Some reflection on the nature of prudence by both Murray and the traditionalists would no doubt have clarified things. But that would also have illuminated Murray's dilemma. For, as I will show in the next chapter, Murray's most mature argument for religious liberty was just as much a modus vivendi argument as that of the traditionalists, a point that did not go unnoticed by the more perceptive Esperantists.

Murray's Case for Religious Liberty within the Context of the Debate at Vatican II

Murray's most mature reflections on religious liberty can only be understood properly by placing them within the context of the debate over religious liberty during the Second Vatican Council. The question of religious liberty was easily the most bitterly disputed issue at the Council. Ultimately, five published drafts were submitted to the Fathers, and these were preceded by two others. Murray did not take part in the pre-Conciliar discussions, nor was he a participant at the first session.

During the preparatory phase of the Council, two distinct drafts were being written and debated. One, presented by the Theological Commission under the presidency of Murray's rival, Cardinal Alfredo Ottaviani, examined the subject of religious freedom as an aspect of the problem of the relation between church and state. Essentially, it set forth the traditional Catholic thesis/hypothesis position. Another, prepared by the Secretariat for the Promotion of Christian unity, under the leadership of Belgian Bishop Emile De Smedt, forcefully asserted that in religious matters the right to follow conscience must be observed not only by the faithful but absolutely by all men and the community of men (Regan 1967, 21). Because of a series of political moves too involved to describe here, the Secretariat was forced to include significant passages from the Theological Commission's draft, resulting in what Regan called a theological "crazyquilt" (27), a bizarre synthesis of the two ultimately irreconcilable positions.

The first published draft of what would eventually result in *Dignitatis humanae* was submitted to the Council during the second session on November 19, 1963. Murray by that time had been invited to participate at the Council as a *peritus*, or expert. The task of presenting the first draft fell to Bishop De Smedt. It was accompanied by a *relatio*, a presentation of the text to the Council as a whole which paraphrases and comments on the text.

Murray's views on the first draft as well as De Smedt's *relatio* are set forth in two published articles, which give considerable insight into his thinking at this time. The first appeared in *America* (1963j) in November 1963 during the second session, and the other in a post-Conciliar article (1966c) that surveyed the legislative history of the text. Additional insights into Murray's thinking about the first draft can be gleaned from an unpublished critique entitled "The Schema on Religious Freedom: Critical Comments" (1963a).

In the article written during the Council, Murray summarized the two essential points in the first schema.

> First, it is asserted that every man by right of nature (*jure naturae*) has the right to the free exercise of religion in society according to the dictates of his personal conscience. This right belongs essentially to the dignity of the human

person as such. Secondly, the juridical consequences of this right are asserted, namely, that an obligation falls on other men in society, and upon the state in particular, to acknowledge this personal right, to respect it in practice, and to promote its free exercise. This is, in a mode of general statement, the heart of the matter. (1963j 704)

Murray, however, rejected this methodology.

The reasons for his rejection are stated most explicitly in the unpublished article. This methodology, said Murray, was most common among the French-speaking theologians who were prone to ground religious liberty primarily on theological and ethical principles, and then evoke political and legal principles as secondary and subsidiary arguments. Among English- and Italian-speaking theorists, it was more common to base religious freedom on both theological-ethical principles and political-legal principles, the two sets being regarded as coordinate and equal in importance. Murray favored the latter primarily because the

structure of argument is more concrete and pragmatic, and more attentive to historical experience," while the "former structure is more abstract and aprioristic, and more concerned to 'found religious freedom in religion itself' (in the Protestant phrase), less inclined to 'legalize religious freedom than to 'theologize' it...." (1963a, 5-6)

Murray also believed that it was "more likely to win acceptance, or at least diminish the area of controversy." On this point, as we will see, he was quite mistaken. It is certainly odd, however, that he would favor the argument that was more concrete and pragmatic given his criticism of a pragmatic approach only a year earlier.

In this article, Murray also commented on and criticized De Smedt's *relatio*. According to Murray, the *relatio* attempted to clear up "confusions and misconceptions with regard to the concept of religious freedom which remain the heritage of the 19th-century conflict between the Church and the laicist ideology that issued from the Enlightenment" (1963j, 704). Murray noted that the *relatio* argued correctly that the "Church must still reject a concept of religious freedom that would be based on the ideology of the outlaw conscience," that is, one which asserted that "the human conscience is not bound by any divine laws, but only by such norms as it individually creates for itself" (704-5). It also correctly rejected "a concept of religious freedom that would be based on the ideology of religious indifferentism, that is, on the notion that all religions are equally true, or equally false" (705). Along the same lines, he insisted that the church reject a concept of religious freedom based "on the ideology of relativism, that is, on the philosophical notion that there is no objective criterion of truth" (705).

If the outline of the *relatio* on which Murray was commenting sounds familiar, it is. Unbeknownst to the readers of *America*, Murray himself had written the initial draft for De Smedt's *relatio*, though, as Murray later put it, he had "re-worked my thing to suit his own style" (cited in Pelotte 1976, 84). In effect, then, Murray was commenting on his own views and seeking to advance the discussion by then criticizing them—a point that should be kept in mind as we proceed.

Murray once again uses the "19th-century ideologies" as his foil. According to Murray, the ideologies to which the *relatio* referred

> falsified the notion of religious freedom, just as they mis-
> conceived the dignity of man. Man is not God; he is only
> the image of God. God alone is the Lord. And man's essen-
> tial dignity consists in his dependence on God alone; man's
> essential freedom requires that he should be governed, in
> the end, *only by the will of God*. From this point of view, the
> true notion of religious freedom begins to appear. (705)

The *relatio* argued that, as a consequence of his "personal dignity," man has the right to be free from social or political institutions, or by the power of human law in his quest for God. Man's quest for God must be free. This itself "is a divine law written in the nature of man, and written even more clearly in the gospel of Christ."

> True religious freedom therefore consists, negatively, in the
> immunity of the human person, from all coercion in what
> concerns his personal relations with God, and, positively,
> in the free exercise of religion within society. (705)

The immediate rejoinder to this line of argumentation is obvious. If it is true that freedom requires that man should be governed "only by the will of God," how can it be that one has a strict and true right to the free exercise of a religion that is opposed to the will of God? Murray had consistently rejected this line of argumentation in the past, and it would have been a major change in his thinking had he accepted it during the Council. And, in fact, Murray is quite clear. "I must confess immediately that I do not find [the conception of religious freedom that is contained in the Conciliar text and developed in the *relatio*] adequate, though I think it is true as far as it goes" (705). Predictably enough, Murray would set his sights on De Smedt's Esperantist argument from freedom of conscience.

In the unpublished article, Murray forcefully spells out his objection to this line of thought. The conclusion of the first draft, Murray argued, goes far beyond the premise.

> [T]he inference is vulnerable to the objection that it sanctions an illegitimate passage from the subjective order of conscience to the objective order of rights. The argument is that this passage is valid only in the case of the right and true conscience. An erroneous conscience creates no objective right that is coactive in the face of legitimate political or legal authority. That is to say, the man of erroneous conscience enjoys no empowerment to act in the public order; and he enjoys no immunity from the repressive action of the public power, employed in the interest of the common good. (1963a, 7)

It's not surprising that Murray would find this argument unpersuasive. But what did Murray mean when he said the argument was true "as far as it goes"? The answer to that question sheds further light on Murray's strategy at this time.

Insight into Murray's strategy is revealed in a private letter in which Murray commented on the *relatio* he had helped to prepare for De Smedt. After saying that the issue could not possibly be treated in the twenty-two pages of the *relatio*, he adds,

> It was a matter of striking off a sort of a story-line. It was also a matter of inviting the conciliar Fathers to improve the Secretariat text, which is not particularly good, by amending it in the sense of *Pacem in terris*, which came out after the text had been composed. (Cited in Pelotte 1976, 84)

In referring to Pope John XXIII's encyclical *Pacem in terris* (April 11, 1963) Murray indicated that he was going to use that document as leverage against the traditional Catholic position. How might this be done?

Pacem in terris stressed two basic themes, the dignity of the human person and the consequent necessity of constitutional limitations on the power of governments. Murray, as we will see, would eventually exploit the necessity of limited constitutional government and make that the primary feature of his argument for religious liberty. Methodologically, the juridical, political, or constitutional question would be primary. But it is also important to note that Murray did *not* take the most obvious tack suggested by *Pacem in terris*.

Quite remarkably, Murray did not make reference to the one statement in *Pacem in terris* that stood out: "Every human being has the right to honor God according to the dictates of an upright conscience (*ad rectam conscientiae suae normam*), and the right to profess his religion *privately and publicly*" (paragraph 14, emphasis mine). Now, Murray was a good enough polemicist to realize that he would have a significant advantage if he could maneuver himself into a position where he had the Pope on his side. In order to take full advantage of the situation, one might certainly expect him to exploit an interpretation of this statement that could be used most effectively against the traditionalists at the Council. It is significant, however, that Murray did not exploit this advantage. He refused to give an Esperantist reading to this statement, which, I believe, suggests a continuation of his unwillingness to speak about a "natural right" to religious freedom.

The crucial issue revolved around two different interpretations of the phrase "*ad rectam conscientiae suae normam.*" For St. Thomas, *recta* means conformity to truth, i.e., to objective moral norms. *Conscientiae recta* and *conscientiae vera* are thus equivalent. Now, if this interpretation were placed on the document, it would mean that only those whose conscience was in accord with the truth would have the "right" to public worship. However, there was another definition within the theological tradition. Following Duns Scotus and Suarez, *conscientiae recta* means sincere or upright, i.e. formed to the best of one's ability, without bad will. In other words, on this view, sincerity as such would be sufficient grounds to support the "right" to public worship. (See Stransky 1967, 20 and Regan 1967, 63ff.)

Which of the two meanings did Pope John XXIII intend? Some theologians claimed the first, while others such as De Smedt, whose argument Murray found inadequate, claimed the second. This probably accounts for the priority it receives in De Smedt's methodology. However, in 1965 Pietro

Pavan, one of the drafters of the encyclical, stated that the Pope deliberately chose *recta* in order *not* to solve the problem (Stransky 1967, 20 at note 11).

In order to gain the maximum polemical advantage against the traditionalists, Murray would have to interpret it in the second way. But that, of course, would commit him to a position hardly distinguishable from that of the Protestants he had been criticizing.

Given the plausible assumption that worship is an action or behavior, it would also seem to commit him to the rather bizarre proposition we encountered in chapter one:

> No one has the right to prevent another person from acting
> in accord with that person's moral system, where that per-
> son's own moral system is as logically consistent and
> coherent as one's own.

As I suggested in the first chapter, that proposition is implicit in any attempt to slip through the horns of the dilemma by way of a relativistic argument. However, it is quite difficult to see why anyone would choose that proposition, particularly someone like Murray, in light of his assertions against "indifferentism." Interestingly enough, despite his willingness to use *Pacem in terris* to his advantage, Murray never took this line, and, in fact, consistently rejected the argument advanced by those who would. That is, Murray would once again reject an argument for the right to public worship from "freedom of conscience." Once again, he rejected an Esperantist strategy.

That Murray would not take the "sincerity line" is revealed in his rejection of De Smedt's argument from conscience. Murray observed that the decree and the *relatio* were quite clear on the issue that the conscience cannot be coerced. However, reiterating a point he made in 1945, he argued that the difficulty begins when it is recognized that "religious freedom is to be a right whose exercise takes place in society—in a civil society that is politically organized, that receives its structure from a juridical order, and that is governed by duly constituted political authority" (1963j, 705). Within organized society, Murray claimed, *no human right, not even the right to religious freedom, is unlimited in its exercise*. This being the case, the essential questions become: What are the principles according to which this right may be justly and legitimately limited? What is the competence of civil government in regard to this right? What are the canons of jurisprudence that must control the use of coercive power in this field? These are difficult questions that cannot be avoided, because the issue of religious freedom "is not simply an ethical or moral problem. It is also a *constitutional* problem" (1963j, 705).

After Vatican II

In a post-Conciliar article Murray spelled out his objection to the argument from conscience more fully.

> The [first] two texts seemed to suppose...that the argument from the freedom of Christian faith and the argument from the rights of conscience were somehow adequate to prove the immunity of the person both from coercive constraint and also from coercive restraint. This, however, is not true. From the necessary freedom of the act of Christian faith—or of any other kind of final religious commitment, even one of atheist tenor—it does indeed follow that no man may be constrained either to believe against his will or to act in a manner contrary to his own beliefs. The argument is obvious and also apodictic. But it is apodictic only because it is impossible to prove that external authority exists that is rightfully empowered to constrain religious belief and action. (1966j, 30-1)

The question of coercive restraint of action complicates matters significantly. Murray simply pointed out that there have been, in fact, governments that asserted the right to repress public manifestations of religious beliefs and practices that were contrary to the established religion of the state. They did so while simultaneously claiming that they had no right to force anyone to accept the established religion. Murray insisted that since there was a school of thought which held that the right to repress the public activities of those who conscientiously acted in a matter in variance with the tenets and practices of Catholicism did not violate the rights of conscience, it was "not sufficient to attend to only the theological and ethical aspects of the issue" (31). Murray wanted to give the constitutional question methodological priority.

It should be noted how closely this parallels Murray's first argument— the one that supposedly failed, and the one Love thought was "confusing." The basic structure of Murray's argument is the same. Someone familiar with his 1945 argument would expect him to bring the question of collective political prudence to the fore. And indeed he does.

> The *political* aspect becomes decisive. It is necessary to confront the question, whether and under what conditions government has the right to restrain citizens from public action according to their own beliefs. In other words, is there some special feature of civil authority that empowers it to disregard and override the claim of the citizen to immunity from coercive interference when he acts in religious matters according to his conscience? Or, in more general terms, what are the functions and the limits of the powers of government in what concerns religion. (31)

Notice how different this strategy is from the Esperantist reading of *Pacem in terris* as well as the freedom of conscience line taken by De Smedt. Observe also how close it is to the modus vivendi argument of the traditionalists. Unlike Murray and the traditionalists the Esperantist interpretation of *Pacem in terris* and De Smedt's views as expressed in the *relatio* are unwilling to ask under what conditions the government might have the right to restrain citizens from acting according to their own religious beliefs. The condition that must hold for the traditionalists was simply the existence of a "Catholic society," or the existence of simple Catholic hegemony. That is the condition under which government could legitimately act to restrain certain kinds of public activity of a "religious manner." In order to decisively defeat the traditionalists, Murray would have to show why and how the instantiation of simple Catholic hegemony is not a sufficient condition. To do that most effectively, however, he would have to posit some ahistorical "right" that would trump the "rights" (and perhaps "duties") of a Catholic society to establish a confessional state if it so desired. An Esperantist interpretation of *Pacem in terris* might have served as that trump. It would also have the advantage of being backed by the Papacy. Murray, however, does not make this move, a point that was not lost on those Esperantists who would.

Now, the first draft of what would eventually be *Dignitatis humanae* was neither seriously discussed nor voted on in the second session. However, as a result of numerous suggestions, a second draft was produced in April 1964. The second schema was sent to the Council fathers on April 2, 1964, and discussion in the Council hall took place during the third session on September 25-28, 1964. It was decided that a third text (*textus emendatus*) should appear as a significantly revised independent document. Murray is generally recognized as one of the primary drafters of this text, which appeared before the third session on November 17, 1964.

In preparation for the third session, Murray distributed to all the American bishops an article detailing his views. The article would eventually be published in *Theological Studies* in December, 1964, and in 1965 as a book entitled *The Problem of Religious Freedom* (hereafter PORF). This article, which is essentially a summary of his previous work, can be read as his advice to the Council—advice that proved highly influential during the third session (Pelotte 1976, 90). Still, despite a desperate petition demanding a vote on the schema, a vote was not taken. Thus, Murray's text became subject to revision. The Pope promised that the discussion on religious liberty would be the first matter discussed the following year in the fourth and final session.

It was. But by then Murray's draft had been altered. Hence, the extent of Murray's stamp on the final document is a matter of disagreement. Debate was followed by the first direct vote (September 22, 1965) on the issue of Religious Freedom—1,997 in favor, 224 against. One final draft incorporated further suggestions made in debate or writing. The final text was approved in November and promulgated on December 7, 1965, at the very end of the Council.[1]

Murray's views had run into considerable opposition at the Council. Therefore, before addressing Murray's proposed argument as reflected in *The Problem of Religious Freedom* and subsequent articles, we must mention two more arguments for religious liberty that he opposed.

The first we already briefly mentioned in our discussion of Murray's methodology. In contrast to Murray, who approached the argument for religious liberty from primarily a juridical, political, or constitutional point of view and then sought to support it with theological and ethical principles, there was another strategy that might appropriately be called "Biblicistic." Basically, it was an attempt to arrive at an argument for religious liberty directly from Scripture. Murray described it as an attempt to "radicate religious freedom in religion itself—concretely, in the Scriptures, and in the traditional doctrine of Christian faith" (1965c, 139). The argument of those who advanced this position was that Murray's argument as reflected in the third draft and in *The Problem of Religious Freedom* was too "juridical," and that it relied too heavily on the Anglo-American constitutional tradition, particularly on the American experience under the First Amendment.

Because many of the French bishops objected to the juridical nature of the third text (*textus emendatus*), their alternative position became referred to as the "French view." One bishop, for instance, thought that it was crucial to remain faithful to the classic Conciliar method of beginning with a doctrinal exposition. It was charged that in restricting the liberty of the person to a civil right, Murray's schema lacked a solid base. The counterproposal to Murray's position insisted that a philosophical and theological definition of free will and moral freedom should be placed at the beginning of the schema, only after which the juridical consequences should be drawn (Regan 1967, 117).

Murray described the "French view" as one which "regards religious freedom as formally a theological-moral concept, which has juridical consequences, scil., within the order of constitutional law" (PORF, 20). This stands in contrast to his own view which "regards religious freedom as formally a juridical or constitutional concept, which has foundations in theology, ethics, political philosophy, and jurisprudence" (PORF, 20). Murray believed that those who simply "quote and argue" from the texts of St. Paul and the Gospels where the message of salvation is presented to man for his free acceptance, and then draw conclusions from these texts were simplistic and unconvincing (1965c, 139; also PORF, 23). He found three problems with this view. For one thing, it risked "setting afoot a futile argument about the rights of the erroneous conscience" (PORF, 22), and this, as we have seen, Murray consistently rejected as irrelevant to the constitutional question. But his two other criticisms of this view reveal just how resistant Murray was to an Esperantist argument for religious liberty. Secondly Murray believed that

> This understanding of religious freedom seems to appear as a piece of theological-ethical theory, arrived at by a process of abstract argument, in a vacuum of historical, political, and juridical experience. The methodology here is vulnerable, in that *it seems to divorce the issue of the rights of the human person from its necessary social-historical context.* (PORF 20-1, emphasis mine)

Finally, this line of argument, Murray thinks, "runs the risk of `overtheologizing' the notion of religious freedom as a human right" (21). He feared that the result might be to propose the legal institution of religious freedom as the 'ideal instance' of constitutional law with regard to public care of religion." A false argument would thus be set afoot because

> traditional philosophies of politics, law, and jurisprudence
> do not recognize any such thing as an ideal instance of con-
> stitutional law. By reason of the very nature of law, the issue
> of ideal never arises. (21)

Ironically, in order to avoid making the American constitutional notion of "free exercise" a new "thesis," or "ideal," he had to temper the demands for an ahistorical argument for religious liberty.

Again, we want to note how similar Murray's argument is to his 1945 argument and therefore similar to that of the traditionalists. In both instances he recognizes the failure of the "ethical" (conscience) and "theological" (or Biblicistic) arguments. In both cases, too, the argument for toleration is "from below." The difference is that the notion of "prudence" is enriched by appeal to the juridical, political, and jurisprudential. It seems to be the type of argument he would have made had he carried out his original 1945 project. Our suspicion at this point is that despite his polemic against the traditionalists, he is, in fact, making their case—just as he did in 1945.

While this may appear as a rather bold assertion given Murray's reputation as a great Catholic defender of religious liberty and one of the principal architects of *Dignitatis humanae*, the similarity of Murray's position to that of the traditionalists did not go unnoticed by Murray's Protestant critics. The Protestant ethicist Philip Wogaman, for instance, insisted that Murray's position, as valuable as it was, nevertheless raises the "old problem of thesis-hypothesis. He has left the door open for the denial of religious liberty in other contexts" (Wogaman 1967, 59; cf. Wogaman 1986, 465-66).

Making the same point a bit more vigorously was Carillo de Albornoz. Carillo, a former Catholic and head of the World Council of Churches secretariat on religious liberty, wrote a scathing review of Murray's *The Problem of Religious Freedom* for *The Christian Century* entitled "Religious Liberty: Intrinsic or Fortuitous?" As the title suggests, Carillo believed Murray's argument for religious liberty rested on "fortuitous" historical circumstances rather than an "intrinsic" right. He was absolutely outraged that Murray could not come up with at least a minimal universal standard of religious liberty (Carillo 1965, 1123), and therefore urged the Council to defend the "French" theological-biblical line against Murray's position.

In his review Carillo cited a number of assertions by Murray to point out that the differences between the French view and Murray's position were not merely methodological, as Murray claimed, but substantive and fundamental. These assertions are worth citing here because Carillo, as a Protestant Esperantist, was pointing out the ambiguity in Murray's position, and thereby highlights the modus vivendi elements in his argument.

> The question, what is religious freedom, is not to be answered a priori or in the abstract. The fact is that religious freedom is *an aspect of contemporary historical experience....* For the theologian, the instant conceptual question is to understand what religious freedom means *today,* in so far as it presents itself as an exigence of the personal and political consciousness of *contemporary* man.
>
> ...religious freedom is not some sort of Platonic idea that has had no history but has been always somehow "there," to be seen by anyone who cared to look at it. Religious freedom is the reasonable affirmation of the *contemporary* man.
>
> The Second View [i.e., Murray's]...posits, *as the basis* for a systematic doctrine of religious freedom, the *concrete* exigencies of the personal and political consciousness of *contemporary* man.
>
> It is not exact to say flatly that the state is incompetent in religious matters, *as if this were some sort of trans-temporal principle, derivative from some sort of eternal law.* The exact formula is that the state, *under today's conditions* of growth in the personal and religious consciousness, is competent to do only one thing in respect of religion, that is, to recognize, guarantee, protect, and promote the religious freedom of the people.
>
> ...the Second View [i.e. Murray's view] goes back to the Jurist for its category of legal discussion. *It is the function of law,* said the Jurist, *to be useful* to the people.... In judging all *past* or *present* realizations of the Catholic state, so called, the historical situation needs to be considered. The historical institutions of establishment and intolerance are to be judged valid, "*in situ.*" The function of the law, said the Jurist, is to be useful to the people. These institu-

tions *might well have been useful* to people, in the condition
of the personal and political consciousness of the people at
that time.... The function of law, as the Jurist said, is to be
useful to men. *Necessity or usefulness* for the common
good—these are the norms of law. [All the emphases are
Carillo's.]

Carillo quickly sets forth the Protestant-Esperantist objection to Murray's
stress on the historically contingent nature of religious freedom.

If the Roman Catholic Church were to adopt such an
insight concerning religious freedom, the ecumenical dialogue would be as impossible as before. This positivist, historical and pragmatic attitude would in fact permit all
situations of intolerance in the past, in the present and
(why not?) in the future to be considered "valid." (1965,
1124)

Actually, Carillo is overstating his case. Murray's view need not validate all
past instances of religious intolerance, simply those instances judged valid
"*in situ.*" Some past instances of intolerance could be judged invalid "*in situ.*"
Whether they were valid or invalid requires a prudential judgment, not an a
priori moralistic declaration, as Carillo wanted to see him give.

Still, Carillo's polemic illuminates Murray's dilemma. It is, in fact, difficult to see why traditional Catholics would object to any of the assertions
just cited. The dilemma is magnified if we keep in mind that Murray wanted
more than a pragmatic argument. One wishes Murray had spelled out why
"pragmatic" had such pejorative connotations. Perhaps a distinction between
"prudent" and "pragmatic" would have clarified things. In any case, given
the lack of such a distinction it seems impossible to reconcile the assertions
cited by Carillo with Pelotte's claim that Murray, in rejecting the so-called
pragmatic arguments of the traditionalists, wanted to set forth a theory that
"would be limited to principles, with no admixture of the historically conditioned, [which] could then be applied in various circumstances with equal
validity" (Pelotte, 1976, 80), or with Cuddihy's claim that Murray wanted an
argument for religious liberty that was "unencumbered to historical contingency and accomodational ad hockery" (1978, 77).

But Murray was not yet finished with the arguments for religious liberty.
He also rejected one final ahistorical argument. Hooper calls this "the argu-

ment from the personal exigence to seek the truth." According to this argument, explains Hooper, "each person must be allowed religious freedom in order to pursue and adhere to what is true. The obligation to seek the truth therefore founds the juridical right to immunity" (Hooper 1986, 148). Unlike the arguments from conscience and Scripture which were ultimately rejected as primary justifications for *Dignitatis humanae*, this argument was accepted in the final text. Richard Regan, who has written the definitive history of the development of *Dignitatis humanae*, argues that this argument displaced Murray's juridical, political, or constitutional argument to a secondary position (1967, 117ff.). This is an entirely plausible interpretation since Murray was hospitalized at the time and unable to participate in the discussion (Pelotte 1976, 98). It also may account for Murray's ambiguous and somewhat defensive attitude toward the argument contained in the final draft (see Canavan 1982, 404-5, and Hooper 1986, 148).

While in one article Murray suggested his own position as reflected in the third document (*textus emendatus*) was retained throughout the final revisions (1966c), he also sought to discount the inclusion of the argument from the exigence to seek the truth in the final document (*textus recognitus*) (Hooper 1986, 148; 1966a, 568-70; 1966d, 680, note 7). In a footnote to the English translation of *Dignitatis humanae*, Murray claimed

> that it was necessary for the Council to present an argument for the principle of religious freedom, lest anyone mistakenly think that the Church was accepting religious freedom merely on pragmatic grounds or as a concession to contemporary circumstances. However, it was not the intention of the Council to affirm that the argument, as made in the text, is final and decisive." (1966d, 680, note 7)

In another article, Murray was more explicit about his rejection of this argument. The argument from the exigence to seek the truth

> fails to yield the necessary and crucial political conclusion, namely, that government is not empowered, except in exceptional cases, to hinder men or religious communities from public witness, worship, practice, and observance in accordance with their own religious convictions. (1966a, 571)

Hooper says that "the fifth schema's moral obligation to search for and adhere to the truth appeared to Murray to be too individualistic and too unhistorical in its starting presuppositions" (Hooper 1986, 151). That may be, but Murray was, despite all his talk about "historical consciousness," still seeking and believed he had found "a new philosophy of society and State" which is "more transtemporal in its manner of conception and statement, less time-conditioned, more differentiated, a progress in the understanding of the tradition" (Stransky 1967, 147). There simply is not, I think, any way to resolve this tension. In any case, Murray was too good a theorist not to reject this argument. It rested on a rather gross *non sequitur* that he had exposed as early as 1945. Just as a monogamist society may grant the polygamist the right to search for the truth but still quite consistently prevent him from marrying more than one wife, so it would be logically proper to allow someone to seek out the truth about God and morality without allowing him to act on a mistake (i.e., by spreading heresy, false worship, idolatry, etc.).

Notes

1. For a detailed exposition of the rather fascinating behind-the-scenes development of *Dignitatis humanae* see Richard Regan's *Conflict and Consensus* (1967).

Chapter Seven

Murray's Constructive Argument for Religious Liberty

Up to this point Murray has been quite clear about the type of religious liberty arguments that he opposed. We know that he was opposed to the traditional thesis-hypothesis doctrine at least partially because its acceptance of constitutional provisions for religious liberty seemed to be less than moral (chap. 3). We also know that he rejected certain Protestant attempts to defend religious liberty on the basis of a free church ecclesiology, liberal Protestant and secularist attempts to ground it in a doctrine of natural rights (chaps. 4 and 5), and Catholic attempts to ground it in Scripture, conscience, and the exigence to seek the truth (chap. 6). Thus far, then, we are left with the rather odd situation that the individual who is thought to have put forth the definitive case for religious liberty is, in fact, the one who has rejected every plausible candidate. Indeed, one gets the impression that Murray is clearer on what he opposed than on what he proposed. What then is his own position? Just what was this so-called "juridical argument" Murray wanted to make for religious liberty?

In this chapter, I suggest that during Vatican II and following, Murray's own argument for religious liberty can best be approached through an examination of two pairs of concepts: (a) historical consciousness and human dignity and (b) public order and the common good.

Human Dignity and Historical Consciousness

Murray credited Pope John XXIII with correctly discerning the "signs of the times," when he stated in *Pacem in terris* that

the aspirations of the minds of men, about which we have
been speaking, also give clear witness to the fact that in
these days men are becoming more and more conscious of
their own dignity. For this reason they feel the impulse to
participate in the process of government and also to
demand that their own inviolable rights be guaranteed by
the order of public law. (Cited in PORF, 17–18)

Murray's strategy was to turn the Pope's comments on the nature of limited
constitutional government to his advantage. In a post-Conciliar article he
spelled out more concretely what this might mean.

The dignity of man has always been a truth. In modern
times, however, there has been a growth in consciousness
of the truth and in sensitivity to its exigencies—not least
perhaps in consequence of the brutal insensitivities that
recent history has displayed. Therefore argument about
human rights, including religious freedom, has to be
informed by historical consciousness, by an awareness that
demands inherent in the nature of man manifest themselves and come to recognition in history, under the impact
of developing human experience. Deductive argument
therefore is not enough. Good moral philosophy, like all
good philosophy, must begin with man's historical experience and undertake to discern in it the intentions of
human nature, the rational imperatives that rise from the
depths of the concrete human person, the dictates of
reason that claim affirmation as natural law. (1965c, 137–
38)

Leaving aside empirical questions about whether in fact the "historical
consciousness" of modern man is now or was then what Murray and John
XXIII said it was, we are concerned with asking what force this argument
might have against the traditionalists?

Murray argued that the demand of the popular consciousness for religious freedom was to be affirmed as true and good. But the traditionalists
were just as willing as Murray to concede that religious liberty was
demanded given the historical fact of religious pluralism. They would also
concede that their case should be "informed" by the popular historical con-

sciousness in the same sense that Murray conceded in 1945 that a good government ought to be "informed" by the popular consciousness of a society or culture that accepts polygamy. What they were not willing to do, however, was claim religious liberty as an "affirmation of natural law" per se. Given his other emphases, perhaps neither was Murray. But if he means that religious freedom is demanded as a requirement of natural law as a determination of prudence, *given the current state of religious pluralism*, then it is hard to see how the traditionalists could object. In fact, Murray's position would seem to collapse into the modus vivendi argument of his traditionalist opposition.

Moreover, in what sense, it may fairly be asked, is the demand for religious freedom a "demand inherent in the nature of man"? Is it a demand inherent in the nature of man as such or is it a demand inherent in the nature of man given the heightened pluralist religious situation of modernity? More pointedly, what about other plausible demands "inherent in the nature of man," particularly the demand for fraternity, community, and solidarity, which might be established and maintained by the institution of religious intolerance? It is hard to see how the rational imperative of the concrete human person for religious freedom could claim an a priori trump on what could also be plausibly claimed as the rational imperative of the human person for solidarity, fraternity, and community, which Murray also wants to assert.

My comments at this point are not intended to reflect sympathy with attempts to override the "right" to religious freedom by appeals to fraternity, solidarity, and community. In fact, I find Murray quite persuasive and absolutely correct if his assertion is simply that, given the highly pluralistic conditions of modernity the guarantee of religious freedom ought to have priority over the state's attempt to ensure fraternity and solidarity. I simply want to point out that the fundamental issue involves the historical conditions that must be in place for freedom to have lexical priority over demands for community and solidarity. And on that issue, both Murray and the traditionalists were agreed. Under modern conditions of religious discord, freedom of religion and the corresponding virtues of toleration and cooperation cannot help but receive priority if the unfortunate effects of religious civil war are to be avoided. But that is also the kind of "pragmatic" argument Murray wanted to avoid.

The problem was that if Murray admitted this outright he would be criticized for advancing a modus vivendi argument that was all too similar to that of the traditionalists. As we have seen, he wants more than a "pragmatic" argument. This leads him to resort to the rather tortured distinction between "classicism" and "historical consciousness."

In *The Problem of Religious Freedom* Murray suggests that the debate among Catholics over the question of religious freedom involves a deeper conflict between "two modes of thought." The traditionalists, according to Murray, expressed an historically insensitive "classicist" mind-set. They "fix the doctrine of the Church on religious freedom in its nineteenth-century stage of conception and statement" and therefore refuse "to consider the fact that the state of the question has altered and the nineteenth-century answer is inadequate" (PORF, 90). Murray accused this view of being archaistic "because all sense of the personal and political consciousness is absent from it" (91).

Again, Murray is distorting the extent to which the traditionalist position was bound to a static view of truth, partly because he has played down the role of the virtue of prudence in their argument. It is simply not the case that they did not take cognizance of the contemporary political consciousness. In fact, that is ultimately the basis upon which they defended religious freedom as a political yet not a metaphysical right. Once this is understood, it becomes quite difficult to see a fundamental difference between, on the one hand, a view that says under the religiously pluralistic conditions of modernity religious freedom should have priority over the solidarity that would be achieved by the confessional state and, on the other hand, a view that says that religious freedom should have priority because the common consciousness of mankind wants it.

In a later article, Murray fleshes out in more detail what he means by this distinction. "Classicism," while not necessarily a theory, is nevertheless an "operative mentality" (cited in Stransky 1967, 143). This "classicism"

> designates a view of truth which holds objective truth, precisely because it is objective, to exist 'already out there now' (to use Bernard Lonergan's descriptive phrase). Therefore, it also exists apart from its possession by anyone. In addition, it exists apart from history, formulated in propositions that are verbally immutable. If there is to be talk of development of doctrine, it can only mean that the truth, remaining itself unchanged in its formulation, may find different applications in the contingent world of historical change. In contrast, historical consciousness, while holding fast to the nature of truth as objective, is concerned with the pos-

> session of truth, with man's affirmations of truth, with the understanding contained in these affirmations, with the conditions—both circumstantial and subjective—of understanding and affirmation, and therefore with the historicity of truth and with progress in the grasp and penetration of what is true. (Cited in Stransky 1967, 141)

Quite frankly, I find this somewhat vague and confusing. Again, it seems to be a caricature of the traditionalist position. For one thing, it's not clear just who holds to a view of the truth that is simply "out there" in a Platonic sense. A true Platonist—Plato, for instance—might believe that such abstract and incorporeal objects as propositions, numbers, and properties "exist out there" independent of minds and their noetic activity. However, it is worth noting that this is, as Alvin Plantinga notes, "realism run amok." Such extreme realism, he says, "is a rare bird in our philosophical tradition" and it is worth noting that no medieval philosopher was a Platonist in this sense (Plantinga 1982b, 68). The traditionalists were no more Platonists than was Murray for believing that his own transtemporal principles of the Gelasian dualism and *concordia* were simply "out there" existing apart from their possession by anyone. Murray, it seems, is arguing with a hyperrealist straw man here.

Moreover, it's not exactly clear what it means for the advocate of historical consciousness to "hold fast to the nature of truth as objective." How, for instance, does this stress on "historical consciousness" fit with the statement which Murray makes in the same article only a few pages later? *The Declaration on Religious Freedom*, Murray claimed, in putting aside the post-Reformation and nineteenth-century theory of civil tolerance, has elaborated a "new philosophy of society and State" that is "more transtemporal in its manner of its conception and statement, less time-conditioned, more differentiated, a progress in the understanding of tradition" (147).

There are, I think, two ways to make sense of these contradictory emphases. One is to point to a hidden premise in Murray's argument: his optimistic view of human development. The other is to see his notion of "historical consciousness" within the context of and correlative to the employment of the notion of "human dignity" in the cause of religious freedom.

Murray favorably cites Pietro Pavan's statement on the declaration: "One must regard it as legitimate to conclude that religious freedom, understood and exercised as a right, answers to a universal conviction. And one must consider it to be a universal persuasion that the emergence of this right in the human consciousness marks a *step forward* in civilization" (cited in 1966a, 566). But the immediate question here is whether it marks a step forward in civilization in that (a) it has been recognized that religious freedom is better than religious civil war, or, (b) that the conditions which call forth the necessity for the priority of religious liberty over, say, religious solidarity, are good per se.

As we have said, Murray is quite reticent to concede the latter. Nevertheless, his optimistic assumptions dovetail quite nicely with his earlier comments about the mature Anglo-Saxon state. By invoking the image of the adult state to characterize Western liberal democracy and coupling this with his claim that the historical development toward that state signified "an intention of nature," one gets the impression that Murray simply believed no further development was possible (see Rohr 1978, 25–26). The impression one gets is that despite his disclaimers, the Anglo-Saxon liberal state has become for Murray what the confessional state was for Leo XIII, the new thesis.

One of Murray's central contentions against the traditionalists was that they took an abstract "ideal instance" of constitutional law, the confessional state of early modernity, and made it obligatory. But in his post-Conciliar writings Murray declares that the achievement of *Dignitatis humanae* was "to bring the church abreast of the developments that have occurred in the secular world. The fact is that the right of man to religious freedom has already been accepted and affirmed by the common consciousness of mankind" (1967f, 282). Now, Murray wanted this new personal and political consciousness to be approved by the authority of the church so that it would effect "a badly needed aggiornamento of the official political philosophy of the Church" (cited in Goerner 1965, 226). But what exactly is an "official political philosophy of the Church?" And how can there be an official political philosophy if the church recognized the relativism of all political forms (see Goerner 1965). And would it not be a violation of the indirect power of the church were clerics such as Murray to proclaim one? Moreover, what does it mean for a cleric or a council of clerics to either validate or invalidate the contemporary popular consciousness (see Goerner 1965, 226)? What if that consciousness changes and makes the conciliar declaration as irrelevant as Murray claims the political thought of Leo XIII to be? What if this historical consciousness is less an awareness of human dignity than, as Rohr says, "a symptom of the growing impertinence of mass man (see Rohr 1978, 21)?

Murray repeatedly denied that he wanted to make the American political system and the First Amendment a "new thesis." His unwillingness to do so created cause for concern among Protestants such as Wogaman, Carillo, and Love. On the other hand, he gives significant credibility to those advocates of the French view who thought he was smuggling American church-state theory into a conciliar document as well as to Cuddihy's charge that Murray, by his appeal to the "contemporary historical consciousness," was engaged in a grand act of legitimizing the Anglo-Saxon American constitutional tradition (Cuddihy 1978, 97-98). At one point, in fact, he explicitly states that

> the political tradition that the Declaration affirms is the political tradition within which the American commonwealth came into being and in which our Constitution and the First Amendment took shape. It is an important endorsement, therefore, of the Anglo-Saxon political tradition, which is the tradition of the United States. (1967, 281)

If this is so, then a document that is taken to be so "progressive" could indeed turn out to be "chauvinistic" or what some might even term "imperialistic." It may forbid a nation whose laity might desire to democratically establish a confessional state, perhaps in opposition to a national clergy committed to the doctrine set forth in *Dignitatis humanae*. Ironically, the claim to validate the contemporary popular consciousness concerning religious liberty results in a type of Anglo-Saxon liberal imperialism that might undercut the "indirect" power of the church in temporal affairs, where Anglo-Saxon notions of liberalism might not have established hegemony.

However, any claim that Murray capitulated to American civil religion must be amended by the fact that total capitulation would require an Esperantist interpretation of the First Amendment that Murray was unwilling to give. Murray's stress on the practical nature of the religion clauses precludes such an interpretation. The tension is there in Murray's argument, but not enough to warrant the claim that he walked through the open door of American civil religion. But the tension does serve as evidence that the tension results from the broader dilemma of religious toleration.

Actually, the difference between the traditionalists and Murray on this point was not over the nature of historical consciousness as such, but ironically in a greater historical sensitivity among the so-called "classicists" for what has been lost in modernity. They refused to state categorically in advance that the conditions which brought about the necessity of the political toleration of religious differences necessarily involve an overall moral improvement in civilization. When the fraternity that is more likely to exist in a religiously unified society fades, it may represent a loss in the types of virtues for which the advantages of religious toleration cannot compensate (cf. Sandel 1983, 31-33).

What is missing, largely as a result of Murray's optimism, is some theoretical insight into the fact that the popular collective consciousness can err, just as the individual conscience does. He recognized this in 1945, when he said that "a high degree of State tolerance may prove a high degree of 'external liberty' as it is called, but it does not prove a high level of moral virtue in the community" (1945e, 271). He does not, however, bring this argument forward during this period. Apart from some similar argument, Murray could fall into a Hegelian affirmation that the real is the rational and the rational is real such that whatever emerges in the historical consciousness of modern man is simply the affirmation of genuine human value and genuine human "rights."

It would be grossly unfair, however, to push Murray down the slippery slope to a full-blooded optimistic historicism. Murray often displayed a strong sense of pessimism about modernity that tended to dilute the type of cultural optimism required by talk about emerging "historical consciousness."[1] We would do well then to consider another reason for Murray's employment of the notion of "historical consciousness."

Once again, the polemical context in which Murray found himself during and after Vatican II provides the answer. I suggest that Murray resorted to the notion of "historical consciousness" largely because he felt obliged to make sense of an argument that had made its way into *Dignitatis humanae* but which he believed was mistaken.

In the unpublished critique of the first schema, Murray said that an argument for religious freedom as a true and strict right from the dignity of the human person

> is vulnerable to the objection…that man is constituted in his true dignity only when he follows the truth, and that he cannot claim public freedom—a true and strict right—in the face of the public power, when he publicly acts out his false convictions. (1963a, 8)

How does Murray handle this problem?

It will be recalled that at the end of chapter 3, I took note of the chief difficulty with the Catholic version of the society-state distinction and the corresponding principle of subsidiarity. One of those problems was that the Roman Catholic Church, as a supernatural institution of grace, can never be a "subsidiary" organization of the state, although other communities, including "religious communities," had to be understood as such. One of the implications of this social ontology is that, as voluntary associations, other societal community structures are to be seen as subsidiary organizations that "stand between" the state and the individual. Given this social ontology, one would expect an argument for the religious liberty of the Catholic Church that is distinct in some respect from that of other churches and religious organizations. One would expect an argument for the freedom of the Catholic Church that was not universalizable, and hence non-Esperantist. And that, in fact, is exactly what we find in Murray's mature argument.

In his footnotes to *Dignitatis humanae* Murray explicitly maintained that the foundation of the right to immunity is different for the Catholic Christian and for other religious bodies.

> The Catholic church claims freedom from coercive interference in her ministry and life on grounds of the divine mandate laid upon her by Christ Himself. It is Catholic faith that no other Church or Community may claim to possess this mandate in all its fullness. In this sense, the freedom of the Church is unique, proper to herself alone, by reason of its foundation. In the case of other religious communities, the foundation of the right is *the dignity of the human person*, which requires that men be kept free from coercion, when they act in community, gathered into Churches, as well as when they act alone. (1966d, 682, note 9)

In other words, the church's right to immunity rests on divine revelation (grace), while the right of other communities is based on the claim that they have "human dignity" (nature).

To understand the implications of this claim, consider the following assertion by Gandhi:

> Current missionary activities are of three kinds, good works, education and religious propaganda. In the India of tomorrow the first two will be welcome but, if the mission-

aries continue to bend their efforts towards religious prose-
lytizing through medical and educational work and so on, I
shall entirely insist that they leave free India. The religions
of India are right for her people; we have no need of spiritual conversion. (Cited in Carillo 1959, 25)

Following the line of argument expressed in the Declaration, Murray might
respond simply by claiming the right to immunity from coercion on the
basis of Christ's mandate to "Go into the whole world and preach the Gospel
to all creatures" (Mark 16:16). But what if a similar Catholic claim were
made? What principle might he use to defeat it?

Suppose a Catholic took a line similar to that of Gandhi and said something like this:

> The religion of this country is not only right for her people;
> it also has the advantage of being the true religion. We have
> no need of spiritual conversion. Moreover, because we do
> not allow the "free exercise of religion" we have a high
> degree of social solidarity and community which Fr.
> Murray admits is a good of the highest order. If some other
> sect or religion wants to evangelize they are not welcome.

Now, Murray believed that religious freedom for other religious communities
was based not on their supernatural status on the basis of divine revelation
but rather on "the dignity of human person." But, as we have already seen,
he also knew quite well that one cannot move immediately from the premise
"all human persons have dignity" to the conclusion "all persons have a right
to the free exercise of religion." Yet this is, in fact, what the "Declaration on
Religious Freedom" seems to do.

Murray's post-Conciliar attempt to make sense of that inference in *Dignitatis humanae* is perhaps the most tortured attempt in all his writings. His
struggle, I think, results from his realism *and* his insistence that religious
freedom not be grounded in skepticism and subjectivism but rather in the
objective moral order. As such, he needs to make freedom to err an objective
requirement of the moral order, and therefore respected by the state as well.
Thus, resident in man's dignity is "the exigence to act on his own initiative
and on his own responsibility. This exigence is of the *objective* order." Hence,
a person's right to be immune from coercion lies in "the values proper to the
human spirit" (1966a, 572, emphasis mine).

Murray is careful to note that *Dignitatis humanae*, like the First Amendment, refuses to affirm that a man has a right to believe or to do what is wrong, for this would be moral nonsense. But then he makes the following assertion:

> Neither error nor evil can be the object of a right, only what is true and good. It is, however, true and good that a man should enjoy freedom from coercion in matters religious. (1966d, 678, note 5)

Murray seems to be arguing that:

> 1.What is true and good and only what is true and good can be the object of a right.

> 2.Freedom from coercion in religious matters is true and good.

> 3.Therefore to be free from coercion in religious matters can be the object of a right.

Now, all parties to the debate accept the major premise. It cannot be otherwise, given Murray's realism. The minor, however, is a matter of degree. Under what condition, we might ask, is freedom from coercion in religious matters true and good? Or in what sense can we say that the minor premise is a proper part of the "moral order"? It, in fact, seems to be a matter of degree, or, as Murray might say, valid *in situ*.

Now, Murray realized that "in order to prove the validity of the moral claim of the human person to immunity from such restraint, it is necessary to show that no valid counterclaim can be entered by government" (1966a, 569). So then, we might ask what valid counterclaim might plausibly be entered by government to override the "right" to be free from coercion in religious matters. Or, under what conditions is freedom from coercion in religious matters true and good?

Suppose a Catholic argued:

> 1. What is true and good and only what is true and good can be the object of a right.

2. Religious diversity undermines societal unity in religious matters.

3. Whatever undermines social unity in religious matters is not true and good.

4. Therefore, religious diversity is not true and good.

Since only what is true and good can be the object of a right (1) and religious diversity is not true and good (4), it would seem to follow that,

5. Religious diversity can not be the object of a right.

Notice that there does not seem to be any premise that Murray would deny outright. Moreover, he consistently affirmed (4) by insisting that pluralism was against the will of God. The crucial question is: since societal unity on religious matters is, for Murray, also true and good, why could that not be the valid counterclaim that can be entered by government?

Now, Murray was not unaware of these difficulties. At one point he admitted that the argument from human dignity is

> only preliminary and partial. It does not yet avail to constitute the right to religious freedom or to any other fundamental human right. It merely lays the foundation for a moral claim on others.... (1966a, 572)

The critical question, according to Murray, is still the concrete juridical or constitutional one, namely "whether some special characteristic or attribute attaches to government that empowers it to repress erroneous religious opinions or practices from public life" (1966a, 573). Thus, Murray seemed to recognize the highly contingent nature of the minor premise in our first syllogism. It could only be asserted "in situ." To make any sense of the argument for religious liberty on the basis of human dignity Murray had to usher in the notion of "historical consciousness."

In effect, his argument entailed an alteration in the priority of the "true and good" that was to be ensured by the state. The good and the true that resulted in immunity from coercion in religious matters was to be given a higher priority than the true and the good that would be achieved by religious social solidarity. However, in order to effect this move he had to appeal not to "the dignity of the human person" as such, but rather to "*the dignity of the human person as affirmed by contemporary human consciousness.*" In other words, given his realism he had to admit the contingent nature of what was to be taken as "true and good" and was thus forced into the type of historically contingent assertion that was criticized by Love, Carillo, and Wogaman. The notion of "historical consciousness" thus must be seen as a polemical counterweight to the notion of "human dignity" in Murray's argument. His appeal to historical consciousness seems restricted to the extent he can use it to defend the right to religious liberty on the basis of human dignity.

However, the arguments from human dignity and historical consciousness are superfluous, and add nothing to Murray's "constitutional" argument. Had Murray simply made the so-called constitutional or juridical argument, it would have been enough. The church should urge religious liberty on the world for the same reason it emerged in the American Constitution: as an article of peace extended to the international situation. Of course, that would not be acceptable to the Esperantists. But then neither would the talk about "historical consciousness."

One final word should be added here. While I have claimed that Murray had recourse to the notion of "historical consciousness" in order to make the argument from human dignity and have argued that this move is subject to serious problems, I nevertheless can find no justification for J. Leon Hooper's bold assertion:

> For Murray, one cannot (and should not) aprioristically claim the eternal validity of any political philosophy or rights theory, or, for that matter, of any ethical theory regarding social reality, familial structuring, common moral affirmations, or even principles of justice themselves. (Hooper 1986, 202)

First, this statement underestimates the extent to which Murray really believed in the superiority of Anglo-Saxon jurisprudence and the corresponding notion of limited constitutional democracy as a "mature" state. But even if we grant that for Murray no political philosophy or rights theory could claim eternal validity, that is simply because of the highly contingent and problematic nature of the consensus that will emerge in any polity. But are we to infer from this that Murray would not rule out a priori some sorts of "familial structuring"? Has Murray come to the point where he would deny that polygamy, for instance, would violate, in his terms, the "objective moral order"? I suspect that Murray would affirm a priori the Western common moral affirmation that monogamy has eternal validity as a familial form. And I suspect that the abandonment of monogamy as a "common moral affirmation" would still indicate a degeneracy in the "common consciousness" just as it did in the 1945 argument. And one suspects that Murray might affirm a priori the common moral notion that "slavery is wrong" or "torture for pleasure is wrong." One simply cannot push Murray down the road to moral relativism or Hegelian rationalism by abstracting his appeal to "historical consciousness" from its polemical context.[2]

From Common Good to Public Order: The Crux of the Matter

The twin concepts of the "common good" and "public order" were more important for Murray's mature argument for religious liberty than his notions of historical consciousness and human dignity. As I argued in chapter 3, the notion of the common good was the one part of the Aristotelian-Thomistic social ontology that would create serious problems for any argument for religious liberty. Murray clearly saw, largely as a result of his debate with the traditionalists, that the state's responsibility for the materially and spiritually good society could be used to override any right claimed in favor of the "free exercise of religion" if the larger society were Catholic. By 1963 Murray was quite clear about the threat posed by an argument for religious liberty based on an appeal to the common good.

> If the term, "common good," is used, it must be qualified to mean only the temporal and terrestrial, secular and civil common good. Only with regard to this limited sector of the common good is the use of legal coercion legitimate. Religion and religious unity are indeed integral elements of the common good of the people; but it does not therefore follow that they are to be protected or promoted by coercive means. (1963a, 5)

Murray further expressed his concerns in the *America* article of 1963. He argued that the first draft "is not sufficiently clear and explicit in its dealing with this problem of social and legal limitation of the right to religious freedom" (1963j, 705). While it did allow restrictions in the name of the common good and the rights of others, Murray found this assertion "too vague."

> An appeal to the common good, as the ground for legal
> restrictions on religious freedom, may be no more than the
> invocation of a *raison d'état,* which is dangerous doctrine.
> Moreover, the allegation of the rights of others, again as the
> ground for restricting religious freedom, may be no more
> than a veiled invocation of the rights of the majority, which
> again is dangerous. (706)

Murray clearly saw how defense of religious freedom on the basis of the
common good would play into the hands of the traditionalists.

Murray found the *relatio* that accompanied the first text more satisfactory than the text itself, because it "adopts the juridical conception of the
state which was developed by Pius XII, and even more sharply emphasized
by John XXIII in *Pacem in terris.*" That Murray would find the *relatio* more
satisfactory is not surprising, given the fact that Murray wrote the draft for
De Smedt in the first place. What comes as a surprise, given Murray's
Thomism, is the way Murray guides the discussion forward.

> These Popes laid aside the more Aristotelian, ethical con-
> ception of the state that is to be found in Leo XIII. The rela-
> tio therefore makes clear that the primary element in the
> common good consists in the legal protection and promo-
> tion of the whole order of personal rights and freedoms
> which are proper to the human person as such. Therefore
> the relatio also makes clear that an infringement of the per-
> sonal rights of man, including notably his right to religious
> freedom, cannot be justified by an appeal to the common
> good. Such an infringement of personal rights would be a
> violation of the common good itself. This is good political
> philosophy. (706)

In addition to the sacred/secular distinction and the society/state distinction, Murray brought forth the ultimately crucial common good/public
order distinction. This, he said, "follows from the distinction between society
and state" (PORF, 29).

> The common good includes all the social goods, spiritual
> and moral as well as material, which man pursues here on
> earth in accord with the demands of his personal and social

nature. The pursuit of the common good devolves upon
society as a whole, on all its members and on all its institutions, in accord with the principles of subsidiarity, legal justice, and distributive justice. Public order, whose care
devolves upon the state, is a narrower concept. It includes
three goods which can and should be achieved by the
power which is proper to the state-the power inherent in
the coercive discipline of public law. The first is public
peace, which is the highest political good. The second is
public morality, as determined by moral standards commonly accepted among the people. The third is justice,
which secures for the people what is due to them. And the
first thing that is due to the people, in justice, is their freedom. (PORF, 29-30)

This principle results in Murray's slogan: "Let there be as much freedom, personal and social, as is possible; let there be only as much restraint
and constraint, personal and social, as may be necessary for the public
order" (31). Stated negatively this implies a rejection of "the opinion that
public care of religion necessarily means, per se and in principle, a political
and legal care for the exclusive rights of truth and a consequent care to
exterminate religious error." Stated positively, it means that the issue of the
public care of religion is not only limited by a necessary care for the freedom
of the church, but also limited "to a care for the freedom of the Church
together with a care for the religious freedom of all peoples and men"
(PORF, 48). The responsibility of the public power for the care of religion is
limited to "the free exercise of religion" which involves a twofold immunity
in religious matters: "a man may not be coercively constrained to act against
his conscience, nor may he be coercively constrained from acting according
to his conscience" (25). Thus, Murray insists that there be a distinction
between the public profession of religion by society (*officium religionis publi-
cae*) and the care of religion by the public power (*cura religionis*) (93).

But, remarkably enough, Murray still regards as legitimate the notion of
a Christian society. Moreover, he still believes "that an obligation to profess
faith in God and to worship Him is incumbent on society—on the people as
such as well as on individuals" (93). He even claims that "the religious unity
of a particular society or people is *a good of the highest order.*"

While Murray claimed that the religious unity of the people is a good of
the highest order, he adds that this is "an order so high that it transcends the

political order" (94). How can he claim that there is a societal good "of the highest order" and yet insist that the state should not promote that good? Murray, quite simply, made a classically liberal move. He simply redefined the role of the state in negative terms as simply the protector of negative rights. That is the only way one can make sense out of his claim—incredible in light of his previous arguments against basing religious liberty on the basis of the liberty of conscience—that a man may not "be coercively constrained from acting according to his conscience" (PORF 25). But this raises two crucial questions: Does this mean that the state is no longer in any sense a "moral entity" but merely a functionalist or instrumentalist agency? Does it imply "indifferentism"?

Murray said that Pius XII and John XXIII "laid aside the more Aristotelian, ethical conception of the state that is to be found in Leo XIII." He clearly approved of this. But he did not seem to see that this had drastic implications for Thomistic or neo-Thomistic political philosophy. Either the state is a moral entity responsible for the common good, or it is not. If it is not, then it would seem to be what George Shea feared: a merely functional or instrumentalist agency that is divorced from what the people who make up that society take to be the common good in religio-moral matters. But if one takes the state to be such, it would seem that one must significantly truncate even the indirect power of the church in temporal affairs. One thus runs the risk, even in a predominantly Christian society, of advocating the naked public square. One of Murray's great fears—that the church would be restricted to the sacristy—would be realized. If, on the other hand, the state is a moral entity and as such is responsible for, and the ultimate guarantor of, the common good, and the common good involves spiritual as well as physical well-being, then there is no a priori way to determine how thick that good will be, nor can it determine what religio-moral actions will be legally prohibited as a violation of that good.

However, the potentially radical nature of Murray's move is muted. While he admits that public order is a narrower concept than the common good, and that only the former devolves upon the state, he includes as an aspect of the public order not only public peace but also *public morality*, as determined by moral standards commonly accepted among the people" and "justice, which secures for the people what is due to the people."

These two aspects of the public order reintroduce into the equation more questions than we can hope to answer. But it does seem arbitrary to claim a priori that the state is incompetent to speak on contentious "religious matters," however much they might be determined by the standards commonly accepted among the people and at the same time consider it appropriate to speak on questions of public morality as determined by commonly accepted standards. Should not the prudential judgments of Murray's "wise man" make public judgments with due consideration of both moral and religious first principles? Should the latter be excluded on moral Esperantist grounds? If not, on what grounds should religious first principles be excluded?

The potentially radical nature of Murray's move can further be seen if we reflect back on the direct/indirect distinction and ask, what if the laity wants a confessional state and the corresponding institution of religious intolerance? if these citizens want, and by due process establish, the institution of religious intolerance of what they take to be heretical or false religions in order to maintain what they take to be true and thus promote social and cultural solidarity based on that truth, it would seem to be a violation of the direct/indirect distinction for a cleric to prohibit it. Murray consistently insisted that the church as mediated through the Christian conscience was to have effects in the temporal order. That means it should, one supposes, have moral effect on temporal activities of government through the agency of its Christian citizens. But now, intent on pushing through an argument for religious liberty immune from traditionalist criticisms, Murray seems to want to seal off the state from the religio-moral desires of the citizens of the larger society.

During the Conciliar debate some of the Council Fathers objected that the document opens up the church to epistemological relativism and religious indifferentism. Murray was anxious to prove that "the charge of religious indifferentism is invalid" (1967f, 280). And evidently, so were many of the Council Fathers. In the final text of the document, they inserted a rather strong statement on "the moral duty of men and societies toward the true religion and toward the one Church of Christ." Murray, when asked why such a statement was included in the final text, answered that it was considered necessary because many of the Fathers felt that earlier versions, including Murray's third version, "had not sufficiently distinguished between the moral order and the juridical order and they felt that some explicit treatment of this was in order lest religious freedom become a pretext for moral anarchy" (1967f, 280). Thus the document even further asserts that "the one true religion subsists in the Catholic and apostolic Church, to which the Lord Jesus entrusted the task of spreading this religion among all men." This profession of Catholic faith, Murray believed, was by no means unecumenical or a contradiction of the principle of religious freedom. Moreover, he believed "that all men of religious conviction of conscience would necessarily admit the fundamental distinction between the moral and juridical orders; and then they can go on to express it in their own theological terms as this declaration expresses it in Catholic theological terms" (1967f, 281-82).

Murray's response, however, is unsatisfactory. The point of disagreement was not on how the juridical-moral distinction was to be theologically justified but rather on the nature of the distinction itself. Even the traditionalist Catholics held to a distinction between the moral and juridical order to some extent. The crucial issue revolved around the extent to which a society should strive to bring the juridical order into harmony with the moral order, which in Catholic thought could not be totally abstracted from its own reverationally grounded truth claims. More precisely, it involved the extent to which a society should strive to bring the juridical order into harmony with the moral order if certain conditions were to hold. The traditionalists simply held that if Catholic hegemony obtained, the state ought to be confessional. Murray conceded to his traditionalist opponents that Catholic-Christian society is a good, indeed a "good of the highest order," but at the same time wanted to remove the state from positive concern for that good. Consistently carried out, this would put the state out of the virtue-creating business altogether. The state would indeed be a purely functional state, a position that Murray, as a Thomist, could not accept.

It is here, in Murray's defense of the limited state, that we can begin to identify the deeper significance of the contemporary debate over the significance of John Courtney Murray, a debate which further serves to illuminate the broader dilemma. The contemporary debate over the meaning of Murray's work is not, of course, directly concerned with the question of religious liberty itself. All parties see that as a settled issue since *Dignitatis humanae*. The tensions in Murray's argument for religious liberty resurface, however, in contemporary Catholic debates over other issues, particularly those that involve the nature and role of the state in the economy and in questions of morality. Most instructive, I think, has been the debate over the extent of state intervention in the economy. Over the past decade, it has become quite commonplace to cite Murray's authority as legitimation for both liberal or interventionist and conservative or noninterventionist positions (McElroy 1989, 174; Novak 1985, 9-16; Hollenbach 1985, 363-66).

From a neoconservative perspective, Michael Novak claims, for instance, that the argument of many Catholics for intervention in the economy is a betrayal of the legacy of John Courtney Murray. Recent attempts

> to commit the church to 'economic rights' has the potential
> to become an error of classic magnitude. It might well posi-
> tion the Catholic Church in a "preferential option for the
> state" that will more than rival that of the Constantinian
> period. (Novak 1985, 10)

Novak is explicitly exploiting Murray's shift away from an emphasis on the
state's responsibility for ensuring the common good to the thinner notion of
guaranteeing public order. In this, he follows Murray in defending a modern
rather than a classical Aristotelian-Thomistic conception of the state.

Contemporary progressive Roman Catholics are not unaware of the
problem and seem to realize that the same argument Murray used to restrict
state intervention in religious matters could easily enough be appropriated
to restrict state intervention in economic matters even should the latter serve
the common good. John Coleman, as we have seen, finds Murray's defense
of a limited state attractive when it produces a strong argument for religious
liberty. Nevertheless, he criticizes Murray's social thought as being too individualistic, a flaw that stems from a failure to appropriate "biblical imagery"
in his social thought.

> My purpose is to point out the relative lack in American
> Catholic social thought, until recent times, of appeals to
> biblical imagery in discussions of the normative founda-
> tions of public life. I also want to suggest that this lacuna
> skews Murray's writings on public issues too strongly in
> the direction of liberal individualism, despite his own
> intentions. (1979, 702)

Coleman argues that the weakness of

> Murray's strategy for public discourse lies in the nature of
> the symbols he uses. There is a sense in which "secular"
> language, especially when governed by the Enlightenment
> ideals of conceptual clarity and analytic rigor, is exceed-
> ingly "thin" as a symbol system. It is unable to evoke the
> rich, polyvalent power of religious symbolism, a power
> which can command commitments of emotional depth.
> The very necessity for seeking a universality which tran-

scends our rootedness and loyalties to particular communities makes secular language chaste, sober, thin. (1979, 706)

Aside from the rather bizarre suggestion that conceptual clarity and analytic rigor are peculiarly Enlightenment ideals, Coleman's analysis is rather sound. Murray did bracket commitments that provided "emotional depth" in public discourse. But it is important to keep in mind why Murray bracketed these "commitments of emotional depth." It was such a commitment coupled with the refusal to bracket them that led the traditionalists to advocate the thesis-hypothesis doctrine in the first place. Murray could not have made his case for religious liberty had he not bracketed those commitments.

David Hollenbach, on the other hand, has argued that there exists an element in Murray's thought that cannot be dismissed as simply a stratagem for gaining a wider audience for Christian moral views in a nonreligious language. According to Hollenbach:

> The relation between the sacred and the secular, as Murray understands it, becomes a relation of unity only within the experience of the individual person, not in the public sphere. The social order can protect this unity, and it can provide the possibility for the realization of this unity within the hearts of persons. The relation between the sacred and secular is attained by the achievement of [citing Murray] a "right order within one man, who is a member of two societies and subject to the laws of both." In the world of institutions, structures, power, and corporate action, however, the dualism is sharply drawn. (1976, 300)

Given this criticism, it is somewhat surprising that in a more recent article Hollenbach takes Novak to task for claiming Murray's legacy. He appeals to the principle of subsidiarity to challenge Novak's argument.

> Both Leo XIII and Murray insisted, of course, that securing economic necessities for all is not, in the first instance, the responsibility of government. Individuals, families and a variety of mediating institutions in society have an obligation to see that people do not go hungry, homeless or jobless. Nevertheless, when the problem exceeds the power of these persons and groups, government can and should

intervene in ways carefully guided by political prudence.
This is the meaning of the principle of subsidiarity so often
stated in Catholic social teaching. Novak admits this also,
but is reluctant to follow through on its implications.
(1985, 366)

And what are these implications?

If government's proper sphere is public order and not the
common good, and if, as Novak appears to believe, the provision of basic economic resources is part of the full
common good rather than part of the more basic condition
of public order, then it makes no sense to sanction any
intervention at all. (1985, 366)

In other words, if mere public order can be achieved without intervention,
then appeals for intervention in the name of the common good are without
warrant.

The core of these progressive objections to Murray's view of the state is
summarized by Charles Curran.

Murray's notion of the state can also be questioned. Again,
from his perspective Murray wants to emphasize the limited nature of the state, so that the matter of religion lies
beyond the competency of the state, while there is still
room for the religious aspect of life.... His criterion of public
order is quite limited. He sees no economic problem that
calls for greater intervention. In my view the state must
have a greater role to play in economic affairs, even while it
adheres to the principle of subsidiarity. There can be no
doubt that Murray is a political conservative with a view of
a very limited state. In contrast John A Ryan is a political
liberal, for he expands the role for the state especially in
terms of its function with regard to social justice. Note that
there is some consistency in Ryan, who also calls for a
greater role of the state in religious matters. (1982, 231–32)

In Curran's comments we find a curious convergence of pre-Conciliar tradi-
tionalism with post-Conciliar progressivism. In fact, Curran seems sympa-

thetic to the charge of the traditionalists at the Council that Murray's concept of the state as presented in the third text (textus emendatus) favored a Manchester liberalism and individualistic capitalism (Curran 232, Regan 1967, 124-25).

I do not wish to enter into the details of this debate, except to say something about how this ironic convergence of traditionalist and progressive criticisms of Murray's work says something about the deeper dilemma. In order to escape the implications of the thesis-hypothesis doctrine, Murray had to argue for a limited state that had no competence in religious matters. Novak's position follows quite consistently from this. McElroy is right to state that both liberal and conservative attempts to appeal to Murray for support of their own political agendas "are extremely dubious, not only because they tend to degenerate into *argumentam ab auctoritate,* but also because Murray did not write enough on economic issues to support either the liberal or conservative agendas in the present day" (McElroy 1989, 174). But it is not unreasonable for a noninterventionalist to claim that the state has little or no competence in economic matters either, unless required for maintaining public order, and to defend that claim by appealing to Murray's mature understanding of the limited state, the common good, and the public order. The trajectory of Murray's mature thought is certainly in that direction. If individual liberty has priority over the common good and can only be trumped by appeal to questions of the public order, then capitalist acts between consenting adults as well as religious acts between consenting adults would seem to be beyond the purview of the state.

But the reverse is also true. if state intervention in economic matters could be justified for the sake of the common good, as the progressives seem to imply, why might not intervention be justified in religious matters? Of course, one could argue for or against economic interventionism as a matter of prudence. But then one would like to know why one could not argue for or against intervention in religious matters on the same basis unless one wanted to escape the modus vivendi horn of the dilemma and speak Esperanto on religious matters while urging a modus vivendi approach on economic ones.

The dilemma for progressive Catholics, as Curran realizes, is to justify on moral grounds a greater degree of state intervention in economic matters in the name of the common good without denying Murray's claim that the state is incompetent in religious matters. "I believe that one could still see an expanded role of the state in economic matters," says Curran, "without denying Murray's position about the role of the state in religious matters"

(232). No doubt one could. But the salient question is whether the justification one gives for each position can be held consistently, and without surrendering the classical Catholic claim that the common good includes both material and spiritual aspects. In any case it seems arbitrary and selective to place the Aristotelian-Thomistic idea of the ethical state and its responsibility for the common good in the background when doing so is useful for a religious liberty argument and yet bring it forward when it is expedient to argue, on ethical grounds, for greater state intervention in the economy.

The neoconservative position confronts a similar problem. What makes the position neo*conservative* is a willingness to use the state to influence what Novak calls the moral/cultural sphere. But it seems arbitrary and selective to place the Aristotelian-Thomistic idea of the ethical state and its responsibility for the common good in the background when discussing economic intervention, and yet bring it forward when certain moral issues, such as abortion, are being considered.[3] Neoconservatives should not be surprised when the Murray slogan, "as much freedom as possible," is appealed to in support of permissive abortion laws. Of course, just as the progressives might argue for or against economic intervention as a matter of collective prudence, one could also argue for or against permissive abortion laws as a matter of collective prudence. But then one would like to know why one could not argue for or against permissive or restrictive laws on religious matters on the same basis unless one wanted to escape the modus vivendi horn of the dilemma and speak Esperanto on religious matters while urging a modus vivendi approach on moral ones. That is certainly an option for one who is willing to completely separate nature from grace, or the supernatural from the natural. But as long as the neoconservatives refuse, as Murray did, to select that option, they, along with Murray, will remain caught in the dilemma.

Notes

1. In *We Hold These Truths* Murray expressed deep concern about the limits of pluralism in American society. "The 'open society' today faces the question, how open can it afford to be, and still remain a society; how many barbarians can it tolerate, and still remain civil; how many 'idiots' can it include (in the classical Greek sense of the 'private person' who does not share in the public thought of the City), and still have a public life; how many idioms, alien to one another, can it admit, and still allow the possibility of civil conversation?" (WHTT, 117). A couple of years later, in an article entitled "The Return to Tribalism" (1962a), Murray's pessimistic streak was even more evident. He was particularly concerned that the rise of "technological secular-

ism" threatened American society. He suggested that if "this country is to be over-thrown from within or from without...it will be overthrown because it will have made an impossible experiment. It will have undertaken to establish a technological order of most marvelous intricacy, which will have been constructed and will operate with-out relation to true political ends; and this technological order will hang, as it were, suspended over a moral confusion; and this moral confusion will itself be suspended over a spiritual vacuum. This would be the real danger, resulting from a type of falla-cious, fictitious, fragile unity that could be created among us" (7). But he considered even more serious "the growth among us of a civil religion that would somehow be a substitute secular faith" in which "the political community becomes a kind of spiri-tual community" and whose "set of democratic values is conceived to be transcendent to all the religious divisions that are unfortunately among us" (7-8). In the end, Murray wondered whether "civil order, civil unity [of] civil peace," was possible with-out what John of Salisbury called "the sweet and fruitful marriage of Reason and the Word of God" (12).

2. Moreover, as Curran (1982, 229) states, "Murray's approach to historical con-sciousness and to development in his discussion of Conciliar definitions about God and Jesus appears to be somewhat different from his approach in the question of reli-gious liberty." Curran is critical of Murray's unwillingness to be consistent here, and seems to believe with John Rohr that if the "archaism" of the traditionalists is a fallacy, "it would seem to follow that any question is legitimate and that one can never write *finis* to a particular issue" (Rohr 1978, 25). As both Rohr and Curran observe, Murray was unwilling to speak of historical consciousness in his understanding of Christol-ogy and the Trinity, the Nicean Conciliar pronouncements being final in these areas.

3. See, for instance, the *Los Angeles Times* editorial, "A Response to Mahoney: Zeal and Politics" (June 6, 1989), and the argument by Mary C. Segers, "Murray, American Pluralism, and the Abortion Controversy" (Hunt and Grasso, 1992, 228-48).

Chapter Eight

Ethicists Between the Horns of the Dilemma: Reinhold Niebuhr, John Rawls, and Stanley Hauerwas

IN THIS CHAPTER I intend to survey the positions on religious toleration adopted by three significant twentieth-century thinkers who have reflected at some length on the subject. In so doing, I hope to suggest that the dilemma with which Murray was confronted was not unique to him or to Catholic thought, but rather plagues all those who enter the debate. Each of these thinkers seems to recognize the dilemma and has proposed a way out. I will suggest that none has succeeded.

Reinhold Niebuhr: Mitigated Skepticism in Support of Religious Toleration

I suggested in the first chapter that an argument for religious toleration grounded in skepticism or relativism will inevitably be self-referentially incoherent. In this section, I want to show how Reinhold Niebuhr's argument for religious toleration is plagued by this difficulty. In both *The Nature and Destiny of Man* and *The Children of Light and the Children of Darkness*, Niebuhr tries to split the difference between the traditional Catholic modus vivendi position and the secularist and liberal Protestant alternative. I will show that Niebuhr's attempt to slip between the horns fails.

In *The Children of Light and the Children of Darkness* (1944) Niebuhr explicitly situated his position on religious toleration between a "religious approach" which attempts to "overcome religious diversity and restore the original unity to culture" (126) on the one hand, and a secularist or bourgeois view on the other.

The first position is represented by Roman Catholicism. According to Niebuhr, this view "accepts religious diversity in a national community only under the compulsion of history" (126). Leo XIII's *Immortale Dei* and Ryan and Boland's *Catholic Principles of Politics* reflect "the chasm between the presuppositions of a free society and the inflexible authoritarianism of the Catholic religion" (128). Even though Ryan conceded that an overwhelming majority would be necessary for the suppression of religious dissidents, Niebuhr thought it perverse that the policy must be maintained despite its irrelevance. And, in *The Nature and Destiny of Man*, Niebuhr claimed that the position of Ryan reflected a "curious and pathetic logic" (2:223 note 3).

The second approach toward the problem of religious diversity is secularism, "which attempts to achieve cultural unity through the disavowal of traditional historical religions" (126). Niebuhr saw this in his own partially secularized American culture, which tended to favor religious toleration, "partly because it does not regard the religious convictions which create religious differences in the community as significant" (129). This "bourgeois secularism" came in two varieties. In its more naive form it manifests itself as "a covert religion which believes that it has ultimate answers to life's ultimate problems." The "historical process" itself is taken to be redemptive (132). The other form of modern secularism "expresses itself in more modest religious terms" and simply holds that "the end of life is the creation of a democratic society" (132). In its more sophisticated form this represents, according to Niebuhr, "a form of skepticism which is conscious of the relativity of all human perspectives. In this form it stands on the abyss of moral nihilism and threatens the whole of life with a sense of meaninglessness" (133).

Unlike the more sophisticated Continental versions of secularism, the American variety has been more naive and hence less dangerous.

> In America the bourgeois mind has not yet faced the ultimate issues, nor been confronted with the inadequacy of its own credos. That is why the secularization of culture still seems an adequate answer in America for both the ultimate questions about the meaning of life and the immediate problem of the unity and harmony of our society. (134)

Niebuhr thought the most pathetic aspect of this secularism or "bourgeois faith" was that "it regards its characteristic perspectives and convictions as universally valid and applicable, at the precise moment in history when they are being unmasked as the peculiar convictions of a special class which flourished in a special situation in Western society" (131). He also objected to this approach to the problem of cultural unity amidst religious diversity and considered it inadequate because it implied a sacrifice of religious profundity. "The achievement of communal harmony on the basis of secularism means the sacrifice of religious profundity as the price of a tolerable communal accord" (136).

This view, one he associates with John Dewey, came under sharp criticism in *The Nature and Destiny of Man* (237ff.). Such a view seems plausible because religious questions historically "have been a particularly fecund source of fanaticism and conflict" (238). Nevertheless,

> the weakness in the modern position is also quite apparent.
> Either it achieves toleration by taking an irresponsible attitude towards ultimate issues; or it insinuates new and false ultimates into views of life which are ostensibly merely provisional and pragmatic. (238)

Lying in wait at the end of the modern view of religious tolerance, Niebuhr believed, were "the twin perils of scepticism and a new fanaticism" (238). The question I want to address is whether Niebuhr ultimately becomes impaled on the skeptical horn of the dilemma.

Because "the real test of toleration is our attitude towards people who oppose truths which seem important to us," religious toleration often results in "an irresponsible attitude towards the ultimate problem of truth, including particularly the problem of the relation of *the* truth to the fragmentary truths of history" (238). Niebuhr thought that this irresponsible attitude may degenerate into complete skepticism. However, absolute skepticism is rare, "because the very lack of confidence in the possibility of achieving any valid truth in history presupposes some criterion of truth by which all fragmentary truths are found wanting" (239).

A new secular fanaticism rather than a complete skepticism, Niebuhr reasoned, is more likely the result of such a stance.

> [T]he belief that the intercourse between fragmentary
> truths will culminate in the realization of the whole truth

becomes itself a religious position as soon as it is changed from a merely provisional and tentative attitude towards the immediate problem of dealing with fragmentary truths, into an answer to the final problem of truth and falsehood. Such a religion can and does maintain tolerance towards all religious beliefs except those which challenge this basic assumption. The idea of progress is the underlying presupposition of what may be broadly defined as "liberal" culture. If the assumption is challenged the whole structure of meaning in the liberal world is imperiled. For this reason the liberal world is intolerant in regard to this element of its creed. It does not argue about its validity, precisely because it has lost every degree of scepticism in regard to it. (239–40)

Historically, such secular fanaticism was manifested in the positions of Hobbes and Bodin. Both thinkers began "with a sceptical and irresponsible attitude towards the religious problem and an aversion to religious controversy." But they did so primarily because religious diversity imperiled "the tranquility of the national state." In a phrase which reminds one of Murray's reference to "secular theologies," Niebuhr called such a position "implicitly religious," because it demands "unconditioned loyalty to the state" without making "the overt claim that the whole meaning of life and existence is fulfilled in the individual's relation to the national community" (241).

So how does Niebuhr propose to slip between the horns of the dilemma? In *The Children of Light and the Children of Darkness* Niebuhr called his proposed tertium quid a "religious" solution to the problem of religious diversity. This solution in contrast to the secularist approach "requires a very high form of religious commitment" (1944, 135). But it also

demands that each religion, or each version of a single faith, seek to proclaim its highest insights while yet preserving an humble and contrite recognition of the fact that all expressions of religious faith are subject to historical contingency and relativity. Such a recognition makes any religious or cultural movement hesitant to claim official validity for its form of religion or to demand an official monopoly for its cult. (135)

In other words, Niebuhr wants a sufficient degree of religious conviction (or commitment) to escape the societal dangers that result from a complete skepticism. But because he also believes that "no toleration is possible without a measure of provisional scepticism about the truth we hold" (1941, 2:239), he also thinks such commitment must be weak enough to create a provisional skepticism that will result in religious toleration. Religious conviction needs to be strong, but not too strong.

"Our toleration of truths opposed to those which we confess," argued Niebuhr, "is an expression of the spirit of forgiveness in the realm of culture. Like all forgiveness, it is possible only if we are not too sure of our own virtue." "Toleration of others," says Niebuhr, "requires broken confidence in the finality of our own truth" (243). The title of the chapter in which this appears is entitled, appropriately enough, "Having, and Not Having, the Truth." In short, he appeals to our lack of final truth as the basis for toleration, the point being that when we realize that we have no final truth we will not be in position to impose our beliefs on those who do not agree with us.

To fully understand and appreciate Niebuhr's comments on religious toleration, one must understand the place it plays within the context of his dialectical theology as a whole, particularly the place it plays in his polemic against liberal optimism. The common thread running through the optimistic anthropologies of modernity arise, according to Niebuhr, from the attempt to locate the source of evil in history rather than in man himself. Because the modern liberal is so certain about his essential virtue he tries to "interpret himself in terms of natural causality or in terms of his unique rationality; but he does not see that he has a freedom of spirit which transcends both nature and reason." Consequently, he is "unable to understand the real pathos of his defiance of nature's and reason's laws." And because he "imagines himself betrayed into this defiance either by some accidental corruption in his past history or by some sloth of reason," he then "hopes for redemption, either through a program of social reorganization or by some scheme of education" (1941, 1:96).

For Niebuhr, errors in the interpretation of human nature are primarily the result of corrupting the dialectic of time and eternity. Man is either perceived as too lofty to be identified with the world or too low to be identified with eternity. But because he, in fact, experiences both natural limitations (body) and the freedom of self-transcendence (spirit), the tension of this dialectic must be maintained at all cost.

> Man is not measured in a dimension sufficiently high or
> deep to do full justice to either his stature or his capacity
> for both good and evil or to understand the total environ-
> ment in which such a stature can understand, express and
> find itself. One might define this total environment most
> succinctly as one which includes both eternity and time.
> (1941, 1:124)

The existential situation of man as a being capable of self-transcendence and
yet bound to history and nature has most adequately been expressed in traditional Christian doctrines. These doctrines provide a vantage point from
which one can view the fallacy of the alternatives.

> Without the presuppositions of the Christian faith the indi-
> vidual is either nothing or becomes everything. In the
> Christian faith man's insignificance as a creature, involved
> in the process of nature and time, is lifted into significance
> by the mercy and power of God in which his life is sus-
> tained. But his significance as a free spirit is understood as
> subordinate to the freedom of God. (1:92)

Throughout his writings Niebuhr comments on a number of traditional doctrines: creation *ex nihilo* (1935, 26), the fall, (1941, 1:179-80), imputed righteousness, justification and sanctification (2:100ff.), the resurrection
(2:294), the second coming of Christ (2:287ff), the wrath of God (2:211),
original sin (2:248ff.) and so forth.

However, in typical neo-Kantian fashion, Niebuhr shifted the emphasis
from the concept of *creation*, the concept of the *fall*, the concepts of *justification and sanctification*, the concept of the *second coming*, the concept of the
wrath of God, and the concept of *original sin*, on the one hand, to the *concept*
of creation, the *concept* of the fall, the *concept* of imputed righteousness, the
concept of the resurrection, the *concept* of the second coming, the *concept* of
the wrath of God, and the *concept* of original sin, on the other. To emphasize
the former is to fall into the "wooden-headed" literalism of orthodoxy. That is
why, shortly after his Gifford Lectures, he would write to Norman Kemp-
Smith, "I have not the slightest interest in the empty tomb or physical resurrection" (Fox 1985, 215). The historical fact of the resurrection of Christ
yields in Niebuhr's theology to the existential significance of the symbol of
the resurrection.

Niebuhr's comments on the *parousia* of Christ in the following passage can be extended to all Christian symbols and myths.

> If the symbol is taken literally the dialectical conception of time and eternity is falsified and the ultimate vindication of God over history is reduced to a point in history.... On the other hand if the symbol is dismissed as unimportant, as merely a picturesque or primitive way of apprehending the relation of the historical to the eternal, the Biblical dialectic is obscured in another direction. All theologies which do not take these symbols seriously will be discovered upon close analysis not to take history seriously either. They presuppose an eternity which annuls rather than fulfills the historical process. The Biblical symbols cannot be taken literally because it is not possible for finite minds to comprehend that which transcends and fulfills history.... The symbols which point towards the consummation from within the temporal flux cannot be exact in the scientific sense of the word. (1941, 2:289)

To literalize these symbols is to rationalize them and a "rationalized myth loses its virtue because it ceases to point to the realm of transcendence beyond history, or, pointing to it, fails to express the organic and paradoxical relationship between the conditioned and the unconditioned" (1968 [1937], 26). In other words, it corrupts the dialectic between time and eternity.

To put it another way, the traditional doctrines of orthodox Christian theism are incorporated into an overarching metaphysical framework which assumes the dialectical relation of time and eternity, the conditioned and unconditioned, the real and the ideal, fate and freedom, or the transcendental and the phenomenal. The symbols, qua symbols, simply express more adequately than their alternatives the existential predicament of the human race. On the one hand, Christian thought allows "an appreciation of the unity of body and soul in human personality which idealists and naturalists have sought in vain" and thus can assert that "man is, according to the Biblical view, a created and finite existence in both body and spirit" (1941, 1:12). On the other hand, Christianity "emphasizes the height of self-transcendence in man's spiritual stature in its doctrine of 'image of God'" (1:150).

The dialectic can only be adequately maintained through a proper understanding of myth and symbol. The Evangelical theologian E. J. Carnell describes the importance of these notions in Niebuhr's thought.

> Ethical fruitfulness [for Niebuhr] is measured by the ability of norms to maintain a tension between what is and what ought to be, between the historical and the transcendental; for unless both of these elements are adequately balanced in one theory, one side of man will be either misunderstood or overestimated or underemphasized. This means that eternity is the absolute and history the relative, and anything in history which is a pointer to the eternal can be no more than a symbol of the eternal. To identify anything in history with eternity is as foolish as it is dangerous. It is foolish because it is impossible for the same thing to be limited and unlimited at the same time, perfect and imperfect; and it is dangerous because it breaks the dialectical relation between time and eternity. It sets the wedge for man to corrupt moral progress by sanctifying as finalities in history what ought rather to be judged by finalities in eternity. (Carnell 1960, 111)

What is true generally for Niebuhr is also true with regard to the question of religious toleration. Religious tolerance results when this dialectic is kept intact and intolerance results when the dialectic is corrupted; that is, when what is taken as final eternal truth is regarded as such in history. The central problem with the liberal optimism of bourgeois culture and its defense of religious toleration was that it failed to understand the true existential situation of mankind and thus could never understand the place of evil in history.

While the liberal optimism of modernity was Niebuhr's main target, it wasn't his only one. He also was critical of orthodox Christianity which "cannot come to the aid of modern man, partly because its religious truths are still embedded in an outmoded science and partly because its morality is expressed in dogmatic and authoritarian moral codes" (1935, 4). While liberalism does injustice to Christianity by interpreting its symbols in favor of the optimistic moral criteria of a bourgeois age, orthodoxy corrupts the dialectic through its "wooden-headed" (1937, 28) literalism. "In each case religion fails because it prematurely resolves moral tension by discovering, or claiming to have realized, the *summum bonum* in some immediate and relative value of history" (1935, 10). Such a view was not only reflected in the intolerance of medieval Roman Catholicism (1941, 2:221–25), but also in the "fanaticism" of the Reformers, particularly the "pretentious" and "obscurantist" ethical system of Calvin and his followers (1941, 2:226–31). Thus the Reformation, as much as medieval Catholicism, was guilty of invoking "premature claims of finality" (2:214). Stated in terms of Christian doctrines and symbols, this intolerance was the result of confusing justification and sanctification in the realm of truth and in the realm of culture (2:229). It resulted in the failure to appreciate what Niebuhr called "the paradox of grace": the having grace and truth (i.e., justification) and yet not-having grace and truth (i.e., sanctification).

Here we confront the importance of myth and symbol against the literalism of orthodoxy. A claim to literal truth in the Christian symbols leads to the claim for final truth in history. But, in accordance with his dialectical understanding of time and eternity, Niebuhr knows that history cannot bear the ideal which explains history. Symbols and myths, as merely "pointers" to the transcendental ideal, are brought forth to escape the difficulty. In the realm of culture, intolerance is the result of claims to final truth in history. The test of

> how genuinely it has entered into human experience is the attitude of Christians towards those who differ from themselves in convictions which seem vital to each. The test, in other words, is to be found in the issue of toleration. (1941, 2:219)

The converse of this is that knowledge of our lack of final truth is a ground for maintaining tolerance.

But there is a rather fundamental objection to this line of reasoning. If no truth is final, then neither is it final that the relation between time and eternity is dialectical or that truth or grace is paradoxical. Since a finite perspective corrupts all truth, it also corrupts the "truth" that all finite truth is corrupted. How, we must ask, given the corruption of all knowledge, does Niebuhr know that tolerance is the test of how well one has grasped the paradox of grace? How does he know that religious tolerance is the final test "of how well this paradox [of grace] of the gospel is comprehended, and how genuinely it has entered into human experience" (2:219)?

If Niebuhr makes a straightforward appeal to an ahistorical objective standard in his defense of toleration, he subverts his understanding of time and eternity as dialectical, for its ambiguity has been overcome at least at this one point in history. Time and eternity are then no longer exclusively dialectical since an ahistorical categorical imperative has entered history ("Be religiously tolerant"). The choice is forced. Either religious tolerance is an absolute norm derived from the agapic demands of the gospel and the dialectic between time and eternity becomes corrupted or it is not an absolute norm that can be derived from the gospel. And, of course, if the obligation to be religiously tolerant is not final, then it cannot be ruled out given the appropriate sociopolitical conditions. If all truth is corrupted because the ideal cannot be embodied in history, then the "truth" which Niebuhr wants to establish, namely, that we ought to be religiously tolerant, is corrupted by the nature of the dialectic as well. Once claims to propositional truth are discarded in favor of a mythical alternative (because the former corrupts the dialectic of time and eternity) one cannot subsequently reintroduce an absolute final norm that is supposedly carried within the myth or symbol (cf. Henry 1976, 63ff).

Consider, for example, the following Niebuhrian propositions:

> (N1) "No toleration is possible without a measure of provisional scepticism about the truth we hold." (1941, 2:239)

> (N2) "Toleration of truths opposed to those we confess is possible only if we are not too sure of our own virtue." (2:243)

> (N3) "Toleration of others requires broken confidence in the finality of our own truth." (2:243)

If, on the one hand, all knowledge is historically contingent, as required by Niebuhr's dialectical theology then N1, N2, and N3 are at best, only provisionally true. But then he must settle for a "provisional" answer to the question of religious tolerance. To put it another way, he then has to settle for a defense of religious toleration subject to the "compulsion of history," a position that he clearly finds morally deficient when he sees it in Catholics. If, on the other hand, N1, N2, and N3 are absolutely true, then it is not the case that all knowledge is historically contingent and his claim that all knowledge is such becomes self-referentially incoherent. To put it bluntly, given the epistemological assumptions at the core of his dialectical theology, Niebuhr has no right to N1, N2, and N3. Thus, he does not escape the dilemma.

John Rawls: Between 'Comprehensive Moral Conceptions' and a Modus Vivendi

The dilemma of religious toleration is also illuminated quite well in the work of the great liberal political philosopher, John Rawls. Rawls has recently defined his project as an attempt to steer a course between "liberalism as a modus vivendi secured by a convergence of self- and group-interests as coordinated and balanced by a well-designed constitutional arrangement—and a liberalism founded on a comprehensive moral doctrine such as that of Kant and Mill" (1987, 23-24).

Rawls' recent work must be set against the backdrop of the communitarian objections to his famous *A Theory of Justice* (1971), the most trenchant and incisive of which is found in Michael Sandel's *Liberalism and the Limits of Justice* (1982). Sandel argued that the liberalism advanced by Rawls' theory of justice presupposed a faulty and ultimately incoherent metaphysics of the self; a self that is freely chosen, self-created, unencumbered by its history and circumstances, and separable from its aims, ends, and attachments.

Sandel argued that to conceive of persons the way Rawls understands the contractors behind the veil of ignorance ignores and distorts the ways personal identity is mediated in community with others and in shared attachments to common goods. Not only does this "deontological liberalism" rest upon a morally impoverished metaphysical anthropology; it is also internally incoherent. In order to attain its own ideal of social justice, it must incorporate certain empirical elements already excluded from the theory. So, for example, Rawls' own difference principle of just economic distribution presupposes the type of identity, community, personal attachments excluded by his conception of persons (1982, 66-103). His Kantianism is compromised, thereby making his theory an incoherent "deontology with a Humean face" (13).

Sandel summarizes his objections as follows:

> Can we view ourselves as independent selves, independent
> in the sense that our identity is never attached to our aims
> and attachments? I do not think we can, at least not with-
> out cost to these loyalties and convictions whose moral
> force consists partly in the fact that living by them is insep-

arable from understanding ourselves as the particular persons we are—as members of this family or community or
nation or people, as bearers for that history, as citizens for
this republic.... To imagine a person incapable of constitutive attachments such as these is not to conceive an ideally
free and rational agent, but to imagine a person wholly
without character, without moral depth. For to have character is to know that I move in a history I neither summon
nor command, which carries consequences nonetheless for
my choices and conduct. (1984, 90-91)

To the extent that we identify ourselves as encumbered selves, Sandel
argues, it is reasonable that we reject the Rawlsian original position, a device
that emasculates convictions and attachments that matter to us the most.

Rawls' general strategy in response to Sandel and other communitarian
critics has been simply to deny that his political philosophy rests upon any
such metaphysical theory. The device of the original position and the veil of
ignorance which played such a large role in *A Theory of Justice*, he now
insists, "has no metaphysical implications concerning the nature of the self;
it does not imply that the self is ontologically prior to the facts about persons that the party are excluded from knowing" (1985, 238). In short, his
theory of liberal justice is "political not metaphysical" (1985).

Because of the highly pluralistic nature of modernity, "no general comprehensive view can provide a publicly acceptable basis for a political conception of justice" (1987, 4; cf. 1985, 230). Therefore, "we try, so far as we
can, neither to assert nor to deny any religious, philosophical or moral views,
or their associated philosophical accounts of truth and the status of values"
(1987, 12-13). In the interest of bypassing long-standing philosophical and
religious controversies, political philosophers must now employ a "method
of avoidance." In this sense, Rawls argues,

a political conception of justice completes and extends the
movement of thought that began three centuries ago with
the gradual acceptance of the principle of toleration and
led to the non-confessional state and equal liberty of conscience. This extension is required for an agreement of a
political conception of justice given the historical and social
circumstances of a democratic society. (1987, 15)

The political conception of justice extends what began three centuries ago by applying "the principle of toleration to philosophy itself" (1985, 223). Rawls is clear that this method of avoidance extends particularly to the controversial liberalisms of Kant and Mill. Because these liberalisms "rest in large part on ideals and values that are not generally, or perhaps even widely shared in a democratic society," they are not, says Rawls, "a practicable public basis of a political conception of justice" (1987, 6). It seems Rawls is now less willing than he is in "A Theory of Justice" to defend a conception of justice that "tries to present a natural procedural rendering of Kant's conception of the kingdom of ends, and the categorical imperative" (1971, 264).

But he is also quite anxious to deflect the charge that his emphasis on a political rather than metaphysical conception of justice is a mere modus vivendi (1987, 9ff.). While agreement on Kantian and Millian liberalism is unattainable in a constitutional democracy, a Hobbesian balance of conflicting interests "even when coordinated and balanced by a well designed constitutional arrangement" (1982, 2) can at best reach an unstable agreement. Under a modus vivendi conception, toleration of different religious, metaphysical, and moral doctrines is only grudgingly accepted. Rawls cites as an historical example of a modus vivendi the situation among Catholics and Protestants in the sixteenth century. At that time, one could not speak of an overlapping consensus on the principle of religious toleration because "both faiths held that it was the duty of the ruler to uphold the true religion and to repress the spread of heresy and false doctrine. In this case, the acceptance of the principle of toleration would be a mere *modus vivendi*" (1987, 11). Opposing groups resorted to tolerance simply because they lacked the power to suppress opposing views. Religious toleration was simply preferred over religious civil war.

According to Rawls, an overlapping consensus results when such things as "liberty of conscience" are taken off the political agenda. He explains what this means as follows:

> [W]hen certain matters are taken off the political agenda, they are no longer regarded as proper subjects for political discussion by majority or other plurality voting. In regard to equal liberty of conscience and rejection of slavery and serfdom, this means that the equal basic liberties in the constitution that cover these matters is fixed, settled once and for all. They are part of the public charter of a constitutional regime and not a suitable topic for on-going public

debate and legislation, as if they can be changed at any time, one way or the other. Moreover, the more established political parties likewise acknowledge these matters as settled. Of course, that certain matters are taken off the political agenda does not mean that a political conception of justice should not explain why this is done. (1987, 14 n. 22)

Thus, an overlapping consensus has what a modus vivendi conception lacks: the political virtue of stability.

But one finds a certain ambiguity in Rawls' description of a modus vivendi. On the one hand, he describes it (as in the above paragraph) as one which lacks constitutional stability. On the other hand, he claims that a modus vivendi would be unacceptable "*even when ordered by a well-framed constitution*" (1987, 2). Even if a modus vivendi conception resulted in a "skillful constitutional design framed to guide self- (family-) and group-interests to work for social purposes by the use of various devices such as balance of powers and the like" (1987, 2 n. 1) it would be unacceptable to Rawls, even though presumably the latter would be stable.

Given this ambiguity one would do well to look elsewhere for the heart of Rawls' distinction between an overlapping consensus and a modus vivendi liberalism. The most telling difference lies in Rawls' belief that a political conception of justice based on an overlapping consensus is, while a modus vivendi is not, a moral conception (1987, 11).

Rawls seems to assume that the type of agreement reached by the Catholics and Protestants in the sixteenth century was not reached on moral grounds. But why should we assume that? Surely, the claim that it is better to accept civil peace at a lower level of social unity rather than continued civil war is itself a moral assertion. Of course, it is not a moral assertion in the Kantian-Rawlsian sense of "rational agents under the conditions of impartiality." But that should not be a problem for Rawls, since he has already conceded that a public conception of justice cannot be so grounded. The problem here is that Rawls seems to take for granted a strong moral-prudential distinction such that the virtue of collective prudence appears to be, at best, nonmoral. That is no doubt why even a well-designed constitutional system grounded in collective prudence is bound to appear as if it were not affirmed on moral grounds.

The advocate of the modus vivendi position should be embarrassed by being nonmoral only if being moral in the Kantian sense is possible, that is, only if she could speak moral Esperanto. To the extent that Rawls wants to keep his theory political rather than metaphysical, and thereby avoid the criticisms of Sandel and other communitarian criticisms of Kantian liberalism, he must adopt a modus vivendi position. But to the extent that he wants to avoid what he takes to be the pitfalls of a modus vivendi approach, he must resort to his Kantian conception of persons, making his theory metaphysical once again. Even Rawls is caught between the horns of the dilemma.

Stanley Hauerwas: A Pacifist/Sectarian Defense of Religious Toleration

In the first chapter I suggested that one way out of the dilemma of religious tolerance was to eschew completely the use of power. The central weakness of this position is that one would have to withdraw oneself or one's community to the margins of the larger society. If a community consistently and completely renounced the use of force or coercion, it could certainly be said of that community that it was truly tolerant of the actions and behavior of the individuals and groups that make up the larger society. And it certainly seems it could do so without resorting to indifference or skepticism about one's own beliefs. Traditionally this has been what has attracted many to the "sectarian," "peace," "anabaptist," or "Mennonite" churches.

The work of Stanley Hauerwas is most relevant in this regard. Over the past fifteen years or so he has urged Christians to surrender the transcendental search for universal foundations of morality. A people's normative frame of reference, he repeatedly insists, is dependent upon and "always gains its intelligibility from narratives" (1981, 115). "All significant moral claims," Hauerwas insists, "are historically derived and require narrative display" (1981, 99).

Taking a cue from Alasdair MacIntyre's *After Virtue*, Hauerwas writes that the "chaotic, fragmented world" of modernity accounts for the two dominant characteristics of recent ethical theory. The first is the "stress on freedom, autonomy and choice as the essence of the moral life." The second is the "attempt to secure a foundation for the moral life unfettered by the contingencies of our histories and communities." Hauerwas argues that the emotivism of contemporary culture stems from the uniquely modern idea that makes freedom itself the content of the moral life. "It matters not *what* we desire, but *that* we desire" (1983, 9). Logically correlative with the emotivism of modern culture is the modern search to find a foundation for ethics.

> Confronted by the fragmented character of our world, phi-
> losophers have undoubtedly tried to secure a high ground
> that can provide for security, certainty, and peace. It is a
> worthy effort, but one doomed to fail, for such ground lacks
> the ability to train our desires and direct our attention; to
> make us into moral people. (1983, 11)

Despite the enthusiasm of many religious thinkers for this search for a
foundation for morality, such a foundation, according to Hauerwas, "cannot
but make religious convictions morally secondary" (1983, 11).

> When the particularity of Christian convictions is made
> secondary to an alleged more fundamental "morality," we
> lose the means to be a peaceable people. For the attempt to
> secure peace through founding morality on rationality
> itself, or some other "inherent" human characteristic, ironi-
> cally underwrites coercion. If others refuse to accept my
> account of "rationality," it seems within my bounds to force
> them to be true to their "true" selves. (1983, 12)

The political institutions of liberal democracy are particularly subject to
Hauerwas' criticism. Hauerwas recognizes that some Christian ethicists
favorably interpret the secular nature of our liberal polity. Even though it
may not be a profound confession of the Lordship of God, the argument
goes, the government's acknowledgment of its incompetence in religion can
at least be brought forth as evidence of an acknowledgment that God limits
all earthly power (1981, 72, 84). Murray is correctly cited as an advocate of
this position (1981, 246 n. 4). However, in contrast to Murray's rather favorable assessment of liberal democracy, Hauerwas sees it less as a natural ally
of Christianity than as a temptation to compromise the distinctive features of
the Christian life.

Remarkably enough, Hauerwas challenges this quasi-positive assessment of the liberal polity to the extent that it is employed to justify Christian
political involvement. He argues that "Christian enthusiasm for the political
involvement offered by our secular polity has made us forget the church's
more profound political task," namely "challenging the moral presuppositions of our polity and society." Christians who look favorably on modern
liberal democracy have acquiesced, Hauerwas argues, in the liberal assumption that a just polity is possible even when the people are not just. One of

the more destructive results of this failure is that "the church has increasingly imitated in its own social life the politics of liberalism" (1981, 73). In
the words of one reviewer of Hauerwas' work, "The unacknowledged narrative of this [political] philosophy produces a people who value individual lib-
erties over the common good of communities" (Beckley 1982, 298). And that
includes the church.

Hauerwas has thus consistently leveled a standard communitarian
charge against liberalism. Liberalism's notions of autonomy and freedom
seep into the virtue-producing institutions of society, corrupt and weaken
them, and subvert the source of liberalism's own strength. Because the
church has been so involved in attempting to manage, control, or influence
public policy, it has failed to "encourage in its members virtues sufficient to
sustain their role as citizens," and thus has failed "our particular secular
polity" (1981, 74).

Recently, Hauerwas has narrowed his criticism of liberal democracy to
the more specific idea of "freedom of religion." He admits it is hard to be
against freedom of religion, but nevertheless argues that it has not been good
for church or society in America. His indictments are sweeping:

> [Freedom of religion] has tempted Christians in America to
> think that democracy is fundamentally neutral, and, per-
> haps, even friendly toward the church." (1991, 69-70)
>
> Because Christians have been so concerned to support
> the social and legal institutions that sustain freedom of reli-
> gion we failed to notice that we are no longer a people who
> make it interesting for a society to acknowledge our free-
> dom. Put differently, in such a context, believer and non-
> believer alike soon begin to think what matters is not
> whether our convictions are true but whether they are func-
> tional. (70-71)
>
> Freedom of religion is a temptation, albeit a subtle one.
> It tempts us as Christians to believe that we have been ren-
> dered safe by legal mechanisms. It is subtle because we
> believe that our task as Christians is to support the ethos
> necessary to maintaining that mechanism.... We thus
> become tolerant allowing our convictions to be relegated to
> the realm of the private. (71)
>
> The inability of Protestant churches in America to
> maintain any sense of authority over the lives of their mem-

bers is one of the most compelling signs that freedom of religion has resulted in the corruption of Christians who now believe they have the right religiously "to make up their own minds...." As a result neither Protestants nor Catholics have the capacity to stand as disciplined people capable of challenging the state. (88)

What should the response of the church be to this situation? In order to develop the "skills of interpretation and discrimination sufficient to help us recognize the possibilities and limits of our society," Christians, he argues, "must be *uninvolved* in the politics of our society and involved in the polity of the church" (1981, 74, emphasis mine).

At the core of Hauerwas' defense of Christian noninvolvement is the claim that under no circumstances should the church resort to "power," "coercion," or "violence," terms which he tends to take, rather uncritically, as synonymous. "The church is that community that trusts the power of truth and charity and thus does not depend on any further power. The world is exactly that which knows not the truth and thus must support its illusions with the power of the sword" (1977, 141).

To be faithful to the Christian story the church must follow Christ's example on how the world is served. It follows from this "that the most effective politics cannot be open to Christian participation exactly because the means required for effective politics are inappropriate to the kind of kingdom we serve as Christians (1977, 133). Thus,

> the Church must again establish that not all professions and roles of a society are open to the Christian's participation.... For the importance of participation can be appreciated only if there is significant non-participation on the part of Christians. (1977, 143)

The task of the church is to be a "paradigmatic community," one whose task is "to pioneer those institutions and practices that the wider society has not learned as forms of justice" (1977, 142). The church is to be a criteriological institution that embodies the truth that is charity as revealed in the person and work of Christ (1977, 143). The hallmark of the church, as distinct from the power of the state, "is its refusal to resort to violence to secure its own existence or to insure internal obedience. For as a community convinced of the truth, we refuse to trust any other power to compel than the truth itself" (1981, 85).

Hauerwas is forthright in challenging the idea that a Christian social ethic should try to make the world more peaceable and just. The church must not try to make the world the Kingdom of God, but simply be faithful to the Kingdom "by showing to the world what it means to be a community of peace" (1983, 103). The primary task of the church is to be (or become) a "community of character" that forms people capable of giving witness to the truth of their convictions. Particularly important is the virtue of patience, which provides a bulwark against the temptation of resorting to coercion, violence, and force in an unjust and sinful world. Such a resort is not an option for Christians. Even if it were to result in only a minimal justice it could not be justified (1983, 104–5).

Now, Hauerwas is quite sensitive to the charge that his position entails a "withdrawal ethic" (e.g., 1983, 102). But to the extent he consistently adheres to a position that rejects the use of force, power, or coercion, this is exactly what his social ethic implies. More importantly, it is here that Hauerwas is confronted with the dilemma. On the one hand, he urges the church to completely eschew the use of force, coercion, and violence. The use of coercive means even toward a minimally just end is ruled out of bounds. On the other hand, he balks when critics suggest that this implies a withdrawal ethic. The only way Hauerwas can escape such a criticism is to compromise on his sweeping rejection of Christian attempts to influence, manage or control society, through coercion, force or violence. But once his pacifism is compromised, the issue then centers around the extent to which Christians should "impose" their conception of the common good on others, which in turn raises the question of the extent to which Christians should tolerate other conceptions of the good within the polity they seek to influence. Hauerwas can escape the charge of advocating a "withdrawal ethic" only by situating himself between the horns of the dilemma of religious toleration, along with the rest of us.

Conclusion

I HAVE ESTABLISHED, I think, that a dilemma exists for a religious believer with strong convictions who wants to make a case for religious tolerance without compromising his convictions. I have also shown how John Courtney Murray exemplified that dilemma. Murray knew that religious liberty was the best bet, in fact the only bet, given the sociopolitical conditions of modernity. In that sense he can be called a liberal. But he was also clearly what Michael Walzer has called a "nervous liberal" (1979). For he was quite aware that the type of secularized lay state he advocated, one that was liberated from the directions of an ecclesiastical hierarchy, could all too easily slide down the slippery slope to a secularist state devoid of all spiritual values.

Murray would agree with Richard Neuhaus that the public square could not remain naked. And he would have shared Neuhaus' belief that absent theologically grounded convictions, secularist ideologies, and *ersatz* religions will inevitably clothe it.

But if the public square is to be clothed, the relevant questions become: Just how thick a garment will it be clothed with? And, of what material will it be made? We should not find it unreasonable that persons with deep religious convictions would not be satisfied with a thin garment if a thicker one could be had. That was the strength of the position of Murray's traditionalist Catholic antagonists.

Murray's dilemma has been captured nicely by one commentator who, after reflecting on Murray's work *On Religious Liberty*, suggested that he would be satisfied with the phrase "In God We Trust" as a public motto, but not with "In Father, Son and Holy Spirit We Trust (Whelan 1985, 370)." Although Murray was a deeply orthodox Trinitarian, I think that is right.

217

Murray was not comfortable with the Catholic triumphalism implicit in the latter phrase. But what is not clear is whether or not he, or anyone else, shouldn't take the latter if he could get it.

I have suggested throughout that the dilemma of religious toleration is a perennial one. Thus, it is not unique to the American situation. But it is highlighted here because at its founding, for the first time in history, a nation explicitly embraced the wonderful, yet conceptually ambiguous notion of *e pluribus unum*. Murray firmly embraced and loved the republic that held to that notion. But this placed him in the rather odd situation that we have explored in this book. Particularly toward the end of his career, Murray was forced to adopt an ambiguous posture on a number of conceptual problems.

But, in the end, Murray probably had no other choice. As Richard Neuhaus says in a chapter of *The Naked Public Square*, titled "The Morality of Compromise," "In a Democracy some issues are best fudged. Some questions cannot be pursued relentlessly to their logical end, except at the price of imperilling public discourse" (114). Neuhaus adds, "Fudging is anathema to the fanatic. That is one reason it is so hard to live with fanatics."

But fudging is not only anathema to fanatics; it is also anathema to academic philosophers and theologians as well, trained as they are to expose conceptual errors and clarify ambiguities even though it might be publicly unacceptable. Perhaps that's why it's so hard to live with philosophers and theologians.

Murray played both roles. As an academic theologian he sought conceptual clarity and analytic rigor. That's what made him such an able polemicist. But as a public philosopher he had to embrace "the morality of compromise." It is not an enviable position to be in. The academic theologian will be criticized for not being "relevant," while the public philosopher or theologian is susceptible to being criticized by the philosophers and theologians of compromising the truth. Some, in fact, do. But Murray didn't. And that, I think, is why the dilemma was particularly acute for him.

Murray was too good a Catholic theologian to try to speak moral Esperanto, but as an American he was forced into employing a simpler dialect of his own Roman Catholic language. One recent interpreter of Murray observed that when he addressed groups who were entirely Christian, Murray would speak of the need to create a "Christian culture" or a society founded on "Christian values." But when such groups included non-Christians, or when writing for American society as a whole, he would speak of creating a "spiritual culture" or a society founded upon the "*res sacrae*" (McElroy 1989, 200–1). The latter reflects the necessity for compromise in public discourse. Such banalities, however, are less than fulfilling for theologians and common folk rooted in richer traditions, for they come all too close to the type of watered-down civil religion Murray found unacceptable. But that, perhaps, is the dilemma a believer must learn to live with if he wishes to engage in public discourse in a pluralistic society.

Bibliography

The following bibliography relies greatly on J. Leon Hooper's exhaustive bibliography of Murray's work in *The Ethics of Discourse*. Those works referred to as "Murray Archives" are located in the Special Collections Room, Lauinger Library, Georgetown University, Washington, D.C. All references to WHTT refer to *We Hold These Truths*.

Works by Murray

Murray, John Courtney

1942   "Current Theology: Christian Co-operation." *Theological Studies* 3 (September): 413–31.

1943a   "Current Theology: Co-operation: Some Further Views." *Theological Studies* 4 (March): 100–11.

1943b   "Current Theology: Intercredal Co-operation: Its Theory and Its Organization." *Theological Studies* 4 (June): 267–86.

1945a   "On the Problem of Co-operation: Some Clarifications: Reply to Father P. H. Furfey." *The American Ecclesiastical Review* 112 (March): 194–214.

1945b   "Current Theology: Freedom of Religion." *Theological Studies* 6 (March): 85–113.

1945c   "Notes on the Theory of Religious Liberty." Memo to Archbishop Mooney, Murray Archives.

1945d   "Freedom of Religion, I: The Ethical Problem." *Theological Studies* 6
         (June): 229-86.

1945e   "The Real Woman Today." *America* 74 (November 3): 122-24.

1945f   "God's Word and Its Realization." *America* 74, supplement (December 8): xix-xxi.

1946a   "The Papal Allocution: Christmas." *America* 74 (January 5: 37-71.

1946b   Review of *Religious Liberty: An Inquiry,* by M. Searle Bates (New York:
         International Missionary Council, 1945). *Theological Studies* 7
         (March): 151-63.

1946c   "How Liberal Is Liberalism?" *America* 75 (April 6): 6-7.

1946d   "Operation University." *America* 75 (April 13): 28-29.

1946e   "Separation of Church and State." *America* 76 (December 7): 261-
         63.

1947a   "Admonition and Grace." Introduction and translation of *The
         Fathers of the Church: Writings of St. Augustine* 2:239-305. New York:
         Cima.

1947b   "Separation of Church and State: True and False Concepts." *America*
         76 (February 15): 541-45.

1947c   "The Court Upholds Religious Freedom." *America* 76 (March 8):
         628-30.

1948a   "Religious Liberty: The Concern of All." *America* 77 (February 7):
         513-16.

1948b   "Dr. Morrison and the First Amendment." *America* 78 (March 6):
         627-29; (March 20): 683-86.

1948c   "The Role of Faith in the Renovation of the World." *The Messenger of
         the Sacred Heart* 83 (March): 15-17.

1948d   "The Roman Catholic Church." *The Annals of the American Academy
         of Political and Social Science* 256 (March): 36-42.

1948e   "The Root of Faith: The Doctrine of M. J. Scheeben." *Theological
         Studies* 9 (March): 20-26.

1948f "Government Repression of Heresy." *Proceedings of the Third Annual Convention of the Catholic Theological Society of America*: 26-98.

1948g "St. Robert Bellarmine on the Indirect Power." *Theological Studies* 9 (December): 491-535.

1949a "On the Necessity for Not Believing: A Roman Catholic Interpretation." *The Yale Scientific Magazine* 23 (February): 11, 12, 22, 30, 32, 34.

1949b "Reversing the Secularistic Drift." *Thought* 24 (March): 36-46.

1949c Review of *Free Speech in Its Relation to Self-Government*, by Alexander Meikeljohn (New York: Harper and Brothers, 1948). *Georgetown Law Journal* 37 (May): 654-62.

1949d Review of *American Freedom and Catholic Power*, by Paul Blanshard (Boston: Beacon Press, 1949). *The Catholic Mind* 169 (June): 233-34.

1949e "Contemporary Orientations of Catholic Thought on Church and State in the Light of History." *Theological Studies* 10 (June): 177-234.

1949f "The Catholic Position: A Reply." *The American Mercury* 69 (September): 274-83; (November): 637-39.

1949g "Current Theology: On Religious Freedom." *Theological Studies* 10 (September): 409-32.

1949h "On the Idea of a College Religion Course." *Jesuit Educational Quarterly* (October): 79-86.

1949i "Law or Prepossessions." *Law and Contemporary Problems* 14 (Winter): 23-43.

1950a "The Natural Law." In *Great Expressions of Human Rights*, 69-104. Ed. Robert M. MacIver. New York: Harper. Later published with minor revisions as the final chapter of *WHTT*.

1950b "One Work of the One Church." *The Missionary Union of the Clergy Bulletin* 14 (March): 5-11.

1951a "Toward a Christian Humanism: Aspects of the Theology of Education." In *A Philosophical Symposium on American Higher Education*, 106-55. Ed. H. Guthrie and G. G. Walsh. New York: Fordham Press.

1951b   "Paul Blanshard and the New Nativism." *The Month*, New Series 5 (April): 214–25.

1951c   "The Problem of 'The Religion of the State.'" *The American Ecclesiastical Review* 124 (May): 327–52. Also published as "The Problem of State Religion," *Theological Studies* 12 (June 1951): 155–78.

1951d   "School and Christian Freedom." *National Catholic Educational Association Proceedings* 43 (August): 63–68.

1952a   "For the Freedom and Transcendence of the Church." *The American Ecclesiastical Review* 126 (January): 28–48.

1952b   "The Church and Totalitarian Democracy." *Theological Studies* 13 (December): 525–63.

1953a   "Leo XIII on Church and State: The General Structure of the Controversy." *Theological Studies* 13 (March): 1–30.

1953b   "Christian Humanism in America." *Social Order* 3 (May–June): 233–44. Edited and republished as chapter 8 of *WHTT*, "Is It Basket Weaving? The Question of Christian and Human Values," 175–96.

1953c   "Leo XIII: Separation of Church and State." *Theological Studies* 14 (June): 145–214.

1953d   "The Problem of Free Speech." *Philippine Studies* 1 (September): 107–24.

1954a   "On the Structure of the Church-State Problem." In *The Catholic Church in World Affairs*, 11–32. Ed. Waldemar Gurian and M. A. Fitzsimons.

1954b   "Leo XIII: Two Concepts of Government: Government and the Order of Culture." *Theological Studies* 15 (March): 1–33.

1954c   "The Problem of Pluralism in America." *Thought* 24: Summer: 164–208. Later published as chapters 1 and 2, "E Pluribus Unum: The American Consensus" and "Civil Unity and Religious Integrity: The Articles of Peace," in *WHTT*, 27–78.

1955a   "Leo XIII and Pius XII: Government and the Order of Religion." Unpublished article, Murray Archives.

1955b   "Special Catholic Challenges." *Life* 39–40 (December 26): 144–46.

1955c   "Catholics in America—A Creative Minority—Yes or No?" *The Catholic Mind* 57 (October): 590-97.

1956a   "Unity of Truth." *Commonweal* 63 (January 13). Later published as "The Catholic University in a Pluralistic Society," in *The Catholic Mind* 57 (May-June): 253-60.

1956b   "St. Ignatius and the End of Modernity." In *The Ignatian Year at Georgetown*. Washington, D.C.: Georgetown University Press.

1956c   "The School Problem in Mid-Twentieth Century." In *The Role of the Independent School in American Democracy*, 1-16. Ed. William H. Conley. Later published as chapter 6, "Is It Justice?: The School Question Today," in *WHTT*, 143-54.

1956d   "Questions of Striking a Right Balance: Literature and Censorship." *Books on Trial* 14 (June-July): 393-95. Later published as chapter 7, "Should There Be a Law?: The Question of Censorship," in *WHTT*, 155-74.

1956e   "Freedom, Responsibility and Law." *The Catholic Lawyer* 2 (July): 214-20.

1956f   "The Bad Arguments Intelligent People Make." *America* 117 (November 3): 120-23.

1957a   "The Christian Idea of Education." In *The Christian Idea of Education*, 152-63. Ed. Edmund Fuller. New Haven: Yale University Press.

1957b   "Church, State and Political Freedom." *Modern Age: A Conservative Review* 1 (Fall): 134-45. Later published as chapter 9, "Are There Two or One?: The Question of the Future of Freedom," in *WHTT*, 197-217.

1958a   "Church and State: The Structure of the Argument." Murray Archives.

1958b   "America's Four Conspiracies." In *Religion in America*, 12-41. Ed. John Cogley. New York: Meridian Books. Later published as "Introduction: The Civilization of the Pluralistic Society," in *WHTT*, 5-24.

1958c   *Foreign Policy and the Free Society* (with Walter Millis). New York: Oceana Publications. Later published as chapter 10, "Doctrine and Policy in Communist Imperialism: The Problem of Security and Risk," in *WHTT*, 221-47.

1958d   "Morality and Modern War." A Paper delivered before the Catholic Association for International Peace, October 28, 1958. Later published as chapter 11, "The Uses of a Doctrine on the Uses of Force: War as a Moral Problem" in *WHTT*, 249-273.

1958e   "The Making of a Pluralist Society." *Religious Education* 53 (November-December): 521-28. Later published as chapter 5, "Creeds at War Intelligibly: Pluralism and the University," in *WHTT*, 125-52.

1958f   "How to Think (Theologically) about War and Peace." *Catholic Messenger* 76 (December): 7-8.

1959a   "*Unica Status Religio.*" Murray Archives.

1959b   "The Liberal Arts College and the Contemporary Climate of Opinion." Murray Archives.

1960a   *We Hold These Truths: Catholic Reflections on the American Proposition.* New York: Sheed and Ward.

1960b   "Morality and Foreign Policy, Part I." *America* 102 (March 26): 729-32.

1960c   "Morality and Foreign Policy, Part II." *America* 102 (March 26): 764-67. Later published as chapter 12, "The Doctrine Is Dead: The Problem of the Moral Vacuum," in *WHTT*, 273-94.

1960d   "On Raising the Religious Issue." *America* 102 (September 24): 702.

1961a   "Hopes and Misgivings for Dialogue." *America* 104 (January 14): 456-60.

1961b   "The American Proposition." *Commonweal* 73 (January 20): 433-35.

1962a   "The Return to Tribalism." *The Catholic Mind* 60: 5-12. Also published as "What Can Unite a Religiously Divided Nation?" *Catholic Messenger* 79 (April 27): 1,4; (May 4, 1961): 4.

1962b   "Federal Aid to Church Related Schools." *Yale Political Review* 1:16, 29-31.

1962c   "On the Structure of the Problem of God." *Theological Studies* 23 (March): 1-26.

1963a   "The Schema on Religious Freedom: Critical Comments." Murray Archives.

1963b   "Remarks on the Schema on Religious Liberty." Murray Archives.

1963c   Foreword to *American Pluralism and the Catholic Conscience*, by Richard J. Regan, S.J. New York: The Macmillan Publishing Company.

1963d   Foreword to *Religious Liberty and the American Presidency: A Study in Church-State Relations*, by Patricia Barrett. New York: Herder.

1963e   *The Elite and The Electorate: Is Government by the People Possible?*, 7-8. Comments to an article by J. William Fulbright. Published by the Center for the Study of Democratic Institutions.

1963f   "Things Old and New in 'Pacem in Terris.'" *America* 107 (April 27): 612-14.

1963g   "Good Pope John: A Theologian's Tribute." *America* 108 (June 15): 854-55.

1963h   "Making the News Good News!" *Interracial Review* 36 (July): 34-35, 130-31.

1963i   "The Church and the Council." *America* 104 (October 19): 451-53.

1963j   "On Religious Liberty." *America* 109 (November): 704-6.

1964a   "The Nature of Theology." Murray Archives.

1964b   "Commentary on the Declaration." To Archbishop Koenig. Murray Archives.

1964c   "On the Future of Humanistic Education." In *Humanistic Education and Western Civilization*, 231-47. Ed. Arthur A. Cohen. New York: Holt, Rinehart, and Winston.

1964d   "The Social Function of the Press." *Journalistes Catholiques* 12 (Janvier-Avril): 8-12.

1964e   "Today and Tomorrow: Conversation at the Council: John Courtney Murray, Hans Kueng, Gustave Weigel, Godfrey Diekmann, and Vincent Yzermans." *American Benedictine Review* 15 (September): 341–51.

1964f   "The Problem of Religious Freedom." *Theological Studies* 25 (December): 503–75. Later published as *The Problem of Religious Freedom*, Westminster, Md.: The Newman Press, 1965.

1964g   "The Problem of Mr. Rawls' Problem." In *Law and Philosophy*, 29–34. Ed. Sidney Hook. New York: New York University Press.

1965a   Memo to Cushing on Contraception Legislation. Undated. Murray Archives.

1965b   Foreword to *Freedom and Man*, 11–16. Ed. John Courtney Murray. New York: P.J. Kennedy.

1965c   "Religious Freedom." In *Freedom and Man*, 131–40. Ed. John Courtney Murray. New York: P.J. Kennedy.

1965d   "This Matter of Religious Freedom." *America* 112 (January 9): 40–43.

1966a   "The Declaration on Religious Freedom." In *Vatican II: An Interfaith Appraisal*, 565–76, 577–85. Ed. John H. Miller. Notre Dame: Association Press.

1966b   "The Declaration on Religious Freedom." In *War, Poverty, Freedom: The Christian Response*, 3–16. Concilium 15. New York: Paulist Press. Reprinted in *Declaration on Religious Freedom*. Ed. Thomas F. Stransky. New York: Paulist Press, 1967.

1966c   "The Declaration on Religious Freedom." *A Moment in Its Legislative History.*" In *Religious Liberty: An End and a Beginning*, 15–42. Ed. John Courtney Murray. New York: Macmillan and Company.

1966d   "Religious Freedom." In *The Documents of Vatican II*, Introduction, 673–74, and text with commentary, 674–98. Ed. Walter M. Abbot and Joseph Gallagher. New York: Fordham University Press.

1966e   "The Vatican Declaration on Religious Freedom." In *The University in the American Experience*. New York: Fordham University Press.

1966f   "The Status of the Nicene Creed as Dogma." *Chicago Studies: An Archdiocesan Review* 5 (Spring): 65-80.

1966g   "The Declaration on Religious Freedom: Its Deeper Significance." *America* 114 (April 23): 592-93.

1966h   "The Issue of Church and State at Vatican II." *Theological Studies* 27 (December): 580-606.

1966i   "Freedom, Authority, Community." *America* 115 (December 3): 734-41.

1967a   "Declaration on Religious Freedom." In *American Participation at the Second Vatican Council*, 668-76. Ed. Vincent A. Yzermans. New York: Sheed and Ward.

1967b   "A Will to Community." In *Theological Freedom and Social Responsibility*, 111-16. Ed. Stephen F. Bayne, Jr. New York: Seabury Press. Also published as "We Held These Truths," *The National Catholic Reporter* 3 (August 23, 1967): 3.

1967c   Review of *Academic Freedom and the Catholic University*, by Edward Manier and John W. Houch (South Bend: Fides Publishers, 1967) *AAUP Bulletin* 53: 339-42.

1967d   "The Death of God." Address at the University of Connecticut, January 10. Murray Archives.

1967e   "Religious Liberty and Development of Doctrine." *The Catholic World* 204 (February): 277-83.

1967f   "Our Response to the Ecumenical Revolution." *Religious Education* 42 (March-April): 91-92.

1967g   Review of *The Garden and the Wilderness: Religion and Government in American Constitutional History*, by M. D. Howe (Chicago: University of Chicago Press, 1965), *Yale Law Review* 76 (April): 1030-35.

1967h   "Freedom in the Age of Renewal." *American Benedictine Review* 18 (September): 319-24.

Other Sources and Secondary Literature

Aristotle

1959   *Politics*. Trans. H. Rackham. Cambridge: Harvard University Press.

Aquinas, Thomas

1975   *Summa Theologiæ*. 61 vols. London: Blackfriars.

Bates, M. Searle

1945   *Religious Liberty: An Inquiry*. New York: International Missionary
        Society.

Baum, Gregory

1966   "Declaration on Religious Freedom—Development of Its Doctrinal
        Basis." *The Ecumenist* 4 (September–October): 121-26.

Beckley, Harlan

1982   "A Social Ethic Emphasizing Family and Church." *Interpretation* 36:
        298-301.

Bennett, John Coleman

1958   *Christians and the State*. New York: Charles Scribner's Sons.

1965   "A Protestant Views Religious Liberty." *Catholic World* 201 (Septem-
        ber 1965): 362-68.

Berger, Peter

1967   *The Sacred Canopy*. Garden City, N.Y.: Paulist Press.

Bevenot, Maurice

1954   "Thesis and Hypothesis." *Theological Studies* 15 (September): 440-
        46.

Bigongiari, Dino, ed.

1953   *The Political Ideas of St. Thomas Aquinas.* New York: Hafner Publishing Company.

Blanshard, Paul

1951   *American Freedom and Catholic Power.* Boston: Beacon Press.

Boonin, Leonard G.

1969   "Man and Society." In *Voluntary Associations.* Ed. J. Roland Pinnock and John Chapman. New York: Atherton Press.

Bowie, W. Russell

1949   "The Catholic Position." *The American Mercury* 69 (September): 261–73; (November): 637.

Bradley, Gerard V.

1992   "Beyond Murray's Articles of Peace and of Faith." In *John Courtney Murray and the American Civil Conversation.* Ed. Kenneth Grasso and Robert P. Hunt. Grand Rapids: William B. Eerdmans Publishing Company: 181–204.

Brink, David

1989   "Moral Realism Defended." In *Ethical Theory: Classical and Contemporary Readings.* Ed. Louis P. Pojman. Belmont, Ca.: Wadsworth Publishing Company: 42–55.

Brown, Robert McAfee, and Gustave Weigel

1960   *An American Dialogue: A Protestant Looks at Catholicism and a Catholic Looks at Protestantism.* Garden City, N.Y.: Anchor Books.

Burgess, Faith E. R.

1971   *Ecclesia et Status: The Relationship Between Church and State According to John Courtney Murray, S.J.* Duesseldorf: Stehle.

Burghardt, Walter J.

1985   "Who Chilled the Beaujolais?" *America* 153 (November 30): 360-63.

Canavan, Francis J.

1979   "The Dilemma of Liberal Pluralism." *The Human Life Review* 5 (Summer).

1982   "Murray on Vatican II's Declaration on Religious Freedom." *Communio* 9 (Winter): 404-5.

Carillo De Albornoz, A. F.

1959   *Roman Catholicism and Religious Liberty.* Geneva: World Council of Churches.

1963   *The Basis of Religious Liberty.* New York: Association Press.

1965   "Religious Freedom: Intrinsic or Fortuitous?" *Christian Century* 82 (September 15): 1122-26.

1967   *Religious Liberty.* Trans. John Drury. New York: Sheed and Ward.

Carnell, Edward J.

1960   *The Theology of Reinhold Niebuhr.* Grand Rapids: Eerdmans.

Cassirer, Ernst

1946   *The Myth of the State.* New Haven: Yale University Press.

Cogley, John

1956   "In Praise of Father Murray." *Commonweal* 65 (December 7): 253.

1973   *Catholic America.* New York: Dial Press.

Coleman, John A.

1976   "Vision and Praxis in American Theology: Orestes Brownson, John A. Ryan, and John Courtney Murray." *Theological Studies* 37 (March): 3-40.

1978   "A Theological Link between Religious Liberty and Mediating Structures." In *Church, State, and Public Policy: The New Shape of the Church-State Debate*. Ed. Jay Mechling. Washington, D.C.: American Enterprise Institute for Public Policy Research.

1979   "A Possible Role for Biblical Religion in Public Life." *Theological Studies* 37 (December): 705.

1982   *An American Strategic Theology*. New York: Paulist Press.

Connell, Francis J.

1941   "Catholics and Interfaith Groups." *The American Ecclesiastical Review* 105 (November): 336-53.

1943   *Freedom of Worship: The Catholic Position*. New York: Paulist Press.

1948   "Christ, the King of Civil Rulers." *American Ecclesiastical Review* 119 (October): 244-53.

1949   "Discussion of 'Governmental Repression of Heresy.'" *Proceedings of the Catholic Theological Society of America* 3 (March): 98-101.

1951   "The Theory of Lay State," *American Ecclesiastical Review*, 125 (July): 7-18

1952   "Reply to Father Murray," *American Ecclesiastical Review* 126 (January): 49-59.

Copleston, F. C.

1953   *Medieval Philosophy*. New York: Harper and Row.

Cord, Robert

1982   *Separation of Church and State: Historical Fact and Current Fiction*. New York: Lambeth Press.

Cox, John F.

1943   *A Thomistic Analysis of the Social Order*. Washington, D.C.: The Catholic University of America Press.

Crick, Bernard

1971   "Toleration and Tolerance in Theory and Practice." In *Government and Opposition* 6: 144–71.

Cuddihy, John Murray

1979   *No Offense: Civil Religion and Protestant Taste.* New York: Seabury Press.

Curran, Charles E.

1982   "John Courtney Murray." In *American Catholic Social Ethics.* South Bend: University of Notre Dame Press.

Dancy, John

1988   "In Praise of Intolerance." Unpublished paper delivered at the Philosophy Colloquium at the University of Pittsburgh.

D'Arcy, Eric

1961   *Conscience and Its Right to Freedom.* New York: Sheed and Ward.

Dawson, Christopher

1938   *Beyond Politics.* New York: Sheed and Ward.

De Smedt, Emile Joseph

1964   "Religious Liberty." In *Council Speeches of Vatican II.* Edited by Hans Kung, Yves Congar, and Daniel O'Hanlon. Glen Rock, N.J.: Deus Books.

Donagan, Alan

1977   *The Theory of Morality.* Chicago: University of Chicago Press.

Dooyeweerd, Herman

1958   *A New Critique of Theoretical Thought.* 4 vols. Amsterdam: H.J. Paris; and Philadelphia: Presbyterian and Reformed Publishing Company.

Dworkin, Ronald

1978   *Taking Rights Seriously.* Cambridge: Harvard University Press.

1985   "Liberalism." In *A Matter of Principle.* Cambridge, Mass.: Harvard University Press.

Fenton, Joseph Clifford

1946a "Time and Pope Leo." *American Ecclesiastical Review* 114 (May): 369–75.

1946b "The Theology of Church and State." *Proceedings of the Catholic Theological Society of America* 2 (June): 15–46.

1950   "The Relation of the Christian State to the Catholic Church according to the *Pontificale Romanum.*" *American Ecclesiastical Review* 123 (September): 214–18.

1951   "The Status of a Controversy." *American Ecclesiastical Review* 124 (June): 451–58.

1952   "Principles Underlying Traditional Church-State Doctrine." *American Ecclesiastical Review* 126 (June): 452–62.

1954a "The Teachings of *Ci Riesce.*" *American Ecclesiastical Review* 130 (February): 114–23.

1954b "Toleration and the Church-State Controversy." *American Ecclesiastical Review* 130 (May): 330–43.

1961   "Doctrine and Tactic in Catholic Pronouncements on Church and State." *American Ecclesiastical Review* 145 (October): 266–71.

Finnis, John

1980   *Natural Law and Natural Rights.* Oxford: Oxford University Press.

Flew, Anthony

1976   *The Presumption of Atheism.* New York: Harper and Row.

Fox, Richard W.

1985   *Reinhold Niebuhr: A Biography.* New York: Pantheon Books.

Giannella, Donald A.

1967   "Religious Liberty, Nonestablishment, and Doctrinal Development."
        Harvard Law Review 80 (May): 1381–1431.

Goerner, Edward A.

1965   *Peter and Caesar: Political Authority and the Catholic Church.* New
        York: Herder and Herder.

Hayek, Friedrich

1976   *Law, Legislation, and Liberty.* 3 vols. Chicago: University of Chicago
        Press.

Harrison, Geoffrey

1982   "Relativism and Tolerance." In *Relativism: Cognitive and Moral,* 229–
        43. Ed. Michael Krausz and Jack W. Meiland. South Bend: Univer-
        sity of Notre Dame Press.

Hauerwas, Stanley

1977   *Truthfulness and Tragedy.* South Bend: University of Notre Dame
        Press.

1981   *A Community of Character: Toward a Constructive Christian Social
        Ethic.* South Bend: University of Notre Dame Press.

1983   *The Peaceable Kingdom: A Primer in Christian Ethics.* South Bend:
        University of Notre Dame Press.

1991   "The Politics of Freedom: Why Freedom of Religion Is a Subtle
        Temptation." In *After Christendom.* Nashville: Abington Press.

Hehir, J. Bryan

1976 "Issues in Church and State: A Catholic Perspective." In *Issues in Church and State: Proceedings of a Dialogue between Catholics and Baptists*, 81-95. Ed. Claude U. Broach. Winston-Salem, N.C.: Ecumenical Institute.

1985 "The Unfinished Agenda." *America* (November): 386-87, 392.

Henry, Carl F. H.

1976 *God, Revelation and Authority: God Who Speaks and Shows*. Vol 1. Waco: Word Books.

Hock, Raymond Anthony

1964 "The Pluralism of John Courtney Murray, S.J., and its Relationship to Education." Ph.D. dissertation: Stanford University.

Hoitenga, Dewey J.

1991 *Faith and Reason from Plato to Plantinga: An Introduction to Reformed Epistemology*. Albany, N.Y.: State University of New York Press.

Hollenbach, David

1976 "Public Theology in America: Some Questions for Catholicism after John Courtney Murray." *Theological Studies* 37 (June): 290-303.

1985 "The Growing End of an Argument." *America* 153 (November): 362-66.

Hollenbach, David, Robin W. Lovin, John Coleman, J. Bryan Hehir

1979 "Theology and Philosophy in Public: A Symposium on John Courtney Murray's Unfinished Agenda." *Theological Studies* 40 (December): 700-15.

Hooper, J. Leon

1986 *The Ethics of Discourse: The Social Philosophy of John Courtney Murray*. Washington, D.C.: Georgetown University Press.

Horton, John

1985   "Toleration, Morality and Harm." In *Aspects of Toleration*, 113-135.
        Ed. Susan Mendus and John Horton. New York and London: Meth-
        uen.

Hunt, Robert P., and Kenneth L. Grasso, Eds.

1992   *John Courtney Murray and the American Civil Conversation*. Grand
        Rapids: William B. Eerdmans Publishing Company.

John XXIII

1963   *Pacem in Terris*. Glen Rock, N.J.: Paulist Press.

Johnson, F. Ernest

1944   "Religious Liberty." *Christendom* 9: 181-94.

Kilcullen, John

1988   *Sincerity and Truth: Essays on Arnould, Bayle and Toleration*. New
        York: Oxford University Press.

Kossel, Clifford George

1984   "Religious Freedom and the Church: J. C. Murray." *Communio* 11
        (Spring): 60-74.

Kraynak, Robert P.

1980   "John Locke: From Absolutism to Toleration." *The American Political
        Science Review* 74 (March): 53-69.

Langon, John

1986   "Prudence." In *The Westminster Dictionary of Christian Ethics*, 514-
        15. Eds. James F. Childress and John Macquarrie. Philadelphia: The
        Westminster Press.

Larmore, Charles E.

1987   *Patterns of Moral Complexity.* New York: Cambridge University Press.

Lawler, Peter Augustine

1982   "Natural Law and the American Regime: Murray's *We Hold These Truths.*" *Communio* 9 (Winter): 368-88.

Leff, Gordon

1958   *Medieval Thought: St. Augustine to Ockham.* Baltimore: Penguin Books.

Leo XIII

1903   *Great Encyclicals of Leo XIII.* New York: Benzinger Brothers.

Lindbeck, George

1961   "John Courtney Murray, S.J.: An Evaluation." *Christianity and Crisis* 21 (November 27): 213-16.

Locke, John

1955   *A Letter Concerning Toleration.* Indianapolis: Bobbs-Merrill.

Love, Thomas T.

1965   *John Courtney Murray: Contemporary Church-State Theory.* New York: Doubleday and Company.

1966   "The Problem of Religious Freedom." *Journal of Church and State* 8 (Autumn): 475-77.

Lukes, Steven

1971   "Social and Moral Tolerance." In *Government and Opposition* 6: 224-28.

McBrien, Richard

1987   *Caesar's Coin: Religion and Politics in America.* New York: The Macmillan Publishing Company.

McClendon, James and James Smith

1978   *Understanding Religious Conviction.* Notre Dame, Ind.: University of Notre Dame Press.

McElroy, Robert W.

1989   *The Search for an American Public Theology: The Contribution of John Courtney Murray.* New York: Paulist Press.

MacIntyre, Alasdair

1981   *After Virtue.* South Bend: University of Notre Dame Press.

1988   *Whose Justice? Which Rationality?* South Bend: University of Notre Dame Press.

Manus, William E.

1985   "Memories of Murray." *America* 153 (November): 366-68.

Marcuse, Herbert

1965   "Repressive Tolerance." In *A Critique of Pure Tolerance,* 81-123. Boston: Beacon Press.

Maritain, Jacques

1951   *Man and the State.* Chicago: University of Chicago Press.

Mechling, Jay, ed.

1978   *Church, State, and Public Policy: The New Shape of the Church-State Debate.* Washington, D.C.: American Enterprise Institute for Public Policy Research.

Mendus, Susan, and John Horton, eds.

1985   *Aspects of Toleration*. London and New York: Meuthen.

Mendus, Susan and David Edwards, eds.

1987   *On Toleration*. Oxford and New York: Oxford University Press.

Mendus, Susan, ed.

1988   *Justifying Toleration: Conceptual and Historical Perspectives*. Cambridge: Cambridge University Press.

Mill, J. S.

1972   *Utilitarianism. On Liberty. Representative Government*. London: Dent.

Miller, William Lee

1987   *The First Liberty: Religion and the American Republic*. New York: Alfred A. Knopf.

Moody, Joseph N.

1961   "Leo XIII and the Social Crisis." In *Leo XIII and the Modern World*. Ed. Edward T. Gargan. New York: Sheed and Ward.

Morrison, Charles Clayton

1947a   "Reply to a Taunt." *Christian Century* 64 (November 19): 1391-93.

1947b   "The Meaning of 'Separation'." *Christian Century* 64 (November 26): 1447-48.

1947c   "Getting Down to Cases." *Christian Century* 64 (December 10): 1512-14.

Nagel, Thomas

1987   "Moral Conflict and Political Legitimacy." *Philosophy and Public Affairs* 16 (Summer): 215-40.

Nash, Ronald

1988   *Faith and Reason: Searching for a Rational Faith*. Grand Rapids: Zondervan Press.

Neuhaus, Richard John

1984   *The Naked Public Square*. New York: Doubleday and Company.

Newman, Jay

1982   *Foundations of Religious Tolerance*. Toronto: University of Toronto Press.

Nicholson, Peter P.

1985   "Toleration as a Moral Ideal." In *Aspects of Toleration*, 158–73. Ed. John Horton and Susan Mendus. London and New York: Methuen.

Niebuhr, Reinhold

1932   *Moral Man and Immoral Society*. New York: Charles Scribner's Sons.

1935   *An Interpretation of Christian Ethics*. New York: Harper and Brothers.

1941   *The Nature and Destiny of Man*. 2 vols. New York: Charles Scribner's Sons.

1944   *The Children of Light and the Children of Darkness: A Vindication of Democracy and a Critique of its Traditional Defense*. New York: Charles Scribner's Sons.

Nisbet, Robert

1973   *The Social Philosophers: Community and Conflict in Western Thought*. New York: Thomas Y. Crowell Company.

Novak, Michael

1985   "Economic Rights: The Servile State." *Catholicism in Crisis* 10: 8–15.

Nozick, Robert

1974   *Anarchy, State, and Utopia.* New York: Basic Books.

Oakeshott, Michael

1975   *On Human Conduct.* Oxford: Clarendon Press.

O'Collins, Gerald S.

1984   "Murray and Ottaviani." *America* 151 (November): 287-88.

Ottaviani, Alfredo Cardinal

1953   "Church and State: Some Present Problems in Light of the Teach-
        ings of Pope Pius XII." *The American Ecclesiastical Review* 128 (May):
        321-34.

Pavan, Pietro

1965   "The Right to Religious Freedom in the Conciliar Declaration." In
        Religious Freedom, 37-52. Concilium 18. New York: Paulist Press.

Pelotte, Donald E.

1976   *John Courtney Murray: Theologian in Conflict.* New York: Paulist
        Press.

Plantinga, Alvin

1982   "Rationality and Religious Belief." In *Contemporary Philosophy of
        Religion*, 255-77. Ed. Steven M. Cahn and David Shatz. New York:
        Oxford University Press.

1982b   "How To Be An Anti-Realist." *Proceedings and Addresses of the Ameri-
        can Philosophical Association* 56, 1 (September 1982): 47-70.

1983   "Reason and Belief in God." In *Faith and Rationality: Reason and
        Belief in God.* Ed. Alvin Plantinga and Nicholas Wolterstorff. Notre
        Dame: University of Notre Dame Press.

Pribilla, Max

1950   "Dogmatic Intolerance and Civil Toleration." *The Month*, New Series
        IV (October): 252-60.

Protestants and Other Americans United

1948   "Separation of Church and State: A Manifesto by Protestants and
        Other Americans United." *Christian Century* 65 (January 21): 79-82.

Rawls, John

1971   *A Theory of Justice*. Cambridge: Harvard University Press.

1980   "Kantian Constructivism in Moral Theory. The John Dewey Lec-
        tures." *Journal of Philosophy* 77 (September): 515-72.

1982   "Social Unity and Primary Goods." In *Utilitarianism and Beyond*.
        Cambridge: Cambridge University Press.

1985   "Justice as Fairness: Political not Metaphysical." *Philosophy and
        Public Affairs* 14: 223-51.

1987   "The Idea of an Overlapping Consensus." *Oxford Journal of Legal
        Studies* 7: 1-25.

1988   "The Priority of Right and Ideas of the Good." *Philosophy and Public
        Affairs* 17: 251-76.

Regan, Richard

1963   *American Pluralism and the Catholic Conscience*. New York: The Mac-
        millan Publishing Company.

1967   *Conflict and Consensus*. New York: The Macmillan Publishing Com-
        pany.

1986   *The Moral Dimensions of Politics*. New York: Oxford University Press.

Rielly, J. E.

1961   "Contemporary Catholic Thought on Church and State: An Analysis
        of the Work of Jacques Maritain and John Courtney Murray." Ph.D.
        dissertation, Harvard University.

Rohr, John A.

1966   "Murray and the Critiques." *Continuum* 4 (Spring): 734-42.

1978   "John Courtney Murray's Theology of Our Founding Fathers' 'Faith': Freedom." In *Christian Spirituality in the United States: Independence and Interdependence*, 1-30. Ed. Francis A. Eigo. Villanova, Pa.: Villanova University Press.

1985   "John Courtney Murray and the Pastoral Letter." *America* 153 (November 30): 373-79.

Rommen, Heinrich

1945   *The State in Catholic Thought: A Treatise on Political Philosophy.* St. Louis: Herder.

1950   "Church and State." *The Review of Politics* 12: 321-40.

Rorty, Richard

1979   *Philosophy and the Mirror of Nature.* Princeton: Princeton University Press.

1987   "The Priority of Democracy to Philosophy." In *The Virginia Statute for Religious Freedom.* Ed. M. Peterson and R. Vaughn. New York: Cambridge University Press.

Runner, H. Evan

1974   *Scriptural Religion and Political Task.* Second revised edition. Toronto: Wedge Publishing.

Ryan, John A., and Moorhouse F. X. Millar

1922   *The State and the Church.* New York: The Macmillan Publishing Company.

Ryan, John A., and Francis J. Boland

1940   *Catholic Principles of Politics.* New York: The Macmillan Publishing Company.

Sandel, Michael

1982   *Liberalism and the Limits of Justice*. Cambridge: Cambridge University Press.

1984   "The Procedural Republic and the Unencumbered Self." *Political Theory* 12, 80-91.

Schall, James V.

1987   *Reason, Revelation, and the Foundations of Political Philosophy*. Baton Rouge: Louisiana State University Press.

Schuck, Michael J.

1991   "John Courtney Murray's Problematic Interpretations of Leo XIII and the American Founders." *The Thomist* 55, 4 (October), 595-612.

Segers, Mary C.

1992   "Murray, American Pluralism and the Abortion Controversy." In *John Courtney Murray and the American Civil Conversation*. Ed. Robert P. Hunt and Kenneth L. Grasso. Grand Rapids, Mich.: W. B. Eerdmans Publishing Company.

Shea, George W.

1950   "Catholic Doctrine and 'The Religion of the State'." *American Ecclesiastical Review* 123 (September): 161-74.

1951   "Catholic Orientations on Church and State." *American Ecclesiastical Review* 125: 405-16.

Skillen, James

1974   "The Development of Calvinistic Political Thought in the Netherlands, with Special Reference to the Thought of Herman Dooyeweerd." Ph.D. dissertation, Duke University.

Skinner, Quentin

1978   *The Foundations of Modern Political Thought.* 2 vols. Cambridge: Cambridge University Press, 1978.

Smith, Elwyn A.

1972   *Religious Liberty in the United States: The Development of Church-State Thought since the Revolutionary Era.* Philadelphia: Fortress Press.

Smith, G. W.

1988   "Dissent, Toleration, and Civil Rights in Communism." In *Justifying Toleration,* 199-221. Ed. Susan Mendus. Cambridge: Cambridge University Press.

Spragens, Thomas A., Jr.

1981   *The Irony of Liberal Reason.* Chicago: University of Chicago Press.

Stackhouse, Max

1984   *Creeds, Society and Human Rights: A Study in Three Cultures.* Grand Rapids: Eerdmans.

Stout, Jeffrey

1981   *The Flight from Authority.* Notre Dame: University of Notre Dame Press.

1988   *Ethics after Babel: The Languages of Morals and Their Discontents.* Boston: Beacon Press.

Stransky, Thomas F.

1967   Vatican Council (Second, 1962-65) *Declaration on Religious Freedom of Vatican Council II.* Promulgated by Pope Paul VI, December 7, 1965. Commentary by Thomas F. Stransky. New York: Paulist.

Sturzo, Luigi

1939   *Church and State.* New York: Longmans, Green and Company.

Taylor, Charles

1988   "Religion in a Free Society." Unpublished paper delivered at the National Symposium on the First Amendment Religious Liberty Clauses and American Public Life, sponsored by the Williamsburg Charter Foundation, Charlottesville, Virginia, on April 11-13, 1988.

Tinder, Glenn

1975   *Tolerance: Toward a New Civility.* Amherst: University of Massachusetts Press.

Tinelly, J. T.

1961   "The Challenge of John Courtney Murray: Can an American Public Philosophy be Stated?" *Catholic Lawyer* 7: 270-96.

Ullmann, Walter

1965   *A History of Political Thought: The Middle Ages.* Baltimore: Penguin Books.

Unger, Roberto Mangabeira

1975   *Knowledge and Politics.* New York: The Free Press.

Walzer, Michael

1979   "Nervous Liberals." *New York Review of Books* 26 (October 11).

1984   "Liberalism and the Art of Separation." *Political Theory* 12 (August): 315-30.

Weber, Paul J.

1982   "James Madison and Religious Equality: The Perfect Separation." *The Review of Politics* 44: 163-86.

1986   "Religious Interest Groups, Policymaking, and the Constitution." In *The Political Role of Religion in the United States.* Boulder and London: Westview Press.

Weigel, George

1985   "John Courtney Murray and the American Proposition." *Catholicism in Crisis* 3 (November): 8-13.

1986a   "John Courtney Murray and the Catholic Human Rights Revolution." *This World* 15 (Fall): 14-27.

1986b   *Tranquillitas Ordinis*. New York: Oxford University Press.

1988   "Religious Freedom: The First Human Right." *This World* 21 (Spring): 31-45.

1989   *Catholicism and the Renewal of American Democracy*. New York: Paulist Press.

Weigel, Gustave

1952   "The Church and the Democratic State." *Thought* 27 (Summer): 164-84.

Whelan, Charles

1985   "The Enduring Problem of Religious Liberty." *America* 153 (November 30): 368-72.

Will, George

1983   *Statecraft as Soulcraft*. New York: Simon and Schuster.

Williams, Bernard

1982   "An Inconsistent Form of Relativism." In *Relativism: Cognitive and Moral*, 171-74. Ed. Michael Krausz and Jack W. Meiland. South Bend: University of Notre Dame Press.

Wills, Garry

1972   *Bare Ruined Choirs: Doubt, Prophecy, and Radical Religion*. Garden City, N.Y.: Doubleday and Company.

Wogaman, J. Philip

1967   *Protestant Faith and Religious Liberty.* Nashville: Abingdon Press.

1986   "Persecution and Toleration." In *The Westminster Dictionary of Christian Ethics*, 464-68. Ed. James F. Childress and John Macquarrie. Philadelphia: The Westminster Press.

Wolf, Donald J.

1968   *Toward Consensus: Catholic-Protestant Interpretations of Church and State.* Garden City: Doubleday and Company.

Wolff, Robert Paul

1965   "Beyond Tolerance." In *A Critique of Pure Tolerance*, 1-52. Boston: Beacon Press.

Wolterstorff, Nicholas

1986   "The Migration of Theistic Arguments: From Natural Theology to Evidentialist Apologetics." In *Rationality, Religious Belief, and Moral Commitment*, ed. R. Audi and W. J. Wainwright. Ithaca, N.Y.: Cornell University Press.

Yanitelli, Victor R.

1951   "Chronicle: A Church-State Controversy." *Thought* 26 (Fall): 443-51.

1952   "A Church-State Anthology: The Work of Father Murray." *Thought* 27 (Spring): 6-42.

Yoder, John Howard

1972   *The Politics of Jesus.* Grand Rapids: Eerdmans.

1984   *The Priestly Kingdom: Social Ethics as Gospel.* Notre Dame: University of Notre Dame Press.

Index

Absolutism
    in jurisprudence, 130-31
    political, 79-81
America
    Catholic prejudices in, 118-19
    civic culture, 58-59, 87-88
    and *Dignitatis humanae,* 179-80
    and Murray, 73-96, 217-19
    and natural rights, 131-32, 140-41
    political rationalism, 79-80
    and secularism, 105-7, 119, 124-25, 181-82, 199-201
America periodical, 5, 130, 186
American Ecclesiastical Review, 5, 137
American Protective Association, 123
Americanist crisis, in Catholic Church, 42
Anti-Catholicism
    of Blanchard, 126
    "camel's nose" metaphor, 105, 134
    in *New England Primer* (1688), 123
    and Protestants, 103-22
Anti-individualism, 88
Anti-theists, 21, 28
Antifoundationalists, 3, 28
Antinomianism, 50. *See also* Law
Aquinas, Thomas, 66, 69, 141. *See also* Thomism
    De Regimine Principum, 95-96
    society-state distinction, 89-94
    and thesis-hypothesis doctrine, 42
Aristotelianism
    of John of Paris, 69
    of Novak, 192
    political theory, 97-98
    and subsidiarity principle, 89-99

Aristotle, *Politics,* 91-92
Articles of Peace, and First Amendment, 117-20, 146
Atheism, 21, 111-12
Atomic Energy Commission, 6
Augustine, and powers of the church, 65
Autonomous man myth, 27

Barber, Benjamin, 15
Bates, M. Searle, 108, 116
Baxter, Michael, xi
Belief. *See also* Foundationalism
    basic, 18
    in God, 20-21
    and human rights, 111-12
Bellah, Robert, 15
Bellarmine, Robert, 64-69, 84
Berger, Peter, 33
Bible, Mark 16:16, 182
Biblical imagery, 192
Bigongiari, Dino, 95-96
Black, Justice Hugo
    Everson v. Board of Education, 127-28
    McCollum v. Board of Education, 129-30
Blanshard, Paul, 123-124
Bodin, Jean, 201
Boland, Francis J., 199
Boonin, Leonard G., 91
Boorstin, Daniel, 120
Boston College, 5
Bowie, W. Russell, 117
Bradley, Gerard, 99n1, xi
Brink, David, 31
Brownson, Orestes, 123
Brunn, Geoffrey, 80
Burgess, Faith E.R., 4
Burke, Edmund, vii, 118

251